TITANIC

A JOURNEY THROUGH TIME

JOHN P. EATON AND CHARLES A. HAAS

The
History
Press

TO THE MEN AND WOMEN of RMS Titanic, Inc., the *Institut Français de Recherches pour l'Exploitation de Mers* (IFREMER), and Atelier LP3 Conservation, who have ensured *Titanic*'s future by preserving her past.

Fine art prints of the E.D. Walker paintings are available from Sumar Publications, 1 Richmond Grove, Lydiate, Merseyside L31 0BL, UK, www.edwalkermarine.com

First published 1999 by Patrick Stephens Ltd, an imprint of Haynes Publishing

This edition first published by The History Press 2017

The History Press
The Mill, Brimscombe Port
Stroud, Gloucestershire, GL5 2QG
www.thehistorypress.co.uk

British Library Cataloguing in Publication Data
A catalogue record for this book is available from the British Library

ISBN 978 0 7509 7007 5

Designed & typeset by The History Press
Printed and bound in India by Thomson Press India Ltd

CONTENTS

FOREWORD

by David F. Hutchings, Author

I IMAGINE THAT, like myself, the readership of this superb volume will have its own '*Titanic* Timeline' that will reflect its interest in the White Star liner *Titanic*.

Personally, my journey began in 1958 when, after nurturing an interest in the ocean liners that then passed my hometown of Cowes on the Isle of Wight on their way to and from Southampton, a (now) old friend suggested that I read Walter Lord's *A Night to Remember*. Three weeks later, the film coincidentally appeared in our local cinema – and I was hooked. For many months afterwards I continually wrote to the Rank Organisation for lobby stills from the film at 2/2 (2 shillings and tuppence) each. A poster was also happily procured along the way! My researches started by questioning my ageing grandmother about *Titanic*: 'Ah! She went out but she didn't come back!' was the sole response to my query.

The year 1962 saw my very first article published in a local newspaper to commemorate the fiftieth anniversary of the liner's sinking; but meanwhile, I had been preparing drawings from photographs from which to make a schoolboy's model.

Fast forward to 1985, and meeting Jack Eaton and Charlie Haas in Southampton during one of their many research trips that would cover three continents in preparation for their mighty tome, the classic *Titanic: Triumph and Tragedy*. It was a meeting that led to a happy and long-lasting friendship.

Three years later, Jack and Charlie introduced me to Walter Lord at his New York apartment and another happy association ensued, mostly through correspondence.

In between, I met several *Titanic* survivors and their families, and was also invited to become one of the first members of the British Titanic Society in 1987.

Another memorable encounter occurred in 1992, when I met the producer of *A Night to Remember*, Bill MacQuitty, again the beginning of another long association. From that initial meeting, I found out that Bill had made his own behind-the-scenes home movie covering aspects of the film's production and, after a short while, I instigated the documentary *The Making of 'A Night to Remember'*, bringing Ray Johnson on board as the documentary's professional 'filmmaker-in-chief'. Bill had written the foreword

to *Titanic: A Journey Through Time*'s first edition. I am honoured to follow his lead. At Bill's memorial celebration at the Hurlingham Club in London, following his passing in February 2004, his family kindly said the making of that documentary had made Bill aware that he and his work had not been forgotten, and had given him a new lease of life.

More pointers on my journey: an invitation to join the 1996 expedition as a speaker on one of two cruise ships during the attempt to raise 'The Big Piece' and another to attend a reception in the House of Lords heralding an emotive exhibition of *Titanic* artefacts at the National Maritime Museum, Greenwich, in 1994, as well as being asked by the current authors to write a foreword to their *Falling Star: Misadventures of the White Star Line Ships*.

Many memorable conventions and events – and the making of some wonderful friends – sprinkle my personal *Titanic* journey with the zest of happy recollection, but with this second edition of *Titanic: A Journey Through Time*, I realise that my personal *Titanic* journey somewhat pales. Jack's and Charlie's own journeys have run in

Titanic's only voyage begins with her departure from Southampton. (E.D. Walker)

parallel after an initial convergence five books; diving to the wreck of *Titanic*; co-founders of the excellent Titanic International Society; and, not least, recipients of New York City's South Street Seaport's prestigious Silver Riband Award for 'their Lifetime of Dedication to the History of the RMS *Titanic*'.

Charlie and Jack have done an admirable job in revising their acclaimed original volume, and within its pages we are introduced first to the main actors – the designers, builders and owners of the mighty ship and those who would sail in her. Subsequent phases of the journey take us through a timeline of shipbuilding, through to the maiden voyage and its passengers, before we are taken step by step through the ensuing disaster and its aftermath.

Not content with leaving us there, the authors guide us through the discovery of the wreck, the revitalised interest in the ship that this incurred, the subsequent artefact exhibitions and, less happily, various legal wranglings over the rights to the recovery of the artefacts.

Jack's and Charlie's narrative is absorbing, and it has given me great pleasure to be invited to write this foreword – yet another marker on my personal *Titanic* journey!

David F. Hutchings
Hampshire
2017

INTRODUCTION TO THE 1999 EDITION

by Robert M. DiSogra, Co-founder and President, Titanic International Society

THERE IS A remarkable consistency in the *Titanic* story that easily can be overlooked. Over the past 14 years, there has been a multitude of new information (and a multitude of old information passed off as 'new') about *Titanic*, her short life at sea, her discovery in 1985 and her subsequent rediscovery through artefact recovery and conservation programmes conducted by RMS Titanic, Inc., the New York-based public company preserving *Titanic*'s history through the educational display of these artefacts worldwide.

Anyone who has had even a minimal interest in this remarkable story has been exposed to the saga in ways that the writers of 1912 could only imagine.

The consistency I allude to is the fifth book about this ship by the internationally acclaimed writing team of John P. Eaton and Charles A. Haas. The reader is encouraged to absorb their first collaboration, *Titanic: Triumph and Tragedy,* now in its second edition. It will orient the reader to what has yet to be learned about what many call the 20th Century's most famous peacetime maritime disaster.

The Eaton-Haas approach combines comprehensive research on three continents, including years of library research, interviews, participation in three RMS Titanic, Inc. expeditions and combing through unpublished documentation, from which they have extracted many of the little known, but historically significant, facts about *Titanic.* This consistency in scholarly research adds to the story's completeness.

But the story of *Titanic* is far from complete. Learning is an ongoing process. Dissemination is a labour of love. Accuracy is synonymous with any Eaton and Haas publication.

Despite being inundated with numerous texts (and pseudo-texts) over the past several years, there continues to be an inherent interest in learning more about this ship and the disaster that befell her. Through all of this information overload, John Eaton and Charles Haas have conservatively watched, listened, taken notes and begun to fill the voids in *Titanic*'s story. Since their last book, they have painstakingly assembled the most detailed and easily readable chronology of *Titanic* ever assembled.

Titanic: A Journey Through Time is the personal diary of RMS *Titanic* that will evoke a variety of all human emotions. As with any diary, some dates are separated by time gaps, yet others are minute-by-minute accounts, from 1912's most compelling events to her current place in history.

Titanic: A Journey Through Time demonstrates that the *Titanic* story is more complex and more poignant than we ever could have imagined. This remarkable book brings our *Titanic* experiences into a unique perspective as we continue to try to understand this event and the impact it has had on the lives of millions throughout the world in the 20th Century.

Robert M. DiSogra
Freehold, New Jersey
December 1998

PREFACE: 1912

THE YEAR 1912 was like many other years at the dawning of the 20th century. After a glorious 63-year reign, the benevolent little lady who had given her name to an era had been dead for 11 years, yet her spiritual heritage continued to dominate the manners and morals of the civilised world in a manner scarcely diminished by the comparatively brief nine-year rule of her son, Edward VII.

Now, since his Coronation in 1910, King George V ruled the British Empire, a domain encompassing nearly one-quarter of the world's habitable land surface, and on which the sun never set. The British Prime Minister, the Right Honourable Herbert Henry Asquith, presided over a Coalition Government whose surplus revenues for the fiscal year ending 31 March exceeded £6.5 million.

Yet throughout the world a hint of change was in the air: German general elections in January saw a loss of conservative Reichstag members in favour of a large majority of Social Democrats; in February a republic was established in China when the Emperor's abdication brought an end to the Manchu dynasty; in their search for equality, suffragettes were on the march in England and America, breaking windows, destroying mail in public letter-boxes and behaving in most unladylike ways; and in England, lengthy and costly coal miners' and dockers' strikes were settled generally in favour of the workers.

Nonetheless, in this year of 1912 people throughout the world clung to the status quo and to traditional ways

HM King George V. (*The Year 1912*)

Rt Hon H.H. Asquith. (*The Year 1912*)

of life. The importance of the British monarchy was reflected by Their Majesties' return from the great Durbar in India on 4 February and the national service of thanksgiving celebrated at St Paul's Cathedral in London only six days before the state opening of Parliament on 14 February. In America, a Republican, William Howard Taft – 54 years old and of English ancestry – was in his fourth and final year of office. (He would be defeated in the November elections by Woodrow Wilson, a Democrat, who would lead the country for eight years.)

Peace in Europe was threatened by war in the Balkans. On 8 October Montenegro declared war on Turkey, followed by Bulgaria, Serbia and Greece, and the invasion of Turkish territory. Many battles were fought until

hostilities between the Balkan States and Turkey were suspended by an armistice signed on 3 December.

Natural disasters in 1912 occurred with no greater nor lesser frequency than in most years. Floods during April in America's Mississippi Valley devastated more than 200,000 square miles, made 300,000 homeless and caused $50 million (£10 million) in property damage and loss; an earthquake on 9 August in Turkey's Dardanelles region killed more than 3,000, while typhoons during September in both China and Japan killed many thousands.

In spite of government safety regulations, colliery disasters in England and America took many lives during 1912: two gas explosions at the Cadeby Pit of the Silverwood Colliery near Conisbrough, Yorkshire, killed 87 miners; in America 156 miners were killed during March by explosions in

HM King George V, accompanied by the Archbishop of York, visits the Silverwood Colliery near Conisbrough, Yorkshire, following the 9 July disaster. (*The Year 1912*)

West Virginia; a disastrous coal mine explosion in Yubari, Hokkaido, Japan, killed 238 miners; and yet another explosion in a coal mine at Gerthe, Germany, took the lives of 103 miners.

The burgeoning cinema theatre industry suffered two setbacks when so-called 'safety' film ignited inside projectors at Villareal de los Infantes, Spain, and at Baraques, Belgium; the resulting fires in each theatre caused panic and loss of life totalling more than 100 patrons.

In horse racing, Tagalie, with jockey J. Reiff up, won the Epsom Derby Stakes in England; Worth won the Kentucky Derby; and Houli, owned by M.A. Fould,

William Howard Taft. (*The Year 1912*)

took French racing's Grand Prix de Paris.

The 1912 Olympic Games were held at Stockholm, while in American baseball, the American League's Boston Red Sox defeated the National League's New York Yankees four games to three in a best-of-seven series. The British tennis team won the prestigious Davis Cup, defeating Australia three games to two. And on 1 April, in their traditional boat race, Oxford defeated Cambridge.

In the 1912 Nobel Prizes, Alexis Carrel, French-born American surgeon and biologist, received the award for medicine, German dramatist Gerhart Hauptmann the award for literature; and American statesman Elihu Root the Peace Prize.

Titanic departing on her maiden voyage (Courtesy of Smithsonian Institution, NMAH/ Transportation)

On 11 April a bill was introduced into the British Parliament that was to have far-reaching consequences. Prime Minister Asquith offered a 'Bill to Amend the Provision for the Government of Ireland', the so-called 'Home Rule Bill', which was passed on its second reading on 9 May by a vote of 362 to 271. A portent of things to come was the great anti-Home Rule demonstration on 27 September at Belfast.

At Southampton, on Wednesday 10 April, the embodiment of British shipbuilding ingenuity and skill, the 46,239-ton White Star liner *Titanic*, departed on her maiden voyage. After a late afternoon stop at Cherbourg and another around noon the following day at Queenstown, Ireland, the ship headed majestically into the North Atlantic toward New York, where she was expected to arrive on Wednesday 17 April.

During 1912 many well-known individuals died: Lord Lister, surgeon and originator of antiseptic surgery, aged 85; Clara Barton, founder of the American Red Cross; Denmark's King Frederick VIII, who became ill while visiting Hamburg, Germany, and died suddenly while walking through the city, lying for hours unrecognised at the city morgue before being identified; on 30 May Wilbur Wright, co-inventor with his brother of the powered heavier-than-air aeroplane; Emperor Matsuhito, Japan's Mikado for 44 years, on 30 July, to be buried in an elaborate state funeral on 13 September; and in contrast, a man whose humble origins belied the great power and influence he was to have in later life, General William Booth, founder of the Salvation Army, who died on 20 August, mourned throughout the world.

In the 'Death Roll of 1912', a section of the American publication *The World Almanac*, appear several entries that, save for a calamitous interruption of *Titanic*'s maiden voyage, need not have been included: 'Astor, John Jacob (47), drowned in the *Titanic* disaster April 15; Butt, Major Archibald Willingham (41), drowned in the *Titanic* disaster April 15; Futrelle, Jacques (42), writer ... Harris, Henry B. (45), theatrical producer ... Hays, Charles Melville (55), President, Grand Trunk Railway ... Millet, Francis D. (66), artist and author ... Stead, William T. (63), British journalist ... Straus, Isidor (67), merchant and philanthropist ...

Each entry bears that designation 'drowned in the *Titanic* disaster April 15', a brief and melancholy count of only some of the prominent men who were lost, only the merest token of the total of 1,513 dead in the era's greatest maritime disaster.

Between 10 April, when *Titanic* so proudly began her maiden voyage, and

Lord Lister. (*The Year 1912*)

Clara Barton. (*The Year 1912*)

HM King Frederick VIII of Denmark. (*The Year 1912*)

General William Booth. (*The Year 1912*)

Isidor Straus. (*The Independent*)

Francis (Frank) Millet. (*The Independent*)

John Jacob Astor (*The Independent*)

William Thomas Stead. (*The Independent*)

Captain Edward John Smith. (*The Independent*)

Major Archibald Willingham Butt. (Authors' collection)

15 April, when the dream ended, many events occurred in particular order; many events preceded *Titanic*'s construction and launch, and many followed the disaster, each in its specific place, each a distinct part of *Titanic*'s incredible story. The sequence of facts can be depicted as flowing along a Time Line, as a succession of episodes of which the sinking is itself but a single scene.

While the birth date of William James Pirrie, *Titanic*'s builder, has been selected as the initial date of this Time Line, it could well have begun on that unknown date when primitive humans first floated a log in a stream and sat atop it to cross in safe and (relatively) dry comfort. And while the sequence ends with on-going current events, there is no true finality to *Titanic*'s story. As long as humans sail the seas, as long as civilisation can remember deeds of valour and heroism, as long as there are dreams of glory and beauty, *Titanic*'s chronicle will never end. Similarly, then, let this Time Line have no true start and, surely, no foreseeable conclusion.

John P. Eaton
Cold Spring, New York

Charles A. Haas
Randolph, New Jersey
1999

ONE

PROLOGUE

Monday, 31 May 1847

IN QUEBEC, CANADA, William James Pirrie, son of William Alexander Pirrie and Elizabeth Montgomery, is born. By 1895 he has become a managing director of the Belfast shipbuilding firm Harland & Wolff and by 1906, as the Rt Hon Viscount Pirrie, is its controlling director.

Sunday, 27 January 1850

EDWARD JOHN SMITH is born at Hanley, Stoke-on-Trent, Staffordshire, England, the son of Edward Smith, a 46-year-old potter, and 42-year-old Catherine Marsh. Starting in February 1867 as an apprentice aboard the *Senator Weber*, a sail vessel, Smith works his way up to command several freighters and liners of Britain's White Star Line, culminating in his command in 1912 of RMS *Titanic*.

Right William James Pirrie. (*The Shipbuilder*)

Far right Edward John Smith. (Authors' collection)

Friday, 12 December 1862

JOSEPH BRUCE ISMAY, first son and second child of Thomas Henry Ismay and Margaret Bruce, is born at Enfield House, Great Crosby, near Liverpool, England. On his father's death in 1899, J. Bruce Ismay assumes the leadership of the Oceanic Steam Navigation Company Ltd, owner and operator of the White Star Line. It is under his operation that the great liners *Olympic* and *Titanic* are constructed.

Monday, 4 April 1864

THE WHITE STAR LINE steamship *Royal Standard*, sailing from Melbourne, Australia, to Liverpool, England, on the return leg of her maiden voyage, is badly damaged and almost sunk in collision with an iceberg at 54°50'S, 145°27'W.

Later bankrupt, the company's assets are sold late in 1867. The purchaser of the company's name, goodwill and flag (a red swallow-tail pennant with a white star) is the Liverpool shipowner Thomas Henry Ismay, who takes his new company and its name to the heights of successful ocean transport business.

Above left Thomas Ismay, at about the time that he purchased the assets of the defunct White Star Line. (Private collection)

Above right Joseph Bruce Ismay. (*The Shipbuilder*)

Left The *Royal Standard* collides with an iceberg, 4 April 1864. (*Illustrated London News*)

Friday, 30 July 1869

THOMAS H. ISMAY, owner of the Oceanic Steam Navigation Company, parent company of his newly acquired White Star Line, places an order with Harland & Wolff, Belfast, Ireland, for the construction of White Star's first four steamships: *Atlantic*, *Baltic*, *Republic* and *Adriatic*.

Wednesday, 6 September 1869

THE OCEANIC STEAM Navigation Company Ltd, White Star's official corporate name, is registered with a capital of £400,000 ($2,592,000) in £1,000 shares.

Saturday, 27 August 1870

WHITE STAR'S FIRST new steamship, Harland & Wolff's yard number 73, is launched at Belfast. Her name: *Oceanic*. The remaining steamships included in the first order from Harland & Wolff, and their launch times, are *Atlantic* (December 1870); *Baltic* (March 1871); and *Republic* (July 1871). The White Star Line's conquest of the North Atlantic has begun.

Above left Designed by Richard Norman Shaw and J. Francis Doyle, the White Star Line's head office was built between 1896 and 1898 for Ismay, Imrie and Company, White Star's parent company. Once known as Albion House, the building at 30 James Street and The Strand, across from Liverpool's Pier Head, now is a luxury hotel. [See 9 September 2013.] (Authors' collection)

Above right Thomas H. Ismay in later years, when his vessels had begun to dominate the North Atlantic passenger service. (Authors' collection)

Right Mr Gustav Wolff and Mr (later Sir) Edward Harland. (Harland & Wolff, Ltd)

Friday, 7 February 1873

THOMAS ANDREWS Jr, son of the Rt Hon Thomas Andrews and Eliza Pirrie, sister of William James Pirrie (qv), is born at Comber, County Down, Ireland.

In 1889 Tom Andrews enters an apprenticeship at his uncle's shipbuilding firm, Harland & Wolff. Working in all parts of the yard, he finally settles in the design department and in 1907 is made a managing director. He is instrumental in *Titanic*'s design and actively oversees the details of her construction at the yard.

1874

THE POEM 'A TRYST' by the New England poet Celia Thaxter is published. In the poem a ship is sunk in collision with an iceberg in a manner resembling *Titanic*'s fate 38 years later.

March 1880

THIRTY-YEAR-OLD Edward J. Smith, after 13 years at sea aboard ships of other companies, joins the White Star Line as fourth, later third, officer aboard their steamship *Cretic*. His rise is rapid and in April 1888 he is given his first transatlantic command, the passenger steamship *Baltic*.

Above Ardara, the home of Thomas Andrews in County Down. (*A Titanic Hero: Thomas Andrew, Shipbuilder*)

Far left Thomas Andrews (Jr) as a young apprentice at Harland & Wolff. (Authors' collection)

Left Celia Thaxter. (Authors' collection)

Monday, 22 March 1886

LONDON'S *PALL MALL Gazette* publishes a story by its editor William Thomas Stead, which describes the loss of a great ship at sea by collision with another vessel. The ensuing large loss of life is attributed to too few lifeboats. Stead concludes his prophetic story with, 'This is exactly what might take place and *will* take place if liners are sent to sea short of boats.'

Friday, 4 May 1888

THE SS *TITANIC*, one of only two vessels in *Lloyd's Register of Shipping* to bear the name other than the ill-fated White Star liner of 1911/12, makes its maiden voyage from Belfast to Glasgow. It is a freight carrier of 1,608 gross tons and 280ft in length, completed in 1888 as yard number 28 by McIllwaine, Lewis & Co. Ltd of Belfast.

Built for H.J. Scott & Co., Belfast, *Titanic* is sold to Smith & Service, Glasgow, prior to her maiden voyage, her name and port of registry remaining unchanged. In 1890 the vessel is sold again, this time to the Ulidian Steam Navigation Co. Ltd, who manage her for 13 years. In 1903 *Titanic* is acquired by Cia de Lota y Coronel, of Valparaiso, Chile, who rename it *Luis Alberto*.

The vessel becomes *Don Alberto* in 1915 and is deleted from *Lloyd's Register* in 1928.

Above left Edward J. Smith, c. 1895. (Authors' collection)

Above right William Thomas Stead as he appeared about 1912. (Authors' collection)

Right *Don Alberto*. (Joseph A. Carvalho collection)

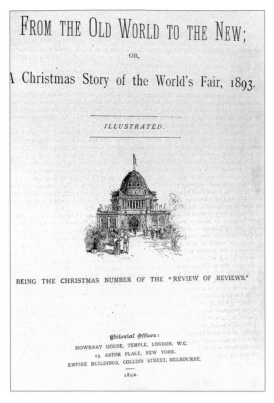

December 1892

IN ITS SPECIAL Christmas Issue for December 1892 the British magazine *Review of Reviews* publishes a fictional article by its editor, William Thomas Stead, describing an imaginary voyage from England to America aboard the White Star Line's ship *Majestic*; the ship's captain is Edward Smith. During the voyage, *Majestic*'s crew rescue survivors from another vessel that has sunk after striking an iceberg. *Majestic* then steers south to avoid the ice field.

May 1898

THE NEW YORK publishing firm of M. G. Mansfield publishes *Futility*, a novel by the American author Morgan Robertson. In the book an Atlantic liner remarkably similar to *Titanic* sinks with great loss of life after striking an iceberg. The fictional ship's name: *Titan*. (See Appendix 7)

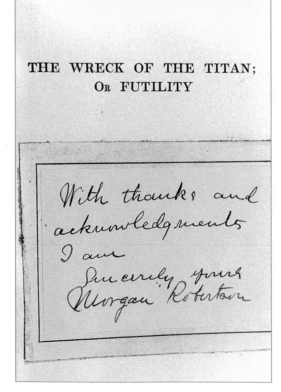

Above left Title page of *Review of Reviews*, December 1892 issue. (Authors' collection)

Above right 'Captain Edward Smith' of the 'White Star Line's ship *Majestic*', as depicted in the magazine. (Authors' collection)

Far left Morgan Robertson. (*Empire State Notables*)

Left Title page of *Futility* inscribed by Robertson. (Authors' collection)

Tuesday, 4 February 1902

FORMED IN 1893, in 1902 the American-owned International Navigation Company of New Jersey – already the owner of three major shipping companies – changes its name to the International Mercantile Marine Company. Financed by the American banker John Pierpont Morgan, the new company raises its capital from $15,000,000 (£3,000,000) to $120,000,000 (£24,000,000) and begins to acquire additional shipping organisations.

On this date IMM reaches an agreement with the White Star Line. The purchase price exceeds £10,000,000 ($50,000,000), £5,000,000 payable in cash on 31 December 1902; it is actually paid on 1 December at J.P. Morgan's London offices.

February 1904

AT THE AGE of 41, and with the approval and encouragement of IMM's creator, Mr J.P. Morgan, Bruce Ismay becomes president of the International Mercantile Marine Company, a post he is to hold until the end of 1912. He does not relinquish chairmanship of the White Star Line to assume the IMM post.

Above Although listed as a director on this International Mercantile Marine Company stock certificate issued in 1902, J. Bruce Ismay did not become president of IMM until 1904. (Authors' collection)

Right John Pierpont Morgan. (Authors' collection)

Wednesday, 10 January 1912

IN A LETTER to Harold Sanderson, president of the International Mercantile Marine's British Committee, IMM president Bruce Ismay expresses the wish to retire from the services of the company at the end of 1912. The retirement date is later modified, by agreement with Mr Sanderson, to 30 June 1913.

On Saturday, 4 December 1912, in a letter to Phillip A.S. Franklin, IMM vice president and company director, Bruce Ismay indicates his intention to resign as IMM's president and as chairman of the Oceanic Steam Navigation Company (White Star Line's owner). In the letter he also resigns his directorship in the International Navigation Company, a Liverpool-based holding company owned entirely by IMM.

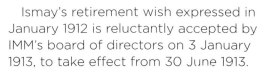

Ismay's retirement wish expressed in January 1912 is reluctantly accepted by IMM's board of directors on 3 January 1913, to take effect from 30 June 1913.

Spring 1912

IN THE AMERICAN publication *The Popular Magazine* appears a story by Mayn Clew Garnett, 'The White Ghost of Disaster'.

The story describes the loss of the *Admiral*, a gigantic liner sailing between Liverpool and New York. *Admiral* sinks with a heavy loss of life due, in part, to a lifeboat shortage. Although published 'after the fact', the story is written months before *Titanic*'s loss and, indeed, is actually in print prior to the April disaster.

Above left Harold Sanderson. (Authors' collection)

Above Phillip A.S. Franklin. (*New York Times*)

Left *Titanic* at Southampton. (Bob Forrest collection)

7 April 1912

IN FAMILY CORRESPONDENCE written aboard *Titanic* at Southampton, Henry Tingle Wilde, soon to be the liner's chief officer, states, 'She is an improvement on the *Olympic* in many respects and is a wonderful ship, the latest thing in shipbuilding.' Four days later, in a letter to his sister posted from Queenstown, Wilde appears to have changed his mind: 'I still don't like this ship ... I have a queer feeling about it.'

TWO

CONCEPTION, CONSTRUCTION, TESTING

April 1907

ON AN APRIL evening, during after-dinner coffee at Downshire House, London SW1, Joseph Bruce Ismay and Lord William James Pirrie conceive *Olympic* and *Titanic*. The order is registered in Harland & Wolff's order book on 30 April 1907, with a third vessel added later.

Wednesday, 11 September 1907

AN EARLIER AGREEMENT between the Oceanic Steam Navigation Company Ltd and the Belfast shipbuilding firm of Harland & Wolff is announced publicly for the first time. It calls for the construction of two large liners to compete with Cunard's *Lusitania* and *Mauretania*.

Above Downshire House. (Authors' collection)

Right The competition: Cunard's *Lusitania*. (Authors' collection)

Wednesday, 22 April 1908

THE WHITE STAR LINE makes its first public announcement of the name for one of the two liners: *Titanic*.

Friday, 31 July 1908

THE CONTRACT LETTER is signed between the Oceanic Steam Navigation Company Ltd and Harland & Wolff for the construction of the proposed liners.

Top More competition: Cunard's *Mauretania*. (Authors' collection)

Middle Soon after the letter of intent is signed, Harland & Wolff's draughtsmen begin laying out the new vessels' lines in the shipyard's mould loft. (*The Shipbuilder*)

Left Inside the draughting room itself (centre, seen here in 1997), dreams and estimates are transferred into realities and costs of working plans. (Authors' collection)

Wednesday, 16 December 1908

THE KEEL IS laid in slipway 2 at Harland & Wolff's Queen's Island yard, Belfast, for yard number 400, *Olympic*, first of the new liners.

Olympic's keel is laid. (Authors' collection/*The Shipbuilder*)

Monday, 22 March 1909

ON NUMBER 3 slipway at the Queen's Island yard, keel blocks are laid for yard number 401, *Titanic*.

Wednesday, 31 March 1909

ON NUMBER 3 slipway, the first keel plate for *Titanic* is laid.

Sunday, 12 December 1909

TITANIC'S STERN FRAME, fabricated at the Darlington Forge Company, Durham, and shipped to Belfast on 10–11 December, arrives at Harland & Wolff's yard.

Wednesday, 5 January 1910

THE ASSEMBLY OF *Titanic*'s stern frame casting begins. The two pieces weigh 70 tons, and have a total height of 68ft 3in.

Top By the summer of 1909, construction of *Olympic*'s double bottom (right) is well under way, while on the adjacent slipway, work on *Titanic* continues. (*The Shipbuilder*)

Middle *Titanic*'s boss brackets. (*The Shipbuilder*)

Left The intricate rivet patterns of the immense liner's hull are seen in this view of *Olympic*. *Titanic*'s ribbing is seen on the left. (*The Shipbuilder*)

Monday, 7 February 1910

TITANIC'S BOSS BRACKETS arrive at Belfast. They will support the new liner's propeller shafts, leading to her triple screws.

Thursday, 21 April 1910

RIVETER CATCH-BOY 15-year-old Samuel Joseph Scott dies after a fall from *Titanic*'s hull.

Above Work on the two sisters continues during the summer of 1910. For the convenience of visitors, the liners are identified by names on painted boards. (Harland & Wolff collection, Ulster Folk and Transport Museum)

Right As *Olympic*'s construction proceeds, a watchman's shack is installed near the bow to protect the liner's increasingly valuable installations. (Authors' collection)

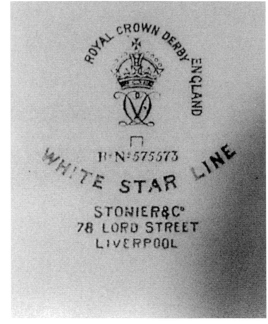

Tuesday, 20 September 1910

THE WHITE STAR LINE orders special chinaware for use aboard *Olympic* and *Titanic*. In keeping with company policy, the ships' names are omitted from all tableware, which is manufactured by Stonier & Co.

Wednesday, 19 October 1910

ALL STEEL PLATES of *Titanic*'s hull are in place.

Above A maker's identification marks the back of a Royal Crown Derby plate destined for the First Class à la carte restaurant, later recovered from the debris field near *Titanic*'s wreck. (Royal Crown Derby Porcelain Co/ Authors' photo © 1993 RMS Titanic, Inc.)

Left Mere days before the event, *Olympic*, poised in her slipway cradle, awaits the installation of cables (on the cart in the centre foreground) that will restrain her during the launch. (Harland & Wolff, Ltd)

Thursday, 20 October 1910

OLYMPIC IS LAUNCHED in the presence of the Lord Lieutenant of Ireland and the Countess of Aberdeen, together with huge harbour crowds.

Monday, 5 December 1910

A SMALL TRAVELLING crane on the overhead gantry collapses while lifting a large iron plate for *Titanic*'s hull. No damage is done to the vessel and no one is injured.

Tuesday–Thursday, 3–5 January 1911

COVERAGE IS PLACED with several underwriters insuring *Olympic* and *Titanic* for £750,000 ($3,750,000) each, with a £150,000 ($750,000) excess deductible.

Monday, 27 February 1911

TITANIC'S RUDDER ARRIVES at Belfast from Darlington aboard *Glenravel*. Its overall length is 78ft 8in, with a maximum width of 15ft 3in.

Top Moments after launch, *Olympic*'s handsome white-painted hull is viewed for the first time by an admiring public. (Authors' collection)

Middle right A travelling crane such as that which collapsed. (*Engineering*)

Right Insurance slip for *Olympic* and *Titanic*. (Courtesy CGU plc)

Far right *Titanic*'s rudder. (Authors' collection)

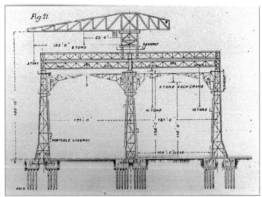

Wednesday, 8 March 1911

CONTRACTS ARE PLACED with the Goldsmith's & Silversmith's Company Ltd of London for *Olympic*'s and *Titanic*'s metallic tableware.

Friday, 5 May 1911

TITANIC'S ANCHOR, one of three carried, arrives at Harland & Wolff from Netherton, Worcestershire.

Top *Titanic*'s hull looms in the distance as a shift ends at Harland & Wolff's Queen's Island yard in Belfast. (Harland & Wolff collection, Ulster Folk and Transport Museum)

Left and below left *Titanic*'s anchors arrive. *Belfast Telegraph*/Harland & Wolff, Ltd)

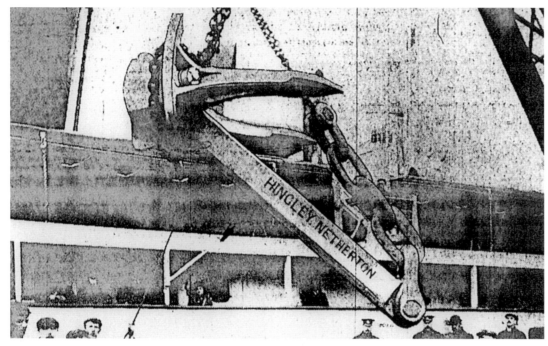

Wednesday, 31 May 1911

TITANIC IS LAUNCHED. During the launch a yard worker, James Dobbin, aged 43, is severely injured by a collapsing hull support. He dies on 2 June at Belfast's Royal Victoria Hospital.

A special report to Harland & Wolff managers dated 10 April 1912 describes deaths and accidents during *Titanic*'s construction. It shows eight fatalities (some of whose details are lacking), 28 severe accidents and 218 slight accidents.

Below left and top right 26 May 1911: *Olympic* and *Titanic* are to be open for public inspection, or may be viewed from the Belfast & County Down Railway steamer *Slieve Bearnagh*. (*Belfast Telegraph*/Authors' collection)

Right *Titanic* is ready for launch. The absence of shipyard activity suggests that the date is Sunday, 28 May 1911. (Harland & Wolff, Ltd)

Below right On 31 May 1911, the day of *Titanic*'s launch, '*Titanic* fever' grips Belfast, as shown by this dated advertisement for the Cromac Brewery, which appeared in the *Belfast Evening Telegraph*.

Pictures showing the progression of *Titanic*'s launch. (Harland & Wolff collection, Ulster Folk and Transport Museum/*The Shipbuilder*/ Private collection/Authors' collection/ *Illustrated London News*/ Peter Pearce collection/ Harland & Wolff, Ltd/*Shipping World*/*Cork Examiner*/*Belfast Telegraph*)

Tuesday, 13 June 1911

A RIVETER, Robert James Murphy, 49, of 6 Hillman Street, Belfast, dies in a 50ft fall from one of *Titanic*'s upper decks.

Right Robert James Murphy. (*Belfast Telegraph*)

Below Collision damage to *Olympic* and HMS*Hawke*. (Authors' collection)

Below right *Titanic*'s original maiden voyage date is announced. (Authors' collection)

"OLYMPIC" (Triple-Screw), 45,000 Tons.
AND
"TITANIC" (Triple-Screw), 45,000 Tons (Launched May 31st, 1911).
THE LARGEST STEAMERS IN THE WORLD.

SOUTHAMPTON-CHERBOURG-QUEENSTOWN-NEW YORK SERVICE
Calling at QUEENSTOWN (Westbound) and PLYMOUTH (Eastbound).

FROM SOUTHAMPTON.			FROM CHERBOURG.		STEAMER.	FROM NEW YORK. CALLING AT PLYMOUTH AND CHERBOURG.		
Date.	Day.	Sailing hour.	Sailing about 4.30 p.m.			Date.	Day.	Sailing Hour.
1911 Aug. 2	Wed.	Noon	1911 Aug. 2		OCEANIC	1911 Aug.12	Sat.	Noon
... 9	Wed.	Noon	... 9		**OLYMPIC**	... 19	Sat.	Noon
... 16	Wed.	Noon	... 16		*ST. PAUL	... 26	Sat.	Noon
... 23	Wed.	Noon	... 23		OCEANIC	Sep. 2	Sat.	Noon
... 30	Wed.	2-30 pm	... 30		**OLYMPIC**	... 9	Sat.	Noon
Sep. 6	Wed.	Noon	Sep. 6		MAJESTIC	... 16	Sat.	Noon
... 13	Wed.	Noon	... 13		OCEANIC	... 23	Sat.	Noon
... 20	Wed.	11-0 am	... 20		**OLYMPIC**	... 30	Sat.	Noon
... 27	Wed.	Noon	... 27		MAJESTIC	Oct. 7	Sat.	Noon
Oct. 4	Wed.	Noon	Oct. 4		OCEANIC	... 14	Sat.	Noon
... 11	Wed.	Noon	... 11		**OLYMPIC**	... 21	Sat.	Noon
... 18	Wed.	Noon	... 18		MAJESTIC	... 28	Sat.	Noon
... 25	Wed.	Noon	... 25		OCEANIC	Nov. 4	Sat.	Noon
Nov. 1	Wed.	2-30 pm	Nov. 1		**OLYMPIC**	... 11	Sat.	Noon
... 8	Wed.	Noon	... 8		MAJESTIC	... 18	Sat.	Noon
... 15	Wed.	Noon	... 15		OCEANIC	... 25	Sat.	Noon
... 22	Wed.	Noon	... 22		*ST. LOUIS	Dec. 2	Sat.	Noon
... 29	Wed.	Noon	... 29		**OLYMPIC**	... 9	Sat.	Noon
Dec. 6	Wed.	Noon	Dec. 6		OCEANIC	... 16	Sat.	Noon
... 13	Wed.	Noon	... 13		*PHILADELPHIA	... 23	Sat.	Noon
... 20	Wed.	Noon	... 20		**OLYMPIC**	... 30	Sat.	Noon
... 27	Wed.	Noon	... 27		*ST. PAUL	1912 Jan. 6	Sat.	Noon
1912 Jan. 3	Wed.	Noon	1912 Jan. 3		OCEANIC	... 13	Sat.	Noon
... 10	Wed.	Noon	... 10		*PHILADELPHIA	... 20	Sat.	Noon
... 17	Wed.	Noon	... 17		**OLYMPIC**	... 27	Sat.	Noon
... 24	Wed.	Noon	... 24		*ST. PAUL	Feb. 3	Sat.	Noon
... 31	Wed.	Noon	... 31		OCEANIC	... 10	Sat.	Noon
Feb. 7	Wed.	Noon	Feb. 7		*PHILADELPHIA	... 17	Sat.	Noon
... 14	Wed.	Noon	... 14		**OLYMPIC**	... 24	Sat.	Noon
... 21	Wed.	Noon	... 21		*ST. PAUL	Mar. 2	Sat.	Noon
... 28	Wed.	Noon	... 28		OCEANIC	... 9	Sat.	Noon
Mar. 6	Wed.	Noon	Mar. 6		*ST. LOUIS	... 16	Sat.	Noon
... 13	Wed.	Noon	... 13		**OLYMPIC**	... 23	Sat.	Noon
... 20	Wed.	Noon	... 20		**TITANIC**	... 30	Sat.	Noon
... 27	Wed.	Noon	... 27		OCEANIC	Apl. 6	Sat.	Noon
Apl. 3	Wed.	Noon	Apl. 3		**OLYMPIC**	... 13	Sat.	Noon
... 10	Wed.	Noon	... 10		**TITANIC**	... 20	Sat.	Noon
... 17	Wed.	Noon	... 17		OCEANIC	... 27	Sat.	Noon
... 24	Wed.	Noon	... 24		**OLYMPIC**	May 4	Sat.	Noon

* American Line Steamer

Sunday, 20 August 1911

THE NEW VESSEL'S steel foremast is placed in position. At its base its diameter is 36 inches, and its overall length is 161ft 6in, with the uppermost 15ft made of wood.

Wednesday, 20 September 1911

OLYMPIC IS DAMAGED during departure from Southampton in a collision with the British Royal Navy cruiser HMS *Hawke* off the Isle of Wight. A large hole is punched into the liner's after starboard side. The accident necessitates cancellation of *Olympic*'s voyage.

Monday, 25 September 1911

WHITE STAR LINE'S Winter 1911/1912 sailing list is released. On it is the date for *Titanic*'s maiden departure, 20 March 1912.

Wednesday, 4 October 1911

OLYMPIC DEPARTS Southampton for repairs at Harland & Wolff's Belfast yard. To make room for *Olympic*, *Titanic* is moved from her berth at the new graving dock and floated to the Alexandra Wharf.

Friday, 6 October 1911

OLYMPIC ARRIVES AT Belfast and lies outside the dock area overnight. By 10.10am on 7 October, the damaged liner is moored and an examination of

A shipyard diving team prepares to examine *Olympic*'s hull for underwater damage. (Harland & Wolff collection, Ulster Folk and Transport Museum)

Gigantic's keel is laid. (Private collection)

her hull begins. A revised official public announcement of *Titanic*'s maiden voyage date is made: 10 April 1912.

Monday, 20 November 1911

OLYMPIC DEPARTS Belfast for Southampton, from where, on 29 November, she departs on the continuation of her interrupted voyage.

Thursday, 30 November 1911

IN SLIPWAY NUMBER 2 the keel is laid of Harland & Wolff's yard number 433, the third vessel in the 'Olympic class', built to provide a weekly, three-ship service between Southampton and New York, instead of the two-ship, fortnightly service originally envisaged. Provisionally named *Gigantic*, the new vessel is later renamed and launched as *Britannic*.

Wednesday, 6 December 1911

BY THIS DATE *Titanic*'s third funnel is in place.

Through the spring, summer and autumn of 1911, *Titanic*'s interiors and electrical installations are taking form. Telephones installed in the bow area (far left) and on the stern docking bridge (left) connect to a communications centre on *Titanic*'s bridge (below left), which also contains telephones to and from the crow's nest and engine room (below). (*The Electrician*)

January 1912

THE WIRELESS CALL letters 'MUC' are assigned by the British Post Office to *Titanic*, which has been fitted with the most powerful Marconi apparatus available. Later the letters are changed to 'MGY'.

This tuner (below), spark gap transmitter (right) and transmitter key (bottom) are 1912 Marconi wireless equipment similar to that installed aboard *Titanic*. (Authors' collection)

Below right The connections of a 1½kw Marconi converter set like that aboard *Titanic*. (*The Shipbuilder*)

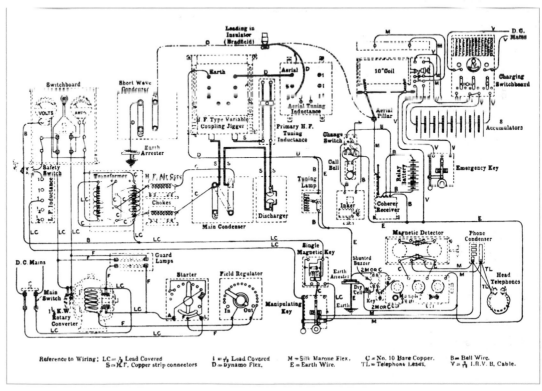

During January and February 1912 *Titanic*'s construction is mainly internal as wiring, interior partitions, air conduits and plumbing are installed. (*Daily Mirror*/Harland & Wolff collection, Ulster Folk and Transport Museum/*Irish Times*)

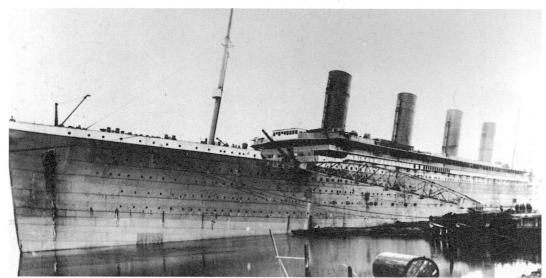

The Welin Davit Company proudly announces that its new double-acting lifeboat davit has been chosen for installation aboard *Olympic* and *Titanic*. (*The Shipbuilder*)

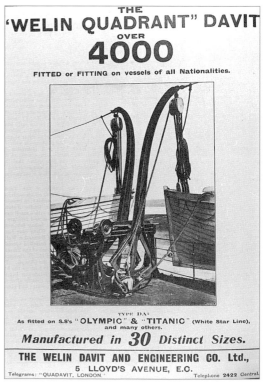

Saturday, 3 February 1912

ASSISTED BY HARLAND & WOLFF's tug *Hercules*, *Titanic* is moved into dry dock.

Saturday, 17 February 1912

TITANIC IS REMOVED from dry dock and moored at the deep water outfitting wharf. Lifeboat installation begins some time after this date and is completed in about three weeks. The resulting boat capacities exceed existing Board of Trade regulations by 17 per cent.

Above right Harland & Wolff's tug *Hercules*. (Harland & Wolff collection, Ulster Folk and Transport Museum)

Right Harland & Wolff's yard vessel *Jackal*, a former British Royal Navy despatch boat, is sometimes used as a tug within the yard; more typically it functions as an auxiliary power source. Tied at the deep water wharf, its onboard generator provides illumination and power to workers outfitting vessels. (Harland & Wolff collection, Ulster Folk and Transport Museum)

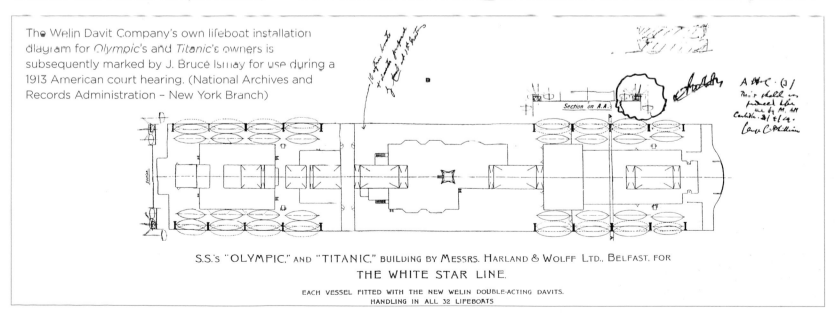

The Welin Davit Company's own lifeboat installation diagram for *Olympic*'s and *Titanic*'s owners is subsequently marked by J. Bruce Ismay for use during a 1913 American court hearing. (National Archives and Records Administration – New York Branch)

Section on A.A.

S.S.'s "OLYMPIC," AND "TITANIC," BUILDING BY MESSRS. HARLAND & WOLFF LTD., BELFAST, FOR
THE WHITE STAR LINE.
EACH VESSEL FITTED WITH THE NEW WELIN DOUBLE-ACTING DAVITS.
HANDLING IN ALL 32 LIFEBOATS

Top Externally, lifeboats are placed under their davits, the hull and funnels are painted (left), and the propellers installed (right). (Harland & Wolff, Ltd/Harland & Wolff collection, Ulster Folk and Transport Museum)

Above Proud of their accomplishment, some of the 15,000 yard workers pose along the hull's towering side. (*Belfast Telegraph*)

Left *Olympic* is dry-docked, and the blade from her port wing propeller is replaced. (Harland & Wolff collection, Ulster Folk and Transport Museum)

Friday, 1 March 1912

OLYMPIC ARRIVES AT Harland & Wolff for the replacement of a blade on her port propeller that was lost on 24 February during an eastbound Atlantic crossing. Windy conditions prevent her from mooring at the yard until Saturday, 2 March.

Wednesday, 6 March 1912

FOLLOWING THE propeller blade replacement, *Olympic* is moved from the dry dock and *Titanic* is taken from the deep water wharf and floated into the dry dock. *Olympic* then moors at the deep water wharf to provide turning space for a bow first departure.

   Begun at 9.30am, the operation takes 2½ hours. Captain Edward J. Smith commands *Olympic*, while Captain Charles A. Bartlett, White Star's marine superintendent, is on *Titanic*'s bridge.

Thursday, 7 March 1912

OLYMPIC DEPARTS HARLAND & Wolff on the morning's high tide. Aboard *Titanic*, still in the graving dock, George Stewart, aged 22, is injured while operating a crane. He is taken to the Royal Victoria Hospital for treatment.

Above right *Olympic* and *Titanic* exchange docks. (Bob Forrest collection)

Right *Titanic* in the graving dock. (Authors' collection)

Wednesday, 20 March 1912

FIRST OFFICER Charles H. Lightoller comes aboard *Titanic*, having been transferred from the *Oceanic*.

Monday, 25 March 1912

TITANIC'S SIGNAL letters – HVMP – are assigned by the Board of Trade, and the final BOT inspection takes place at the Queen's Island yard; *Titanic*'s anchor and all 16 lifeboats under davits are tested to the satisfaction of the Board of Trade's surveyor, Francis Carruthers.

At Southampton, Captain Herbert J. Haddock, a senior White Star Line captain, signs on as *Titanic*'s master.

Wednesday, 27 March 1912

Joseph Groves Boxhall, Herbert John Pitman, Harold Godfrey Lowe and James Paul Moody report aboard.

Titanic's hull is insured for £1,000,000 ($5,000,000) at a premium cost of £20,000 ($100,000) against damage or loss during her sea trials. The Atlantic Mutual Insurance Company is the largest American insurer, underwriting $100,000 (£20,000) of the total.

Although still in need of final details, the luxurious amenities for *Titanic*'s First Class passengers are now near completion. The Palm Court (from *Olympic*, top), with its doors open to the smoke room, and the à la carte restaurant (also from *Olympic*, above) will be finished at Southampton during the week before the maiden voyage. (Harland & Wolff collection, Ulster Folk & Transport Museum)

Left *Titanic*'s hull is insured. (Atlantic Mutual Insurance Companies)

Friday, 29 March 1912

A BELFAST CREW of 79 firemen, stokers and others is signed on for sea trials and the visit to Southampton on Saturday, 30 March 1912.

A select number of guests, mostly journalists, are granted an inspection trip aboard the moored *Titanic* in Belfast.

Sunday, 31 March 1912

TITANIC IS SWUNG around to face seaward.

Monday, 1 April 1912

THE TRIALS ARE postponed within an hour of the scheduled departure time, due to windy weather.

At Belfast, Captain Edward John Smith formally takes over command of *Titanic* from Captain Herbert J. Haddock.

Top left A drawing for a 1912 Colman's Mustard advertisement depicting *Titanic*'s deluxe, extra-charge restaurant as it will appear once in operation. (Authors' collection)

Top right The sea trials crew sign on. (Public Record Office of Northern Ireland TRANS 2A/45/381C)

Middle *Titanic* faces seaward, having been turned during the night of 31 March. However, the morning of 1 April finds a stiff breeze that cancels the departure for trials. (Authors' collection)

Right On 1 April the trials are postponed. (*Daily Sketch*)

Tuesday, 2 April 1912

TITANIC DEPARTS QUEEN'S Island at 6am, assisted by the tugs *Huskisson*, *Herculaneum*, *Hornby* and *Herald*. Aboard are 41 officers and senior crew, and several Harland & Wolff officials including Thomas Andrews and his assistant, Edward Wilding. Harold Sanderson represents the owner, and Francis Carruthers the Board of Trade. Below are 78 boiler room crew, one having deserted during the one-day delay.

After the tugs cast off, trials are conducted in Belfast Lough: a series of start-and-stop tests and circle turnings of several diameters, then finally a 40-mile trip down the Irish Sea to test *Titanic*'s sea-going capabilities.

Returning to Belfast around 6pm, the new liner is certified by the Board of Trade ('good until 1 April 1913') and turned over by her builder to her new owner.

After taking aboard some additional kitchen equipment and some special chairs for the First Class reception area, as well as fresh food supplies, *Titanic* departs Belfast a few minutes after 8pm.

Titanic undergoes sea trials. (Public Record Office of Northern Ireland D/2460/42B/ David F. Hutchings collection/Private collection)

THREE

THE INLAND VOYAGE: SOUTHAMPTON, CHERBOURG AND QUEENSTOWN

Wednesday, 3 April 1912

SOME 570 MILES are logged between Belfast and Southampton. During the passage *Titanic* reaches a speed of 23¼ knots, the highest she would ever attain.

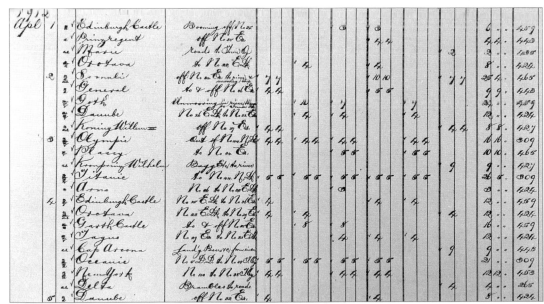

Top left A respected shipping newspaper's columns erroneously report that on 10 April *Titanic*'s departure point will be Liverpool. (*Liverpool Gazette*)

Top right During the crossing from Belfast to Queenstown, Marconi operators Jack Phillips and Harold Bride are constantly at work, fine tuning the wireless apparatus. Freak atmospheric conditions enable them to communicate with Tenerife, more than 2,000 miles away, and with Port Said, more than 3,000 miles distant. (Authors' collection)

Right Under the date 3 April 1912, the Alexandra Towing Company's log shows the tugs used in *Olympic*'s departure from Southampton, and those despatched to service *Titanic*'s midnight arrival there. (Red Funnel Group)

Thursday, 4 April 1912

SHORTLY AFTER midnight, assisted by five Red Funnel tugs, *Titanic* moors at Berth 44 at the White Star Dock at Southampton. During the forenoon Henry Tingle Wilde, *Olympic*'s chief officer, reports aboard at Captain Smith's request. Wilde, though not yet a member of *Titanic*'s staff, is assigned general supervisory duties in preparing the ship for sailing.

Friday, 5 April 1912

GOOD FRIDAY. *TITANIC* is decked out in flags, dressed as a salute to the citizens of Southampton who, because of the urgent need to complete interior decoration and sailing arrangements, are not allowed to visit the vessel. The liner is heeled as part of the stability test required by the Board of Trade.

Top The morning light of 4 April brings with it a view of the arrangement of *Titanic*'s stern mooring lines. (Authors' collection)

Left In this photo taken during *Titanic*'s stay at Southampton, workers put the finishing touches of paint to the liner's two forward funnels. The ship's wireless antenna has been retouched for emphasis. Early in the morning the ship would be dressed – her flags strung out her entire length. (Authors' collection)

Below Good Friday: *Titanic* is again decked in flags. (Authors' collection)

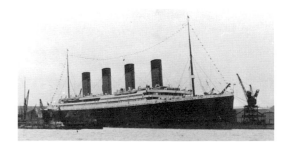

Saturday, 6 April 1912

RECRUITMENT OF general crew for all departments begins in the union hiring halls in Southampton. Following a prolonged coal strike that had idled most ships, positions aboard *Titanic* are highly sought-after.

Between the date of her arrival at Southampton and the morning of her departure, *Titanic* takes aboard supplies and cargo.

Ship's and catering department's stores are drawn from White Star's vast storage facilities near the dock as well as goods received at the dockside.

In accordance with prevailing custom, automobiles are usually dismantled and crated. This is probably the way First Class passenger William Carter's red 35hp Renault touring car (similar to that at right) was loaded — the only car aboard *Titanic*. (Authors' collection/Courtesy of Michael Malamatenious)

Far right *Titanic* is moored at Berth 44 in Southampton. Two weeks later chief officer Henry T. Wilde's premonition would prove correct. (Bob Forrest collection)

Tuesday, 9 April 1912

HENRY TINGLE WILDE is appointed *Titanic*'s chief officer by White Star's Marine Superintendent Captain Charles A. Bartlett. *Titanic*'s former chief, William Murdoch, and first officer Charles Lightoller are reduced one rank. Second officer David Blair is transferred out; he returns to *Oceanic*.

David Blair, shown later in his career, is moved from his position as *Titanic*'s second officer when Wilde is appointed chief officer. (*White Star Magazine*)

Wednesday, 10 April 1912

6.00am: *Titanic*'s crew begin to come aboard.
7.30am: Captain Edward J. Smith comes aboard, as does the Board of Trade inspector Maurice Clarke.
8.00am: *Titanic*'s flag, the Blue Ensign, is hoisted at the stern as the crew commences its muster and signs the Articles of Agreement, the standard employment contract.
9.00am: A standard lifeboat drill is held. In keeping with Board of Trade regulations, two boats are manned, swung out and lowered: Starboard 11, with fifth officer Harold Lowe in charge, and Starboard 15, with sixth officer

Sailing Day! A toilet soap advertisement appearing in a publication on the same date celebrates the event. (Authors' collection)

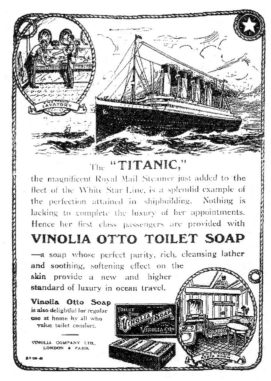

At 9am on the morning of sailing, ocean mails are delivered to the pier under supervision of Post Office officials, and are hoisted aboard in cargo slings to be stowed in the ship's post office sorting rooms. (*White Star Magazine*)

James Paul Moody in charge. The drill is completed by 9.30am.
9.30am: The boat train carrying Second and Third Class passengers from London arrives alongside *Titanic*. Passengers begin embarkation through separate gangways and entrances.
11.15am: Trinity House pilot George Bowyer reports aboard and goes to the bridge to consult with Captain Smith and his officers.
11.30am: The First Class passengers' boat train from London's Waterloo station arrives at the dockside, and its passengers embark.
Noon: Moments after midday *Titanic* slips her mooring and leaves the pier,

Below For more than a week, *Titanic*'s huge funnels had towered over her Southampton pier. Now it is Sailing Day, and the ship's triple-chambered whistles announce in their mighty voices the hour of departure. (Authors' collection)

Right The tug *Vulcan* (centre) struggles to pull the wayward *New York*'s stern away from *Titanic*'s side. (*L'Illustration*)

Middle right Another tug pushes *Titanic* outward. Spectators lean forward, expecting a collision. (*Daily Mirror*)

Below right Another view of the near collision. (Southern Newspapers plc)

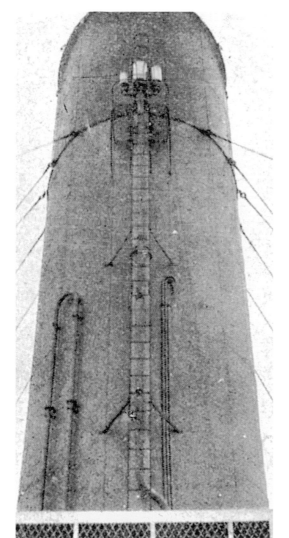

assisted by six Red Funnel tugs. A near collision with the American Line vessel *New York*, caused by displacement of water as *Titanic* passed, is narrowly averted by quick thinking on the part of Captain Gale, master of the tug *Vulcan*. *Titanic*'s departure is delayed by almost an hour as the wayward *New York* is cleared. When *Titanic* departs

Above Quick thinking avoided the collision. (Authors' collection)

Left Delayed about an hour by the *New York* incident, *Titanic* at last moves slowly into Southampton Water on her way to Cherbourg. (*Daily Graphic*)

Below For some 31 *Titanic* passengers, the voyage aboard the world's largest liner terminates in Cherbourg or Queenstown. Known as the 'Cross Channel' passengers, their names appear on the liner's ticketing list. They are accompanied by two dogs and a canary. (National Archives and Records Administration – New York Branch)

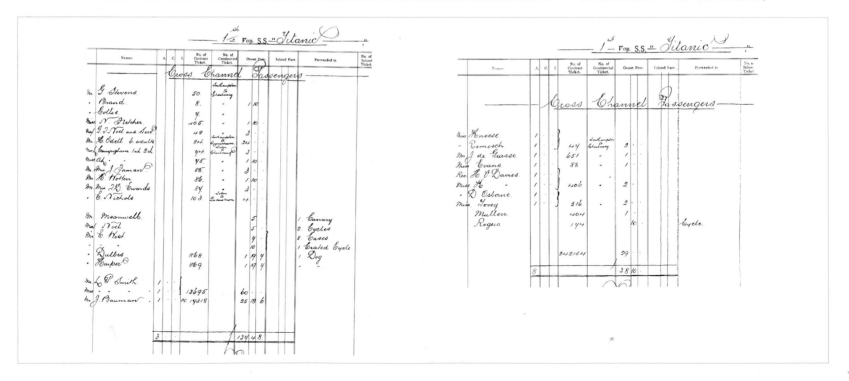

Southampton she has aboard a total of 1,846 persons, including 24 'Cross Channel' passengers to Cherbourg and seven staying aboard only as far as Queenstown.

A fire in coal bunker number 6 that began when coal was taken aboard at Belfast has smouldered ever since, including the entire period that *Titanic* is at Southampton. Crewmen have been assigned round the clock at Southampton in an effort to extinguish it, and they are still at work as the liner sails. *Titanic* passes down Southampton Water and rounds the Isle of Wight via the Spithead route. Although the pilot vessel is routinely at its station, descendants of pilot George Bowyer state that he does not leave *Titanic* until she reaches Cherbourg.

6.35pm: The late afternoon sun fills the sky as *Titanic* arrives at Cherbourg and anchors beyond the breakwater, having logged 88 miles. Via White Star's tenders *Nomadic* and *Traffic*, 15 First and nine Second Class passengers are disembarked, as is Southampton pilot George Bowyer; 142 First, 30 Second and 102 Third Class passengers are taken aboard.

8.10pm: *Titanic* departs Cherbourg for Queenstown, gliding off the Grande Rade, through the west passage and into the English Channel.

Top Gare St Lazare, Paris, is the starting point for the boat train to Cherbourg via the (French) Western State Railway. (Authors' collection)

Middle The boat train departs Paris at 9.40am and arrives at Cherbourg at 3.45pm. (Authors' collection)

Right After a journey of 6 hours the boat train arrives at Cherbourg's Gare Maritime, alongside the simple terminal building. (Authors' collection)

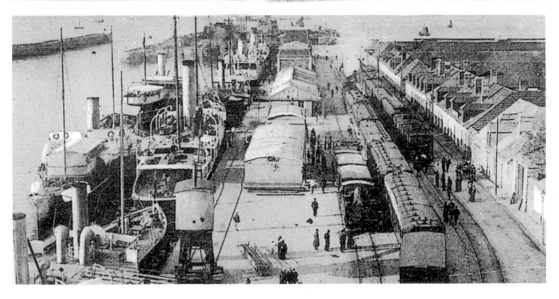

Until recently, it was believed that *Titanic* arrived at Cherbourg in darkness. This 1912 postcard demonstrates clearly that the rays of the early evening sun lit her first moments in the French port. (Authors' collection)

Once formalities have been concluded, *Titanic*'s First and Second Class passengers board the tender *Nomadic* (seen to the left of the station building) for the journey to *Titanic*, lying beyond the breakwater (seen in the distance). (Authors' collection)

Nomadic carrying troops during the First World War. (Authors' collection)

Third Class passengers embark aboard the smaller, simpler tender *Traffic*. (Authors' collection)

As embarkation of the continental passengers continues, smoke issues from the fourth funnel, indicating that the galley stoves are in operation during the dinner hour. The lights of the harbour's breakwater are visible in the background. (Bob Forrest collection)

After a stay of less than 2 hours, the glittering liner departs Cherbourg for Queenstown. (Authors' collection)

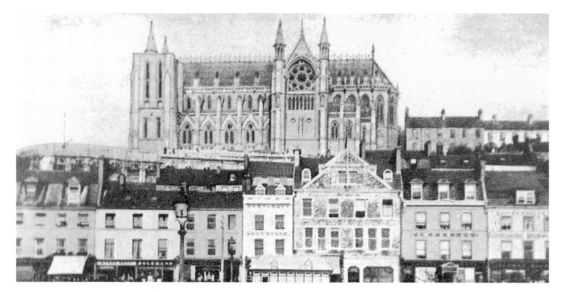

Thursday, 11 April 1912

TITANIC CROSSES THE English Channel, rounds Land's End, proceeds up Sl George's Channel and takes aboard the Queenstown pilot at the Daunt's lightship.

Top St Colman's Cathedral dominates the Queenstown skyline. (Authors' collection)

Left Too large to enter Queenstown Harbour, *Titanic* anchors about 2 miles off Roche's Point, and awaits the arrival of the tenders. (Authors' collection)

Below left Because the boat train is slightly late, the tenders *America* and *Ireland* (shown here) leave their usual docking position at the White Star wharf, Scott's Quay, and instead embark *Titanic*'s passengers alongside Queenstown's railway station. (Authors' collection)

Below The tender *Ireland* begins its half-hour journey to *Titanic*'s side. (Authors' collection)

11.30am: The new White Star liner arrives at Queenstown, anchoring off Roche's Point. She has logged 315 miles on her journey.

Via the Clyde Shipping Company's Queenstown tenders *America* and *Ireland*, seven First Class passengers disembark. *Titanic* then takes aboard seven Second Class and 113 Third Class passengers together with 194 sacks of mail for America. One crewman, fireman John Coffey, a Queenstown native, deserts.

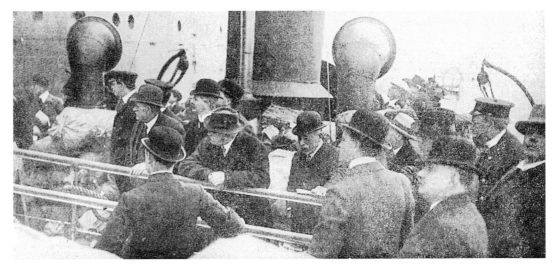

Top A gangway is rigged from the tender's deck to *Titanic*'s lower entranceway in Queenstown Harbour. (*Cork Examiner*)

Middle left Hugh McElroy, purser, and Captain Edward J. Smith oblige a newspaper photographer who boards the liner at Queenstown for a brief visit. (Private collection)

Middle right Second Officer Charles Lightoller supervises as several seamen prepare to seal the gangway door for the last time. (*Cork Examiner*)

Right *Titanic*'s screws turn as she begins to leave Queenstown. (*Cork Examiner*)

As *Titanic* departs, Third Class passenger Eugene Daly goes to the stern and plays the dirge 'Erin's Lament' on his bagpipes. (*Cork Examiner*)

After the ship's departure, the Board of Trade's Survey of an Emigrant Ship is filed at Queenstown, clearances having been given while the ship was at Belfast and Southampton. (Crown Copyright material in the Public Record Office, reproduced by permission of the Controller of Her Majesty's Stationery Office; PRO MT9/920/4 M23780)

1.30pm: *Titanic* departs Queenstown for New York. Aboard (as best as can be determined) are 324 First Class passengers, 284 Second Class passengers, 709 Third Class passengers and 908 crew (those engaged in any working capacity). The total complement of 2,225 represents just two-thirds of the ship's capacity.

Titanic has been designated a 'Royal Mail Ship' by British and American postal authorities. As she departs Queenstown she has on board 1,758 bags of mail loaded at Southampton, 1,412 loaded at Cherbourg and 194 loaded at Queenstown, a total of 3,364.

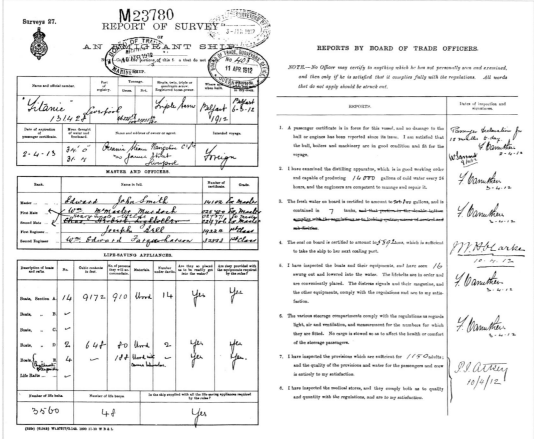

FOUR

THE ATLANTIC CROSSING

Friday, 12 April 1912

TITANIC LOGS 386 MILES between noon on Thursday 11 April and noon on Friday 12 April. The following routine was observed daily (except Sunday) aboard all White Star Line ships while at sea:

9.00am: Inspection of crew and all compartments by department heads.
10.00am: Department heads report to Captain Smith in his quarters.
10.30am: The Captain inspects the entire vessel, 'bridge to engine room'.

Noon (including Sundays): The ship's whistles and engine room telegraphs are tested.

Aboard *Titanic*, the routine is varied slightly, the 9.00am daily inspection lasting until 11.00am.

Right North Atlantic lane routes had been established by an agreement between the principal steamship companies dated January 1899. (National Archives and Records Administration – New York Branch)

NORTH ATLANTIC LANE ROUTES

As agreed to by the principal Steamship Companies, take effect from January 15th, 1899, and now issued general information.

WESTBOUND.

FROM 15th JANUARY TO 14th AUGUST, BOTH DAYS INCLUSIVE.

Steer from Fastnet, or Bishop Rock, on GREAT CIRCLE course, but nothing South, to cross the meridian of 47° West in Latitude 42° North, thence by either *rhumb line*, or Great Circle (or even North of the Great Circle, if an easterly current is encountered), to a position South of Nantucket Light-Vessel, thence to Fire Island Light-Vessel, when bound for New York, or to Five Fathom Bank South Light-Vessel, when bound for Philadelphia.

FROM 15th AUGUST TO 14th JANUARY, BOTH DAYS INCLUSIVE.

Steer from Fastnet, or Bishop Rock, on GREAT CIRCLE course, but nothing South, to cross the meridian of 49° West in Latitude 46° North, thence by *rhumb line*, to cross the meridian of 60° West in Latitude 43° North, thence also by *rhumb line*, to a position South of Nantucket Light-Vessel, thence to Fire Island Light-Vessel, when bound to New York, or Five Fathom Bank South Light-Vessel, when bound for Philadelphia.

EASTBOUND.

At all seasons of the year, steer a course from Sandy Hook Light-Vessel, or Five Fathom Bank South Light-Vessel, to cross the meridian of 70° West, nothing to the northward of Lat. 40° 10'.

FROM 15th JANUARY TO 23rd AUGUST, BOTH DAYS INCLUSIVE.

Steer from 40° 10' North, and 70° West, by *rhumb line*, to cross the meridian of 47° West in Latitude 41° North, and from this last position nothing North of the GREAT CIRCLE to Fastnet, when bound to the Irish Channel, or nothing North of the GREAT CIRCLE to Bishop Rock, when bound to the English Channel.

FROM 24th AUGUST TO 14th JANUARY, BOTH DAYS INCLUSIVE.

Steer from Latitude 40° 10' North and Longitude 70° West, to cross the meridian of 60° West in Latitude 42° 0' North, thence by *rhumb line* to cross the meridian of 45° West in Latitude 46° 30' North, and from this last position nothing North of the GREAT CIRCLE to Fastnet, when bound to the Irish Channel, and as near as possible to, but nothing North of the GREAT CIRCLE to Bishop Rock, always keeping South of the Latitude of Bishop Rock, when bound to the English Channel.

GENERAL INSTRUCTION.

When courses are changed at the intersections of meridians any time before or after noon, you will note in your logs both distances to and from the meridians, that the ship has sailed from noon to noon, and not the distance from the position at noon the day before to the position at noon the day after the meridian is crossed.

N.A.O. page 559.

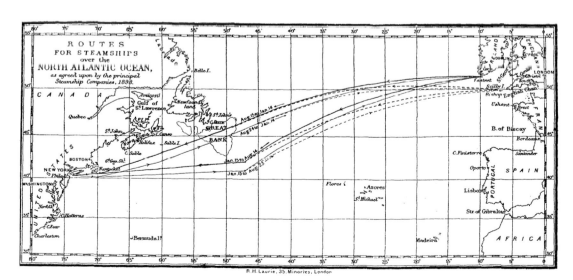

ROUTES FOR STEAMSHIPS over the NORTH ATLANTIC OCEAN, as agreed upon by the principal Steamship Companies, 1898.

R.H.Laurie, 35, Minories, London

Left In 1912, because of severe ice conditions, these lanes are shifted further south than those shown. (National Archives and Records Administration – New York Branch)

11.00am: A wireless message is received by *Titanic* from the eastbound *Empress of Britain* (wireless call letters 'MPB') reporting ice at 43°28'N, 49°36'W.

Noon: *Titanic*'s whistles and telegraphs are tested.

8.00pm: A wireless message received from the eastbound French liner *La Touraine* (wireless call letters 'MLT') describes an ice field and two large bergs in a path ahead and directly along *Titanic*'s course.

11.00pm: At about this time *Titanic*'s wireless apparatus fails due to a problem in the secondary circuit. The problem is corrected shortly before 5am on Saturday, 13 April.

Saturday, 13 April 1912

TITANIC LOGS 519 miles from noon on Friday 12 April to noon on Saturday 13 April.

9.00–11.00am: Daily inspection takes place.

Noon: The ship's whistles and telegraphs are tested.

Left At 11am on 12 April the Canadian-Pacific liner *Empress of Britain* sends an ice warning to *Titanic*. (Authors' collection)

Below *La Touraine* of the Compagnie Générale Transatlantique. (Authors' collection)

Right White Star's company regulations emphasise safety of operation. A copy of these regulations is posted in the wheelhouse of each company ship. (National Archives and Records Administration – New York Branch)

Below right As required by White Star Line regulations, Captain Smith conducts a daily inspection of his vessel between 9.00 and 11.00am. He is shown here leading an inspection aboard his earlier command, *Adriatic*. (Authors' collection)

WHITE STAR LINE.

The Managers are desirous of impressing upon Commanders the importance of strictly adhering to the Company's Regulations, and attention is particularly called to the following points:—

1.—The vital importance of exercising the utmost caution in Navigation, *safety outweighing every other consideration.*

2.—*Over-confidence*, a most fruitful source of accident, should be especially guarded against.

3.—It cannot be too strongly borne in mind that any serious accident affects prejudicially not only the welfare of the Company, but also the prospects and livelihood of the Commanders and Officers of the Ships; and, as every consideration is shown to those placed in positions of responsibility, the Company relies upon faithful and efficient service being given in return, so that the possibility of accidents may be reduced to a minimum. The Company assumes the entire risk of insurance on its vessels, their freights, and on a considerable portion of the cargoes carried by them; whilst the large sum which is paid annually to its Officers as a bonus for absolute immunity from accidents is additional evidence of anxiety to subordinate all other considerations to the paramount one of *safety in navigation.*

4.—No thought of making competitive passages must be entertained, and time must be sacrificed or any other temporary inconvenience suffered, rather than the slightest risk should be incurred.

5.—Commanders should be on deck and in full charge during Thick Weather, in Narrow Waters, or when near the Land. A wide berth must be given to all Headlands, Shoals, and other positions of Peril; cross bearings must be taken wherever possible, *and the use of the ordinary deep sea lead* not neglected when approaching land in thick or doubtful weather, more particularly in view of the fact that signals on shore are not always reliable.

6.—The attention of Commanders is particularly directed to Articles 16 and 23 of the "Regulations for preventing Collisions at Sea," viz:—

Article 16.—Every Ship shall, in a Fog, Mist, Falling Snow, or Heavy Rain Storms, go at a moderate speed, having careful regard to the existing circumstances and conditions.

Article 23.—Every Steam Ship, which is directed by these rules to keep out of the way of another vessel, shall, on approaching her, if necessary, slacken her speed, or stop or reverse.

7.—The Regulations as to Inspection of Watertight Doors, and Fire and Boat Drill are to be carefully observed; Rigid discipline amongst Officers maintained and the Crew kept under judicious control. Convivial intercourse with Passengers is to be avoided.

8.—It is expected that all details connected with the working of the Steamers will be mastered by the Commanders, and any suggestions tending to improvement are invited, and will receive every consideration.

LIVERPOOL, *Jan* 1st, 1901.   MANAGERS.

Chief Engineer Joseph Bell. (*The Truth About the Titanic*)

Between noon and 1pm: Chief engineer Bell reports to Captain Smith that the fire in coal bunker 6 has been extinguished.

10.30pm: Morse signals are exchanged with the eastbound steamer *Rappahannock*, which reports that an extensive ice field lies ahead, along *Titanic*'s course. The message is acknowledged by Morse lamp from *Titanic*'s bridge.

Sunday, 14 April 1912

TITANIC LOGS 546 miles between noon on Saturday 13 April and noon on Sunday 14 April.

9.00–11.00am: Daily inspection takes place.

Between 9.00 and 11.40am *Titanic* is in wireless contact with the eastbound *Caronia* (wireless call letters 'MBA'), which transmits a report relayed by the eastbound *Noordam* ('MHA') describing ice at 42° extending from 49° to 40"W, directly ahead in

Titanic's path. The message is delivered to Captain Smith, who posts it on the bridge for his officers.

10.30am: Captain Smith leads divine services in the First Class dining saloon.
Noon: The ship's whistles and telegraphs are tested.
1.42pm: A message is received from the westbound Greek steamer *Athinai* ('MTI'), relayed by the eastbound *Baltic* ('MBC'), warning of ice in the vicinity of 41°45'N, 49°52'W. Delivery of this message to the bridge is delayed while Bruce Ismay, to whom Captain Smith has handed the message, keeps it to show several friends, until around 7.10pm, when the Captain requests its return.

Officers' Watches aboard *Titanic*

	Time	Senior Officer	Junior Officers
(13 April)	Noon - 1 pm	First Officer William M. Murdoch	Fourth Officer Joseph G. Boxhall / Sixth Officer James P. Moody
	1 pm - 2 pm		
	2 pm - 3 pm		
	3 pm - 4 pm	Chief Officer Henry T. Wilde	Third Officer Herbert G. Pitman / Fifth Officer Harold G. Lowe
	4 pm - 5 pm		
	5 pm - 6 pm		Fourth Officer Joseph G. Boxhall / Sixth Officer James P. Moody
	6 pm - 7 pm		
	7 pm - 8 pm	Second Officer Charles H. Lightoller	
	8 pm - 9 pm		Third Officer Herbert G. Pitman / Fifth Officer Harold G. Lowe
	9 pm - 10 pm		
	10 pm - 11 pm		
	11 pm - Midnight	First Officer William M. Murdoch	
14 April	Midnight - 1 am		Fourth Officer Joseph G. Boxhall / Sixth Officer James P. Moody
	1 am - 2 am		
	2 am - 3 am		
	3 am - 4 am	Chief Officer Henry T. Wilde	
	4 am - 5 am		
	5 am - 6 am		Third Officer Herbert G. Pitman / Fifth Officer Harold G. Lowe
	6 am - 7 am		
	7 am - 8 am	Second Officer Charles H. Lightoller	
	8 am - 9 am		Fourth Officer Joseph G. Boxhall / Sixth Officer James P. Moody
	9 am - 10 am		
	10 am - 11 am		
	11 am - Noon	First Officer William M. Murdoch	
	Noon - 1 pm		Third Officer Herbert G. Pitman / Fifth Officer Harold G. Lowe
	1 pm - 2 pm		
	2 pm - 3 pm		
	3 pm - 4 pm	Chief Officer Henry T. Wilde	Fourth Officer Joseph G. Boxhall / Sixth Officer James P. Moody
	4 pm - 5 pm		
	5 pm - 6 pm		
	6 pm - 7 pm		Third Officer Herbert G. Pitman / Fifth Officer Harold G. Lowe
	7 pm - 8 pm	Second Officer Charles H. Lightoller	
	8 pm - 9 pm		Fourth Officer Joseph G. Boxhall / Sixth Officer James P. Moody
	9 pm - 10 pm		
	10 pm - 11 pm		
	11 pm - Midnight	First Officer William M. Murdoch	
15 April	Midnight - 1 am		Third Officer Herbert G. Pitman / Fifth Officer Harold G. Lowe
	1 am - 2 am		
	2 am - 3 am		
	3 am - 4 am	Chief Officer Henry T. Wilde	
	4 am - 5 am		
	5 am - 6 am		

'Regular sea watches must be kept from the time the ship leaves the port of departure until she reaches the port of arrival.' (Ship's Rules, White Star Line)

The division of the watches is specified by company regulations. (Authors' collection)

Cunard Line's *Caronia* and Holland-America Line's *Noordam*. (Authors' collection)

Afternoon: The eastbound British steamer *Portland*, with no wireless aboard, reports at a later date that during the afternoon of 14 April she sighted *Titanic* but did not signal.

In a transmission to the United States Hydrographic Office, Washington DC, *Titanic* relays a wireless message from the German liner *Amerika* warning of icebergs. The position of the ice described in the message lies south of *Titanic*'s course.

5.50pm: A few minutes earlier than anticipated, *Titanic* reaches 42°N, 47°W, a navigation reference point called 'The Corner', and alters course from S62'W to S86°W, with a compass heading of N71'W ('S86° true').

7.00pm: The air temperature is 43°F. Around this time, soon after sunset, the shutters in the wheelhouse are closed so that the compass light and light from the course board within the wheelhouse will not interfere with the night vision of those on the bridge.

7.15pm: *Baltic*'s ice warning is finally posted on the bridge by Captain Smith. First officer Murdoch orders lamp-trimmer Samuel Hemming to secure the forward hatch cover and the skylight over the crew's galley to prevent any glow from interfering with the crow's nest watch.

7.30pm: The air temperature has dropped to 39°F.

The Leyland freighter *Californian* ('MWL') transmits a report of ice at 42°3'N, 49°9'W to its fleet mate *Antillian*. The transmission is overheard by *Titanic*.

At about 7.35pm, second officer Lightoller, as officer of the watch, assisted by third officer Pitman, takes a set of stellar observations, which are then written on a chit, attached to the

HYDROGRAPHIC OFFICE,
WASHINGTON, D. C.

DAILY MEMORANDUM

No. 1013.   April 15, 1912.

NORTH ATLANTIC OCEAN

OBSTRUCTIONS OFF THE AMERICAN COAST.

Mar. 28 – Lat 24° 20', lon 80° 02', passed a broken spar projecting about 3 feet out of water, apparently attached to sunken wreckage.—EVELYN (Sb) Wright.

OBSTRUCTIONS ALONG THE OVER-SEA ROUTES.

Apr 7 – Lat 35° 20', lon 59° 40', saw a lowermast covered with marine growth.—ADRIATICO (It. ss), Cevasou.

ICE REPORTS.

Apr 7 – Lat 45° 10', lon 56° 40', ran into a strip of field ice about 3 or 4 miles wide extending north and south as far as could be seen.   Some very heavy pans were seen.—ROSALIND (Br ss), Williams.

Apr 10 – Lat 41° 50', lon 50 25', passed a large ice field a few hundred feet wide and 15 miles long extending in a NNE direction.—EXCELSIOR (Ger ss), (New York Herald)

COLLISION WITH ICEBERG – Apr 14 – Lat 41° 46', lon 50° 14', the British steamer TITANIC collided with an iceberg seriously damaging her bow; extent not definitely known.

Apr 14 – The German steamer AMERIKA reported by radio telegraph passing two large icebergs in lat 41° 27', lon 50° 08'.—TITANIC (Br ss).

Apr 14 – Lat 42° 06', lon 49° 43', encountered extensive field ice and saw seven icebergs of considerable size.—PISA (Ger ss).

J. J. KNAPP

Captain, U. S. Navy
Hydrographer.

R.M.S. "TITANIC."

APRIL 14, 1912

HORS D'ŒUVRE VARIÈS
OYSTERS

CONSOMMÉ OLGA   CREAM OF BARLEY

SALMON, MOUSSELINE SAUCE, CUCUMBER

FILET MIGNONS LILI
SAUTÉ OF CHICKEN, LYONNAISE
VEGETABLE MARROW FARCIE

LAMB, MINT SAUCE
ROAST DUCKLING, APPLE SAUCE
SIRLOIN OF BEEF CHATEAU POTATOES

GREEN PEAS   CREAMED CARROTS
BOILED RICE
PARMENTIER & BOILED NEW POTATOES

PUNCH ROMAINE

ROAST SQUAB & CRESS
COLD ASPARAGUS VINAIGRETTE
PÂTE DE FOIE GRAS

Above *Amerika*'s ice report is distributed to other vessels the following day; the report also contains news of *Titanic*'s collision with an iceberg. (National Oceanic and Atmospheric Administration)

Above *Titanic*'s First Class passengers enjoy a luxurious meal. (*Daily Mirror*)

Below *Amerika*'s wireless message relayed by *Titanic*. (Joseph A. Carvalho collection)

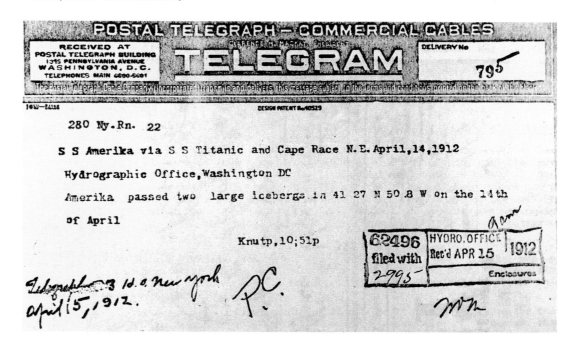

POSTAL TELEGRAPH – COMMERCIAL CABLES

TELEGRAM

RECEIVED AT
POSTAL TELEGRAPH BUILDING
1315 PENNSYLVANIA AVENUE
WASHINGTON, D. C.
TELEPHONES MAIN 6600-6601

DELIVERY No

795

280 Ny. Rn. 22

S S Amerika via S S Titanic and Cape Race N.E. April, 14, 1912

Hydrographic Office, Washington DC

Amerika passed two large icebergs in 41 27 N 50.8 W on the 14th

of April

Knutp, 10;51p

62496
filed with
2-995

HYDRO. OFFICE
Rec'd APR 15 1912
Enclosures

navigation chart and tacked on to the chart later in the evening by Captain Smith. (During the subsequent American and British investigations, no one could recall the 7.35pm position.)

8.00pm: On the bridge, fourth officer Joseph Boxhall and sixth officer James Moody report for their 4-hour watch; third officer Herbert Pitman and fifth officer Harold Lowe go off watch.

8.30pm: In the Second Class dining saloon, a 'hymn sing-song' is conducted by Rev Ernest Courtenay Carter, vicar of St Jude's Parish in London's East End. Some 100 passengers participate; a young Scottish engineer, Robert Douglas Norman, provides piano accompaniment. Among the hymns is 'Eternal Father, Strong to Save', whose soon-to-be-prophetic refrain includes the words 'Oh, hear us when we cry to Thee for those in peril on the sea'.

8.40pm: As officer of the watch, Lightoller orders the ship's carpenter, John Maxwell, to attend to the fresh water supply lest it freeze.

8.55pm: Captain Smith arrives on the bridge from a dinner party he has attended in the à la carte restaurant. He converses with Lightoller and checks the navigational data.

9.00pm: The air temperature has dropped another degree, and is now 33°F.

9.20pm: Captain Smith retires to his cabin after leaving word to be called immediately at the first appearance of haze.

9.30pm: Lightoller sends a message to the lookouts in the crow's nest to be alert for ice throughout the night.

9.40pm: *Mesaba* ('MMV'), westbound, transmits an ice warning addressed to *Titanic* describing ice 42°N to 41°25'N, and 40°W to 49°09'W. Because of the volume of commercial traffic being handled by *Titanic*'s wireless operators,

Antillian. (Authors' collection)

the message is spiked and never sent to the bridge.

10.00pm: The air temperature is 32°F. First officer Murdoch relieves second officer Lightoller as officer of the watch. Lee and Fleet relieve Jewell and Symons in the crow's nest. Inside the shuttered wheelhouse, quartermaster

Mesaba. (Authors' collection)

Lookout Frederick Fleet. (*Washington Evening Star*)

Robert Hichens relieves quartermaster Alfred Olliver at the wheel.

10.55pm: Stopped in ice at 42°5'N, 50°7'W, north of *Titanic*'s course, the Leyland freighter *Californian* ('MWL')

transmits an ice warning to *Titanic*. *Californian*'s wireless operator, Cyril Evans, is cut off by *Titanic*'s senior operator, John George Phillips, before the position is transmitted.

11.40pm: Through a slight haze on the horizon, lookout Frederick Fleet spots something 'about the size of two tables' directly ahead. It quickly resolves itself into an iceberg. He immediately sounds the crow's nest bell three times, and telephones the bridge, where sixth officer James P. Moody takes the call and relays the message 'Iceberg right ahead' to the officer of the watch, William Murdoch.

Murdoch orders the engines full astern and the helm hard astarboard to make a hard port turn around the berg. (Quartermaster Hichens, at the wheel, later testifies that he was never given an order to countermand the 'hard astarboard' position of the ship's wheel.) Murdoch also quickly activates the lever that closes the liner's watertight doors.

Titanic brushes against an iceberg at a position hastily and tentatively identified as 41°46'N, 50°14'W. At a speed of approximately 20 knots, contact lasts for about 10 seconds, enough time to tear a series of six intermittent stabs and punctures extending along almost 250ft of the liner's forward starboard plating about 15ft above the keel, and breaking off rivet heads, permitting the sea to enter through the seams. Seawater enters the vessel's forepeak, number 1 hold, number 2 hold, number 3 hold (mail and baggage hold), and number 6 boiler room, and penetrates about 6ft beyond the bulkhead of number 5 boiler room.

Murdoch instantly orders standby quartermaster Olliver to note the time of the collision, then orders Moody to enter the time in the ship's log.

Boxhall, who has briefly left the bridge to visit the officers' quarters, returns to the bridge at the moment of impact.

FIVE

DISASTER

BETWEEN *TITANIC*'S COLLISION with the iceberg and transmission of the first wireless distress signals, many diverse activities ensued aboard the doomed liner. Of *Titanic*'s surviving officers, fourth officer Joseph Groves Boxhall, in testimony at both the American and British inquiries, provided the most detailed description of responses in and around the bridge to the emergent condition.

When pressed at the British inquiry, Boxhall was reluctant to state the specific times when the first 20 or 30 minutes' actions had occurred. But to Boxhall's statements can be added those of quartermasters Rowe and Olliver, owner J. Bruce Ismay, and officers Lightoller and Pitman, all elicited under oath at Washington and London.

If time intervals appear brief it should be borne in mind that activities and their sequence are based upon sworn testimony. Due consideration has been given to shipboard distances, and when necessary the time intervals have been maximised to account for these. With the distinct probability that specific events occurred at different relative times aboard *Titanic* and *Californian*, it is difficult to understand why this factor was not examined more closely during both the American and British hearings. The only basis for estimating these relative times is, again, sworn testimony.

What happened is factual. When it happened can be variable. As Walter Lord so aptly states in *A Night to Remember*, 'It is a rash man indeed who would set himself up as the final arbiter of all that happened on that incredible night that *Titanic* went down.'

IN THE FOLLOWING ACCOUNT, up to five different times are given for each event. The principal time given is '*Titanic* Standard Time', in which midnight equals 12.00.

TCT is '*Titanic* Corrected Time', which is 23 minutes slow and represents a time resulting from the setting of the liner's clocks back 23 minutes at midnight (to account for the westbound time loss). Testimony in the American and British inquiries shows that while some clocks were reset, others were not.

CTT is '*Californian* "True" Time', the time being kept aboard the Leyland liner, 12 minutes slow.

GMT is Greenwich Mean Time, 3hr 14min fast.

NYT is 'New York Time' (Eastern Standard Time), 1hr 50min slow.

Sunday, 14 April 1912

11.40pm (CTT 11.28pm; GMT 2.54am; NYT 9.50pm): Collision with the iceberg. Captain Smith comes quickly to the bridge from his quarters and receives Murdoch's report. Standby quartermaster Olliver is despatched immediately to find the ship's carpenter.

First Class passenger George Rheims.
(*Philadelphia Press*)

A for identification

The huge liner drifts to a stop in about a half mile. The ship's telegraphs indicate 'Stop'.

11.41pm (CTT 11.29pm; GMT 2.55am; NYT 9.51pm): Boxhall is sent by Captain Smith to assess the damage in the forward area. He goes directly to the lowest passenger deck forward, between numbers 2 and 3 hatches, G deck. During his return to the bridge he inspects all decks in the vicinity of the impact, but sees no damage.

George Rheims steps from an A deck men's room and sees the retreating iceberg, which he later sketches for a public inquiry. (National Archives and Records Administration – New York Branch)

Joseph Scarrott, a *Titanic* able-bodied seaman, sees the berg after the collision and later supervises a sketch of it. (*The Sphere*)

Captain Smith emerges from his cabin adjacent to the bridge. 'What have we struck?' he demands. (*Daily Sketch*)

Murdoch responds, 'An iceberg, sir. I hard-astarboarded and reversed the engines, and I was going to hard-aport around it, but she was too close. I could not do any more. I have closed the watertight doors.' (Harland & Wolff collection, Ulster Folk and Transport Museum)

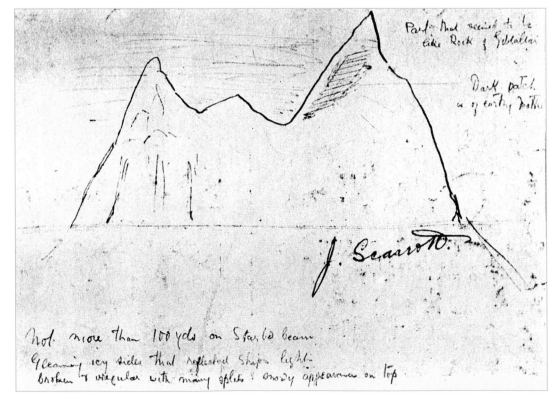

Fourth officer Joseph G. Boxhall (*Daily Mirror*)

Thomas Andrews. (*A Titanic Hero. Thomas Andrews, Shipbuilder*)

J. Maxwell, ship's carpenter. (*Daily Mail*)

On the bridge, Captain Smith moves the telegraphs to 'Half-speed ahead'. The engines run for 3 to 4 minutes.
11.45pm (CTT 11.33pm; GMT 2.59am, NYT 9.55pm): The engines are stopped. Thomas Andrews, a managing director of Harland & Wolff and the ship's designer, comes to the bridge at Captain Smith's request.
11.47pm (CTT 11.35pm; GMT 3.01am; NYT 9.57pm): Boxhall reports back to Captain Smith who orders him to find the ship's carpenter and have him sound the ship. Ismay arrives on the bridge and is told by Captain Smith that the ship is badly damaged. Ismay returns below.

11.48pm (CTT 11.36pm; GMT 3.02am; NYT 9.58pm): Captain Smith and Andrews leave to inspect the damage. Boxhall meets the carpenter on his own way to the bridge to report damage forward and below.
11.49pm (CTT 11.37pm; GMT 3.03am; NYT 9.59pm): Mail clerk John R.J. Smith, on his way to the bridge, meets Boxhall and tells him of water in the mail hold. Boxhall descends to E deck, finds the watertight door closed, and crosses over the working alleyway to the mail room stairs; descending to G deck, he sees water in the mail hold, rushing in and rising rapidly.
11.57pm (CTT 11.45pm; GMT 3.11am; NYT 10.07pm): Boxhall arrives back on the bridge. Captain Smith and Andrews also return to the bridge after their tour of inspection. Andrews calculates that the ship has only a short time to remain afloat.

John R. Jago Smith, one of *Titanic*'s two British postal workers. (*Southampton and District Pictorial*)

J. Bruce Ismay. (Private collection)

Lookouts Hogg, Evans, Fleet and Lee.
(Authors' collection/*Lloyds Deathless Story/
Daily Sketch*)

Chief officer H.T. Wilde. (Authors' collection)

11.59pm (CTT 11.47pm; GMT 3.13am; NYT 10.09pm): Ismay returns to the bridge where he is advised of the ship's doom. Boxhall arouses Pitman and Lightoller in their nearby cabins.

Monday, 15 April 1912

Midnight (TCT 11.37pm; CTT 11.48pm; GMT 3.14am; NYT 10.10pm): Captain Smith orders all officers and boat crews to be mustered. The ship's clocks are intended to be set back 23 minutes (to 'TCT'), the first of two such adjustments that slow the vessel's onboard time a total of 47 minutes during the day's first two watches; apparently some departments make the adjustment, while others do not. The engine room watches change. Lookouts Hogg and Evans relieve Fleet and Lee in the crow's nest.

12.02am (TCT 11.39pm; CTT 11.50pm; GMT 3.16am; NYT 10.12pm): Captain Smith orders chief officer Wilde to have the boats uncovered. Boxhall assists with the initial uncovering of the portside boats, augmenting second officer Lightoller's activities. First officer Murdoch is in charge of preparing and lowering the starboard boats, assisted by fifth officer Harold Godfrey Lowe. The order is given to muster passengers.

12.04am (TCT 11.41pm; CTT 11.52pm; GMT 3.18am; NYT 10.14pm): Third officer Pitman goes to the forward well deck to see the ice deposited there by the berg. He meets a group of firemen emerging from their quarters on F deck who tell him that their bunks are flooded.

12.07am (TCT 11.44pm; CTT 11.55pm; GMT 3.21am; NYT 10.17pm): Seeing that the officers and boat crews are

Radio officer J.G. Phillips. (GEC-Marconi)

mustered and manning the boats, Boxhall goes to the chart room to work out the ship's position; he takes it to Captain Smith on the bridge.

12.10am (TCT 11.47pm; CTT 11.58pm; GMT 3.24am; NYT 10.20pm): Captain Smith himself takes the message to the wireless room and tells operator Phillips to stand by to send the distress call when given the word.

12.14am (TCT 11.51pm; CTT 12.02am; GMT 3.28am; NYT 10.24pm): Captain Smith again goes to the wireless cabin and tells Phillips to send the signal for distress. (*Titanic*'s wireless call letters are 'MGY'.)

12.15am (TCT 11.52pm; CTT 12.03am; GMT 3.29am; NYT 10.25pm): The first distress signal is transmitted: 'CQD,

Top and Middle *La Provence* and *Mount Temple*. (Authors' collection/Courtesy of the Mariners Museum, Newport News, Va)

Below The land station at Cape Race, Newfoundland. (Canadian Marconi Co)

Right *Ypiranga*. (Authors' collection)

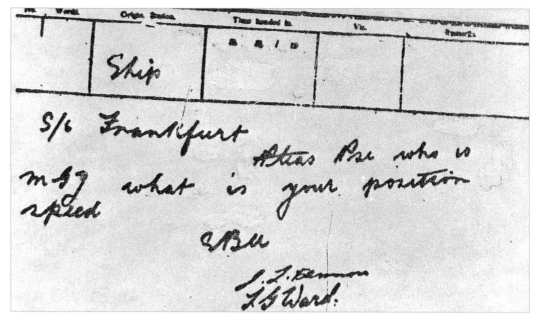

Top left Quartermaster Robert Hichens. (*Daily Sketch*)

Top right Quartermaster Walter J. Perkis. (Authors' collection)

Above left J.G. (Jack) Phillips. (Authors' collection)

Above right Harold Cottam. (*Daily Mirror*)

41°46'N, 50°24'W'. It is heard by *La Provence* (wireless call letters 'MLP') and *Mount Temple* ('MLQ'), and by the land station at Cape Race, Newfoundland ('MCE').

12.18am (TCT 11.55pm; CTT 12.06am; GMT 3.32am; NYT 10.28am): *Titanic*'s CQD, repeated 10 times, is heard by *Ypiranga* ('DYA').

12.23am (TCT 12.00 midnight; CTT 12.11am; GMT 3.37am; NYT 10.33pm): The helmsman, quartermaster Robert Hichens, is relieved by quartermaster Walter J. Perkis. Boxhall, who has been re-calculating *Titanic*'s position, takes the corrected position to the bridge and shows it to Captain Smith, who tells him to take it to the wireless cabin.

12.25am (TCT 12.02am; CTT 12.13am; GMT 3.39am; NYT 10.35pm): Cape Race ('MCE') logs a message from *Titanic* reporting that the vessel has moved 5 or 6 miles. Boxhall takes the corrected position, 41°46'N, 50°14'W, to the wireless cabin, where Phillips immediately begins transmitting it. The corrected position is heard by the wireless operator aboard *Carpathia* ('MPA'), Harold Cottam, and by Cape Race.

Frankfurt ('DFT') inquires of *Birma* ('SBA'), 'Who is MGY?'. (Frank P. Aks collection)

Birma quickly responds, '... MGY is the new White Star liner *Titanic Titanic* O[ld] M[an].' (Frank P. Aks collection)

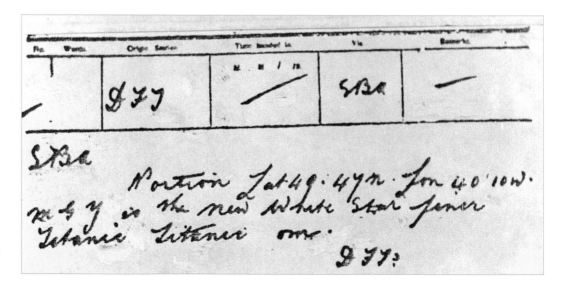

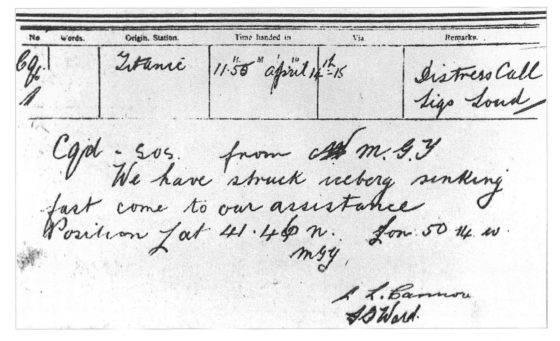

Returning to the bridge, Boxhall first sights the masthead lights of a nearby vessel about half a point off *Titanic*'s port bow, about 5 miles away.

12.26am (TCT 12.03am; CTT 12.14am; GMT 3.40am; NYT 10.36pm): *Ypiranga* ('DYA') hears *Titanic*'s CQD repeated 15 to 20 times. The message: 'Here corrected position 41.46N, 50.14W. Require immediate assistance. We have collision with iceberg. Sinking. Cannot anything hear [sic] for noise of steam.'

12.27am (TCT 12.04am; CTT 12.15am; GMT 3.41am; NYT 10.37pm): *Titanic* sends the following message: 'I require assistance immediately. Struck by iceberg in 41.46N, 50.14W.'

12.30am (TCT 12.07am; CTT 12.18am; GMT 3.44am; NYT 10.40pm): *Titanic* gives her position to *Frankfurt* ('DFT') and says, 'Tell your captain to come to our help. We are on the ice.'

Caronia ('MRA') alerts *Baltic* ('MBC'), then relays *Titanic*'s CQD: '*Titanic* struck iceberg, requires immediate assistance.'

Mount Temple ('MLQ') hears *Titanic* calling CQD, and transmits: 'Our captain reverses ship. We are about 50 miles off.'

Birma ('SBA') receives *Titanic*'s call for assistance. Following her inquiry, 'What is the matter?', *Birma* sends her own location ('100 miles away') and says that she will reach the distress position by 6.30am.

Top *Titanic*'s distress message. (*The Sphere*)

Middle left *Frankfurt*. (Authors' collection)

Middle right *Baltic*. (Authors' collection)

Right *Mount Temple*. (Courtesy of the Mariners Museum, Newport News, Va)

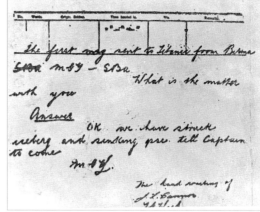

Birma (above left), in response to *Titanic*'s plea (above), sends a message of assurance (left) saying that she can be at the scene in 7 hours. (Courtesy of the Mariners Museum, Newport News, Va/Frank P. Aks collection)

Below *Prinz Friedrich Wilhelm*. (Authors' collection)

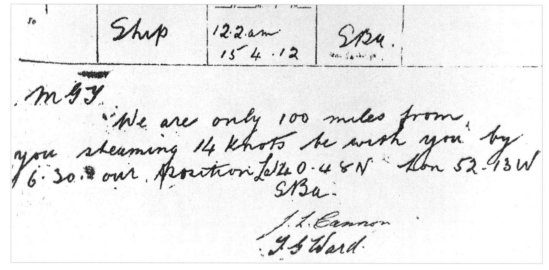

After receiving Captain Smith's permission, Boxhall orders quartermaster Rowe to signal the nearby vessel whose masthead lights appear to be 5 or 6 miles off, using *Titanic*'s powerful Morse lamp.

12.36am (TCT 12.13am; CTT 12.24am; GMT 3.50am; NYT 10.46pm): *Prinz Friedrich Wilhelm* calls *Titanic*, who asks, 'Are you coming to our aid?' *Prinz Friedrich Wilhelm*: 'What is the matter with you?' *Titanic*: 'We have collision with iceberg. Sinking. Please tell your captain to come.' *Prinz Friedrich Wilhelm*: 'OK, will tell.'

12.38am (TCT 12.15am; CTT 12.26am; GMT 3.52am; NYT 10.48pm): *Mount Temple* ('MLQ') hears *Frankfurt* ('DFT') give *Titanic* their position, 39°47'N, 52°10'W.

12.40am (TCT 12.17am; CTT 12.28am; GMT 3.54am; NYT 10.50pm): *Olympic* ('MKC') hears *Titanic* signalling another ship, saying something about striking an iceberg, but is not sure (because of

TCT – 'Titanic "Corrected" Time', 23 minutes slow.
CTT – 'Californian "True" Time', 12 minutes slow.
GMT – Greenwich Mean Time, 3hr 14min fast.
NYT – 'New York Time', 1hr 50min slow.

atmospherics and many stations working) whether it is *Titanic* that is in danger.

There is little, if any, water in boiler room 5 until water pressure causes the collapse of the forward starboard bunker door. The water's inrush causes the sinking vessel to lurch slightly downward.

12.45am (TCT 12.22am, CTT 12.33am; GMT 3.59am; NYT 10.55pm): The first lifeboat, starboard 7, is lowered with 28 aboard, seaman George A. Hogg in charge. Boxhall, assisted by quartermaster Rowe, fires the first rocket.

Olympic. (Authors' collection)

Seven more rockets are fired during the next 55 minutes at 5 to 10 minute intervals, until about 1.40am. Quartermaster Rowe, using the Morse lamp, tries repeatedly to signal the nearby ship, which appears to be approaching.

Titanic calls *Olympic*. CQD changes to SOS.

12.50am (TCT 12.27am; CTT 12.38am; GMT 4.04am; NYT 11.00pm): Again signalling CQD, *Titanic* says, 'I require immediate assistance. Position 41°46'N, 50°14'W.' The message is heard by *Olympic* and also received by *Celtic* ('MLC').

12.53am (TCT 12.30am; CTT 12.41am; GMT 4.07am; NYT 11.03pm): *Caronia* signals *Baltic* that *Titanic* is transmitting SOS and CQD, 41°46'N, 50°14'W, and wants immediate assistance.

12.55am (TCT 12.32am; CTT 12.43am; GMT 4.09am; NYT 11.05pm): Port lifeboat 6 is lowered with 28 aboard, quartermaster Hichens in charge. Starboard boat 5 is lowered with 41 aboard, third officer Pitman in charge.

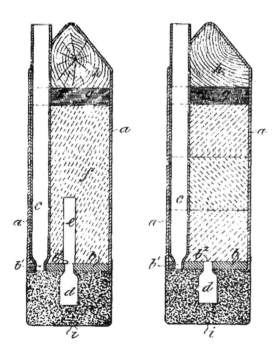

Designed by Mr George Trench and patented by him in 1888, the signal rockets used aboard *Titanic* were manufactured by the Cotton Powder Co. Ltd of London, according to regulations set by the British Board of Trade's Marine Department. (Science Museum, Kensington)

Left Feature film star Dorothy Gibson and her mother board boat 7 on the starboard side. (*New York Morning Telegraph*)

Above Aboard boat 5 as it is lowered are Washington 'Bobo' Dodge Jr and his mother, Ruth. Later, at sea, both are transferred to boat 7. (*New York Tribune/San Francisco Examiner*)

1.00am (TCT 12.37am; CTT 12.48am; GMT 4.14am; NYT 11.10pm): *Titanic* transmits a distress call and position, and *Cincinnati* ('DDC') responds. Assistance from *Cincinnati* is not needed, as shortly afterwards *Olympic* ('MKC') answers the distress call.

Titanic responds to *Olympic*, giving her position as 41°46'N, 50°14'W, and saying, 'We have struck an iceberg.'

Water enters E deck, appearing first at the foot of the grand staircase.

1.02am (TCT 12.39am; CTT 12.50am; GMT 4.16am; NYT 11.12pm): *Titanic* calls *Asian* ('MKL') and says, 'We want immediate assistance.' *Asian* receives *Titanic*'s position and requests a repeat call.

Virginian ('MGN') tries to contact *Titanic* without success. Cape Race ('MCE') advises *Virginian* to tell her captain that *Titanic* has struck an iceberg and requires immediate assistance.

1.10am (TCT 12.47am; CTT 12.58am; GMT 4.24am; NYT 11.20pm): Port boat 8 is lowered under Captain Smith's personal direction. It carries 24 women passengers and four male crew members. Its capacity is 65.

Starboard 'emergency' boat 1 is lowered under first officer Murdoch's direction. With a capacity of 40, it leaves with 12 aboard, seven of whom are crew. Among the five passengers are Sir Cosmo and Lucy, Lady Duff-Gordon.

Titanic notifies *Olympic* ('MKC'): 'We are in collision with berg. Sinking head down. 41°46'N, 50°14'W. Come as soon as possible.'

Top left *Cincinnati*. (Authors' collection)

Top right *Asian*. (Authors' collection)

Middle *Virginian*. (Authors' collection)

Left Following their rescue, the occupants of emergency boat 1 pose together on *Carpathia*'s deck. (*Daily Mirror*)

1.15am (TCT 12.52am; CTT 1.03am; GMT 4.29am; NYT 11.25pm): *Baltic* ('MBC') to *Caronia* ('MRA'): 'Please tell *Titanic* we are making toward her.'

1.20am (TCT 12.57am; CTT 1.08am; GMT 4.34am; NYT 11.30pm): Under the direction of chief officer Wilde, port boat 10 is lowered, seaman Edward John Buley (late of the Royal Navy) in charge. With a capacity of 65, there are 55 aboard: 41 women, seven children, five crew and two stowaways.

Starboard boat 9 is lowered under the direction of first officer Murdoch, with 56 aboard and bosun's mate Albert Haines in charge.

Cape Race notifies *Titanic* that *Virginian* is 170 miles north and is on the way to assist.

1.25am (TCT 1.02am; CTT 1.13am; GMT 4.39am; NYT 11.35pm): Second officer Lightoller directs the lowering of port boat 12; seaman John Poigndestre is in charge, with 43 aboard.

Starboard boat 11 is lowered under first officer Murdoch's direction, quartermaster James Humphreys in charge. The boat's capacity of 65 is exceeded by the 70 aboard.

Almost simultaneously, Murdoch orders boat 13 lowered, a total of 64 aboard. The boat is almost swamped by a discharge of water being pumped from the ship's interior near the sea's surface. The boat is pushed off from the waterflow and the descent is completed.

Caronia advises that *Baltic* is on the way to assist. (Leaving her eastbound course for Liverpool, *Baltic* steams 134 miles westward toward *Titanic* before being advised that her assistance is no longer required.)

Olympic transmits that her position as of 4.24am GMT (1.10am *Titanic*

Assisting with the loading of boat 8 is Howard B. Case, managing director of the Vacuum Oil Co. Ltd, London. After assuring the women's and children's safety, Mr Case stands back as the boat is lowered. His heroic behaviour is later praised by survivors. (*Illustrated London News*)

Virginian. (Authors' collection)

Left During the loading of boat 8, Isidor and Ida Straus make their gallant decision to remain together. (*Daily Sketch*)

TCT – *Titanic* "Corrected" Time', 23 minutes slow.
CTT – *Californian* "True" Time', 12 minutes slow.
GMT – Greenwich Mean Time, 3hr 14min fast.
NYT – 'New York Time', 1hr 50min slow.

'Standard' time) is 40°52'N, 61°18'W. She asks, 'Are you steering southerly to meet us?' *Titanic* replies, 'We are putting off the women in the boats.' The nearby ship, sighted earlier, now shows her stern light and appears to be steaming away.

The last rocket is fired (per testimony of quartermaster George Thomas Rowe, British Inquiry, p419).

1.27am (TCT 1.04am; CTT 1.15am; GMT 4.41am; NYT 11.37pm): Transmitting generally, *Titanic* repeats, 'We are putting the women off in the boats.'

1.30am (TCT 1.07am; CTT 1.18am; GMT 4.44am; NYT 11.40pm): After directing port boat 14's loading, fifth officer Lowe joins 51 passengers and 9 crew already in it.

Titanic repeats her earlier message to *Olympic*. 'We are putting passengers off in small boats.'

1.35am (TCT 1.12am; CTT 1.23am; GMT 4.49am; NYT 11.45pm): The loading and lowering of port boat 16 is directed by sixth officer James Paul Moody. With master-at-arms Henry Bailey in charge, the boat carries 40 Second and Third Class women and children and six crew members.

Olympic asks, 'What weather have you?' *Titanic* responds, 'Clear and calm.' Then, 'Engine room getting flooded.'

Mount Temple hears *Frankfurt* ask *Titanic*, 'Are there any boats around you already?' There is no reply.

Above During their lowerings, boats 13 and 15 are in near vertical collision. (*Graphic/Sphere*)

Left '... cannot last much longer.' (*The Sphere*)

'We are sinking fast ...' (Sphere)

First officer Murdoch directs the loading and lowering of starboard boat 15. Fireman Frank Dymond has charge of the 70 persons aboard.

1.37am (TCT 1.14am; CTT 1.25am; GMT 4.51am; NYT 11.47pm): *Baltic* advises *Titanic*, 'We are rushing to you.'

1.40am (TCT 1.17am; CTT 1.28am; GMT 4.54am; NYT 11.50pm): The last of eight distress rockets is fired from *Titanic*. (Mersey, in Annex 2 to his *Report*, gives the time as 'about 1.45 o'clock', although this would not have enabled quartermaster Rowe, who was assisting with firing the rockets, to join collapsible boat 'C', in which he left.)

The forward well deck is awash.

Chief officer Wilde directs the loading and lowering of collapsible boat C. With reportedly no one else in sight, chief officer Wilde permits Bruce

Fifth officer Harold Godfrey Lowe. (Private collection)

Chief officer Henry T. Wilde. (Authors' collection)

William Carter. (*New York Tribune*)

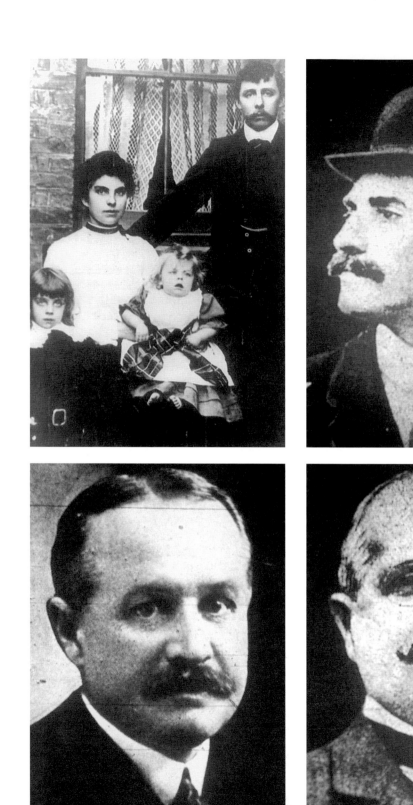

Top left Among the 27 women and children in collapsible C are Frank J.W. Goldsmith (lower left) and his mother Emily. His father, Frank John Goldsmith (right) is lost. (Authors' collection)

With no thought to their own safety or survival, John B. Thayer (far left), John Jacob Astor (above left) and George D. Widener (left) assist their wives into boat 4, then step back. Harry Elkins Widener (above) bids his mother farewell, then he too steps back. The men stand quietly together as boat 4, with 40 women and children aboard – the last conventional lifeboat to leave *Titanic* – is lowered. (*Philadelphia Inquirer/Philadelphia Public Ledger*)

TCT - 'Titanic "Corrected" Time', 23 minutes slow.
CTT - 'Californian "True" Time', 12 minutes slow.
GMT - Greenwich Mean Time, 3hr 14min fast.
NYT - 'New York Time', 1hr 50min slow.

Ismay and William Carter to board. With quartermaster George Rowe in charge, the boat carries 39 persons, 27 of whom are women and children.

Cape Race advises *Virginian* by wireless: 'Please tell your captain this: "The *Olympic* is making all speed to *Titanic* but his [*Olympic*'s] position is 40°32'N, 61°18'W. You are much nearer to *Titanic*. [Later this is given as 170 miles north of *Titanic*.] The *Titanic* is already putting off women in the boats and says the weather there is clear and calm. The *Olympic* is the only ship we have heard say 'Going to the assistance of *Titanic*'. The others must be a long way from *Titanic*."'

1.45am (TCT 1.22am; CTT 1.33am; GMT 4.59am; NYT 11.55pm): The last signals are heard by *Carpathia* from *Titanic*: 'Engine room full up to bunkers.'

With the foredeck under water, port boat 4, quartermaster Walter Perkis in charge, is lowered after a delay in loading, with 42 on board. Eight swimmers are picked up from the sea, two of whom die in the boat.

1.47am (TCT 1.24am; CTT 1.35am; GMT 5.01am; NYT 11.57pm): *Caronia* hears *Titanic*, but the signals are unreadable.

1.48am (TCT 1.25am; CTT 1.36am; GMT 5.02am; NYT 11.58pm): *Asian* hears *Titanic*'s SOS and answers, but receives no response.

1.50am (TCT 1.27am; CTT 1.38am; GMT 5.04am; NYT 12.00 midnight): *Caronia* hears *Frankfurt* communicating with *Titanic*. (*Frankfurt*, according to her position, was 172 miles from *Titanic* at the time that the first SOS was sent – 39°47'N, 42°10'W at 12.30am.)

Olympic's signal 'Going to assistance of *Titanic*' is heard by *Virginian* and Cape Race.

Water begins to wash over the fo'c'sle deck.

1.55am (TCT 1.32am; CTT 1.43am; GMT 5.09am; NYT 12.05am): Boiler room 4 begins to flood, causing the bow to sink noticeably deeper. Propeller blades begin to rise above the surface. The fo'c'sle deck is awash. The sinking process slows slightly.

2.04am (TCT 1.41am; CTT 1.52am; GMT 5.18am; NYT 12.14am): The forward expansion joint pulls open.

2.05am (TCT 1.42am; CTT 1.53am; GMT 5.19am; NYT 12.15am): The after cables holding funnel number 1 snap, causing the funnel to fall forward toward the starboard side. The starboard bridge wing is crushed; several people in its path, both onboard and in the water, are killed.

As the bow dips lower, water gently edges into the reception room and First Class dining saloon on D deck, and invades the First Class corridors on B deck.

Collapsible boat D is carefully lowered, filled almost to capacity.

2.08am (TCT 1.45am; CTT 1.56am; GMT 5.22am; NYT 12.18am): A deck is under water.

2.10am (TCT 1.47am; CTT 1.58am; GMT 5.24am; NYT 12.20am): Captain Smith relieves wireless operators Harold Bride and Jack Phillips; however, they remain at their posts.

The break-up process begins, due to stresses deep within the hull.

2.17am (TCT 1.54am; CTT 2.05am; GMT 5.31am; NYT 12.27am): *Virginian* hears *Titanic* call 'CQ', but is unable to read him 'Titanic's signals end very abruptly, as [though] power is suddenly switched off, his spark rather blurred and ragged. Called *Titanic* and suggested he should try emergency set, but heard no response.'

As the bow plunges, the bandsmen, unable to play any longer on the sloping deck, cease their music.

Caronia. (Authors' collection)

Nearer, my God, to Thee.

PROPRIO DEO.   ARTHUR S. SULLIVAN.

mf

= 40. Near-er, my God, to Thee, Near-er to Thee; E'en though it

be a cross That rais-eth me: Still all my song shall be, Near-er, my

God, to Thee, Near-er to Thee! Near-er to Thee! A-men.

There are many witnesses to the music played by *Titanic*'s orchestra during the sinking vessel's final clamorous moments. Some say the last tune was 'Autumn'; a larger number agree on 'Nearer, my God, to Thee.' But there has never been a consensus on the hymn's tune. Interviewed after the disaster by the *London Daily News*, Mr Elwand Moody, a close friend of *Titanic*'s bandleader Wallace Hartley, stated, 'When I speak of "Nearer, my God, to Thee", I mean Sullivan's setting. That would be what the orchestra played on the sinking *Titanic*.'

At the solemn ceremonies attending Wallace Hartley's funeral at Colne, Lancashire, on 18 May 1912, Sir Arthur Sullivan's setting of the hymn is sung twice, once at the chapel service, once at the graveside. (Authors' collection)

A 1912 postcard commemorating the disaster bears Sir Arthur Sullivan's setting of the hymn. (Authors' collection)

Nearer, my God, to Thee, Nearer to Thee!
E'en though it be a cross that raiseth me;
Still all my song shall be,
Nearer, my God, to Thee, Nearer to Thee!

Almost simultaneously, collapsible boats A and B float off the boat deck. **2.18am** (TCT 1.55am; CTT 2.06am; GMT 5.32am; NYT 12.28am): As the bow sinks, *Titanic*'s stern rises into the starlit sky at an angle estimated at approximately 25°. There is a roar as the shell plates buckle and movable objects inside the vessel fall. The ship's lights blink once, then go out. **2.20am** (TCT 1.57am; CTT 2.08am; GMT 5.34am; NYT 12.30am): The bow sinks. The superstructure and hull rupture just aft of number 3 funnel. Still attached to the bow section by the keel, the stern rises into the sky, then settles back as the keel bends. The water-filled bow drags the stern back into near-alignment, again raising it almost to the perpendicular. As the stern fills, both sections begin the descent to the ocean floor. Just beneath the surface, perhaps about 100ft down, the keel snaps, parting the stern from the bow.

Olympic is in contact with *Hellig Olav* ('DHO'), whose signals are very strong, and asks if he has heard anything from

TCT – *'Titanic* "Corrected" Time', 23 minutes slow.
CTT – *'Californian* "True" Time', 12 minutes slow.
GMT – Greenwich Mean Time, 3hr 14min fast.
NYT – 'New York Time', 1hr 50min slow.

Titanic. *Hellig Olav* replies, 'No. Keeping strict watch, but hear nothing more from *Titanic*.'

2.20am is the official time of *Titanic*'s sinking in the vicinity of 41°46'N, 50°14'W, as given by *Carpathia* in a message to *Olympic*.

2.22am (TCT 1.59am; CTT 2.10am; GMT 5.36am; NYT 12.32am): Although *Titanic* has disappeared, her sinking continues. Based upon studies made on the sunken wreck in 1996, a respected naval architect, William H. Garzke, reports that a third section of the ship, 56–60ft long, from boiler room 2 to the forward half of the reciprocating engine room, peels away at this time. 'This section was the result of a buckling failure in the inner bottom and explains why only half of the reciprocating engines remain in the stern section,' he writes.

Titanic's stern rises. (Authors' collection/Simon Fisher)

Hellig Olav. (Authors' collection)

SIX

ADRIFT IN THE LIFEBOATS

TIMES IN THIS CHAPTER are approximate, and are 'Titanic Standard Time' (see Chapter 5).

Monday, 15 April 1912

2.20am: As Titanic goes under, collapsible boats A and B float off the boat deck. Boat A swamps as it reaches the water; it remains upright but half-submerged. Boat B overturns as it is swept clear by a wave created by the collapse of the forward funnel.

John B. Thayer Jr. (New York Herald)

2.30am: Boat 14, fifth officer Lowe in command, rounds up and ties together boats 10, 12, 4 and collapsible D. Lowe transfers several occupants of collapsible D to boat 12, then divides about 50 of his own boat's occupants among other boats.

From his precarious perch atop overturned collapsible B, First Class passenger John B. Thayer Jr witnesses Titanic break into two pieces. Later, based on Thayer's descriptions, Carpathia passenger J.P. Skidmore draws a series of sketches depicting Titanic's final hours. (Philadelphia Bulletin)

Boat 5, third officer Pitman in charge, starts to return to the wreck but turns away at the request of several female passengers.

Boat 2, in command of fourth officer Boxhall, drifts about without returning to the wreck, as does boat 1, with Sir Cosmo Duff-Gordon and his wife Lucy aboard. Quartermaster Hichens, in charge of boat 6, flatly refuses to return to the wreck.

2.40am: At the order of quartermaster Walter J. Perkis, who is in charge, the men at the oars of boat 4 stop rowing when they are about 900ft from the wreck and search for survivors. Eight swimmers are taken aboard from the 28°F water, but of these, steward Sidney C. Siebert dies in the boat and seaman William Lyons dies aboard the rescue ship *Carpathia*.

3.00am: After selecting six oarsmen from among the crew in other boats, as well as one passenger volunteer, Charles Williams, Lowe makes for the floating debris in search of survivors. He picks up only four, including First Class passenger William F. Hoyt, who dies soon after rescue. During the hours of darkness, boats 6 and 16 tie up together, as do boats 5 and 7, which also exchange occupants in order to trim the smaller craft.

3.35am: Those in *Titanic*'s boats see a distant flash to the south-east, and hear a far-off 'boom'; it is a rocket from *Carpathia*, fired under the orders of Captain Rostron to reassure *Titanic*'s passengers.

4.03am: The green flare from the first of *Titanic*'s lifeboats is sighted from *Carpathia*'s bridge.

4.10am: Boat 2 is alongside *Carpathia*, and its occupants are taken aboard.

4.45am: Boat 13 is picked up.

4.50am: In dawn's increasing light, collapsible A's distress can be seen

Above After the ship has sunk, fireman Harry Senior reports seeing Captain Smith, in the water, bringing a baby to one of the lifeboats, while entrée cook Isaac Maynard (below left) says that he actually accepted a baby from Captain Smith's arms. (*Illustrated London News*/Private collection)

Above Fifth officer Lowe. (*Illustrated London News*)

Left First Class passenger Charles Williams. (Authors' collection)

clearly. Fifth officer Lowe's boat 14 takes collapsible D in tow and, sail raised, heads for collapsible A. One woman, Rosa Abbott, and eight men are transferred from boat A to collapsible D.

Aboard collapsible A, one of the men, Third Class passenger Edvard Lindell, dies before he can be taken aboard *Carpathia*. Earlier, his wife Elin is unable to lift herself into the boat from the icy water. Already in the boat, Edvard has no strength to help her over the gunwale. He clings desperately to her wrist, but as his own strength ebbs, he has to relinquish his grasp. As Elin's hand loosens from Edvard's, her wedding ring slips from her finger and falls to the boat's flooring. Edvard is buried from *Carpathia*'s deck at 4.00am the next day, Tuesday.

The lifeboat, collapsible A, is one of the boats cast adrift. It is discovered on 13 May (qv) by the liner *Oceanic*. In the boat's bottom is Elin Lindell's wedding ring, an inscription identifying it as her property. It is later returned to her family.

Top As *Carpathia*'s lights come up over the horizon, the occupants of *Titanic*'s lifeboats begin to burn green company flares to attract attention. (E.D. Walker)

Middle Sail furled, and collapsible D in tow, boat 14 under fifth officer Lowe's skilful command, heads for *Carpathia*'s sheltering side. (National Archives and Records Administration – New York Branch)

Far left Third Class passenger Rosa Abbott. (Michael A. Findlay collection)

Left Edvard and Elin Lindell. (Claes-Göran Wetterholm collection)

5.10am: Boat 7 comes up to *Carpathia* and discharges its occupants to the liner's decks.

5.20am: Lowe casts collapsible A adrift, sea cocks open. Left aboard the drifting boat are the remains of First Class passenger Thompson Beattie (from Winnipeg, Manitoba), an unidentified seaman and an unidentified fireman.

At sunrise, the enormity of the disaster becomes visible. Only drifting lifeboats and icebergs can be seen. (*L'Illustration*)

SEVEN

RESCUE AT SEA AND RETURN TO NEW YORK

Thursday, 11 April 1912

Noon (New York time): The 13,600-ton Cunard liner *Carpathia* departs New York's North River Pier 54 for Gibraltar and Mediterranean ports. The nine-year-old vessel has on board 743 passengers – 128 First, 50 Second and 565 Third Class – six officers and 320 crew. The voyage's first 3½ days are uneventful.

Carpathia. (Joseph A. Carvalho collection)

RESCUE AT SEA

THE FOLLOWING TIMES are '*Titanic* Standard Time' (see Chapter 5).

Monday, 15 April 1912

12.25am: While preparing for sleep, *Carpathia*'s wireless operator, Harold Cottam, intercepts *Titanic*'s call for assistance and immediately notifies Captain Arthur H. Rostron. Rostron quickly calculates that *Carpathia* is

58 miles south-east of the stricken *Titanic* and orders his own vessel's course to be changed to N52°W.

12.35am: Extra stokers are assigned to the engine room as *Carpathia*'s speed is increased to 'Full ahead'. Rostron

Harold Cottam. (Authors' collection)

Carpathia's simple wireless 'shack' was located on an after deck. (*New York Times*)

assembles his officers and issues orders, mustering the entire crew to receive survivors.

Carpathia's speed is increased to 17½ knots, some 3½ knots faster than customary.

2.40am: From *Carpathia*'s bridge a green flare is sighted a half point on the port bow, far ahead, but it quickly vanishes.

2.45am: Rostron orders signal rockets to be fired at 15-minute intervals, and for Cunard company signals (a blue light and two roman candles, each throwing out six blue balls to a height not exceeding 150ft) to be displayed.

3.15am: During *Carpathia*'s approach from the south-east, when about 12 miles from *Titanic*'s distress position – 41°46'N, 50°14'W – the masthead light of a nearby vessel is seen from the bridge. Captain Rostron later testifies that he saw only the masthead light, while one of his officers tells of seeing the vessel's red port light as well.

3.30am: Entering the area of ice, *Carpathia* must dodge and repeatedly turn to avoid striking passing bergs.

Rostron orders the ship's speed to be reduced to 'Half ahead', then to 'Slow'.

4.00am: Arriving at what he estimates is the site of *Titanic*'s wireless distress signals, Captain Rostron orders the liner's engines to be stopped.

4.03am: The green light from *Titanic*'s boat 2 is sighted about 300 yards directly ahead. Her engines stopped, *Carpathia* has barely enough way to dodge a passing iceberg and swing around to take aboard survivors through the shelter deck's open gangway.

4.10am: The first survivors come aboard. *Titanic*'s fourth officer, Joseph Boxhall, reports to Captain Rostron on the bridge that *Titanic* sank at 2.20am.

4.20am: As dawn breaks, one by one *Titanic*'s boats and collapsibles appear in the emerging light.

5.00am: There is sufficient light to see to the horizon. Rostron later reports sighting two steamships to the north, perhaps 7 or 8 miles distant: one a four-masted steamer with one funnel, the other a two-masted steamer with one funnel.

Carpathia arrives. (Authors' collection)

Dawn reveals *Titanic*'s boats. (*Graphic*)

6.00am: A breeze rises, and low waves wash with increasing frequency into the overloaded boats. Collapsible B's stability is maintained only by a delicate balancing manoeuvre by its standing occupants, led by second officer Lightoller. In response to shrill blasts from his officer's whistle, boats 4 and 12 row up to the rapidly submerging collapsible. Five survivors scramble into boat 4, eight into boat 12. Lightoller, last to leave, heaves the body of an unidentified fireman into boat 12 before he comes aboard. (Jack Phillips, *Titanic*'s senior wireless telegraphist, is known to have been pulled from the water in a very weakened state and placed aboard collapsible B, yet his body is not removed at the time of the boat's abandonment. A witness, fireman John Haggan, later states that he observed a body rolling off into the water at the stern during the night; it is likely that this was Phillips.)

One by one the boats gather at *Carpathia*'s side, and the survivors come aboard:

6.15am: Collapsible C. Among those aboard is J. Bruce Ismay.

7.00am: Boat 14, with collapsible D in tow.

7.30am: Boat 4.

Top Collapsible D. (National Archives and Records Administration – New York Branch)

Middle left One by one, *Titanic*'s lifeboats come alongside Carpathia and discharge their pitiable contents. (*Harper's*)

Middle right Boat 6 arrives. (National Archives and Records Administration – New York Branch)

Left One of the last *Titanic* lifeboats reaches *Carpathia*'s side. (Authors' collection)

8.00am: Boat 6, at 12.55am the first boat to leave *Titanic*'s port side, arrives.

In his cabin, Bruce Ismay prepares a message to Islefrank, New York – one of the White Star Line's American cable addresses: 'Deeply regret advise you *Titanic* sank this morning after collision with iceberg resulting in serious loss of life. Full particulars later. Bruce Ismay.'

The message, handed to *Carpathia*'s chief steward, is taken to Captain Rostron, who approves its transmission. Clocked in at 9.58am, it is sent that afternoon via *Olympic* to Cape Sable and Halifax. Astray in a tangle of official and unofficial red tape, the message is not received at New York until about 9.00am, Wednesday, 17 April. Shortly after 8.00am Captain Rostron orders *Carpathia*'s house flag to be lowered to half-mast.

8.20am (6.30am New York time): The eastbound White Star liner *Baltic* receives an unofficial message from *Carpathia*: 'The *Titanic* has gone down with all hands, as far as we know, with the exception of 20 boatloads, which we have picked up. Number not accurately fixed yet. Can not see any more boats about at all.'

The message is given to *Baltic*'s commander, Captain Joseph B. Ranson, who decides not to forward it to any other wireless land or ship station.

8.30am: Boat 12, which departed *Titanic*'s port side at 1.25am with 43 aboard, arrives alongside *Carpathia* bearing more than 70 survivors, transfers from collapsibles D and B having been made at sea. Second officer Lightoller is the last to disembark, the final *Titanic* survivor to board *Carpathia*.

Arriving along the ice field's western edge, *Californian* approaches *Carpathia* and pulls up nearby.

Right *Californian* arrives on the scene at 8.30am on the morning of 15 April. (Mr & Mrs George A. Fenwick)

Below and below right Thirteen lifeboats are lifted aboard *Carpathia*. (National Archives and Records Administration – New York Branch/*Harper's*)

Thirteen of *Titanic*'s lifeboats are lifted aboard *Carpathia*'s deck. Boats 4, 14 and 15 and collapsibles B, C and D are cast adrift and quickly sink. (Fifth officer Lowe had set collapsible A adrift during the night.)

ON BOARD *CARPATHIA*

8.50am: Captain Rostron orders *Carpathia*'s course set westward toward New York. *Californian* remains to search the disaster site for additional bodies.

9.00am: At Captain Rostron's suggestion, a service of remembrance and thanksgiving is conducted in the Second Class dining saloon, led by *Carpathia* passenger Rev Roger B. Anderson, a member of the Episcopal Order of the Holy Cross.

Following the service and throughout the morning a roster of survivors is compiled. *Carpathia*'s chief purser, Ernest G.F. Brown, and second purser, Percy B. Barnett, prepare the list of surviving passengers, while *Titanic*'s second officer, Charles H. Lightoller, prepares that for deck and engine department survivors. The list of cooks, stewards and messmen is done by *Titanic*'s chief Second Class steward, John Hardy.

Noon: *Carpathia* passes the eastbound Russian-Asiatic Line steamer *Birma*.

Above As *Carpathia* departs from the wreck site, Captain Rostron (right) confers on deck with two of *Titanic*'s surviving officers, fourth officer Joseph Boxhall (left) and second officer Charles Lightoller (centre). (*New York Evening Mail*)

Above In addition to *Carpathia*'s own complement of 1,069 passengers and crew, Captain Arthur Rostron must now cope with an additional '705 living survivors' from the lost *Titanic*. (*The Independent*)

Below *Carpathia*'s Second Class dining saloon. (Authors' collection)

Above Father Roger Anderson. (*Daily Mirror*)

Top *Birma*. (Authors' collection)

Middle During late morning and the afternoon, *Titanic*'s stunned and exhausted survivors gather on *Carpathia*'s decks. (*Harper's*)

Bottom *Carpathia*'s passengers share blankets and clothing with the survivors. (*Illustrated London News*)

3.50pm: *Carpathia* establishes radio contact with *Olympic*, whose powerful transmitter is used to relay messages to land stations. Ismay's message and those prepared earlier by Rostron are sent.

Wireless contact between the two liners continues until about 10.00pm when distance weakens the signals into silence. During the 7-hour period, in addition to the company messages, the names of 322 First and Second Class survivors are also transmitted.

4.00pm: *Carpathia*'s engines are stopped, her flag already at half-mast. From her deck, the bodies of four victims who died in the boats are committed to the deep. Both Catholic and Episcopal clergy officiate. The solemn burial ritual is conducted for *Titanic* bedroom steward Sidney C. Siebert and an unidentified fireman. Also committed are the bodies of Third Class passenger Edvard Lindell, taken

dead from collapsible D, and First Class passenger William F. Hoyt, who succumbed following rescue by boat 14. Burial takes place at 41°14'W, 51°24'W.

A dense fog enshrouds *Carpathia* during the evening as she heads for New York; the fog continues well into Tuesday morning.

DATELINE NEW YORK

THE FOLLOWING TIMES are New York times (EST).

David Sarnoff. (Authors' collection)

The *New York Times*'s city room fills with reporters covering the unfolding story of *Titanic*'s accident. (NYT Pictures/NYT Permissions)

Monday, 15 April 1912

Midnight (1.50am '*Titanic* Standard Time'), New York, NY: For the past 50 minutes, a young wireless operator, David Sarnoff, has been glued to the earphones of his station ('MHI'). There, atop the Wanamaker Department Store at 9th Street and Broadway, at about 11.10pm (New York time), he detects the faint, distant signals of *Olympic*'s first

Above A young *Carpathia* passenger, identified as Marjorie Sweetheart – seen here with Captain Rostron – gives all her spare clothing to some of *Titanic*'s children. (*Daily Mail*)

exchange of wireless signals with the sinking *Titanic*. He acknowledges receipt of the message and asks *Olympic* for further details. He notifies the press. He then remains at his station almost continuously during the next three days, receiving lists of *Titanic*'s saved and lost.

Midnight, Montreal, Canada: Harold Strange, the *Montreal Gazette*'s marine reporter, receives a telephone call from George Hannah, marine superintendent at Montreal for the Allan Steamship Line. He tells Strange that his office has just received via land line from Cape Race a wireless message from the captain of the Allan Line steamship *Virginian* requesting permission to change course and go to the aid of the liner *Titanic*, calling for assistance after striking an iceberg.

Strange immediately reports the story to Ted Slack, the *Gazette*'s managing editor, who decides not to run it at this time. However, because of an arrangement the *Gazette* has with *The New York Times* to share important stories, Slack sends the despatch to the *Times* via their direct, leased land line.

For Carr Van Anda, the *Times*'s night managing editor, this bulletin is the first of several indications that something has happened to *Titanic*. He assigns a feature story about the occurrence, utilising the *Times*'s front page.

The rest is history.

12.40am, Cape Race, Newfoundland: An urgent telephone call is received from the Associated Press in New York requesting confirmation of *Virginian*'s earlier messages. After a pause for coordinating its message logs, Cape Race responds by land-line. The end of the message contains the ominous words: 'The last signals from *Titanic* were heard by *Virginian* at 12.27am [New York time, 2.17am 'Titanic

Standard Time]. The wireless operator on *Virginian* says these signals were blurred and ended abruptly.'

It is not unlikely that soon after confirmation of *Titanic*'s cessation of communication, the telephone (Rector 2100) rings at the offices of the White Star Line, 9 Broadway, as members of the press request additional information.

Nor is it totally unreasonable to imagine that White Star's night executive officer quickly places a telephone call to Plaza 3585, the residence of Mr Phillip Albright Small Franklin, vice president of International Mercantile Marine and general manager of White Star's American operations.

The evidence that these particular telephone calls were made is speculative. But the point is apparent

P.A.S. Franklin. (*New York Times*)

that no later than 2.30am (New York time) there was confirmed news that something had happened to *Titanic*; the White Star Line did have a New York office to which inquisitive reporters could make inquiries; and Mr Franklin did have a telephone at his home to which the company could make reports.

8.00am, New York, NY: New York's downtown financial centre stirs. Made curious by the newspapers' early morning editions, a crowd begins to gather in Bowling Green, across Broadway from the White Star office; it grows larger as the day passes.

In keeping with the customs of the day, crowds seeking news – any news – about the latest messages regarding *Titanic* gather around outposts of White Star influence: Pier 59, North River, at 19th Street, and the White Star freight offices at 17 Battery Place.

Crowds also form around the bulletin boards that adorn the outside facades of newspaper offices: Newspaper Row, opposite City Hall Park; Herald Square; and Times Square. They see no details, only meagre bulletins.

Unconfirmed rumours abound. Confusion reigns.

10.30am, New York, NY: Thomas J. Stead, assistant to the Cunard Line's general manager at New York, states that *Titanic*'s loss was known by his company as early as 10.00am, but that they had made no public announcement. Mr Stead later says that he had only repeated what he had been told by a friend, whose name he refuses to give, and denies that the company had any official involvement.

A rumour that financier J.P. Morgan is told of the disaster at about this same time is later emphatically denied by Mr Morgan's office.

10.45am, New York, NY: While attending a board of directors' meeting of the

Union Typewriter Company, Timothy L. Wodruff, former lieutenant governor of New York State, calls the White Star office, inquiring about *Titanic*'s status. He receives the news, which he imparts to other men present at the meeting, that, 'The *Titanic* had struck an iceberg and that, although she was still afloat, she would probably sink within half an hour.'

2.00pm, Cape Race, Newfoundland: A message that describes some details of *Titanic*'s loss, prepared by *Olympic*'s Captain Herbert J. Haddock and transmitted about half an hour earlier, is received in full by the Marconi station at Cape Race. The message is sent by land-line from Cape Race to White Star's New York office, where it should have arrived by 2.30pm.

3.00pm, New York, NY: According to a report circulating in real estate circles, a meeting of men prominent in the management of the Astor estate is held to discuss the news received by the Astor office at 1.00pm that John Jacob

In Bowling Green, opposite the White Star Line's offices at 9 Broadway, and on the sidewalk outside the offices, crowds gather, curious to learn the latest news. Throughout the day the crowds continue to grow. (Private collection/*Philadelphia Inquirer*)

Rumours of *Titanic*'s sinking with great loss of life bring a constant stream of visitors to White Star's 9 Broadway offices. (Authors' collection)

Astor has drowned in the *Titanic* disaster.

Charles A. Peabody, president of the Mutual Life Insurance Company, who is reported to have attended the meeting, later strongly denies that such a conference had ever been held, and maintains that the Astor family remained uninformed until 7.00pm, when the general public announcement was made.

Top Once inside, visitors view company lists of *Titanic's* passengers. (National Archives and Records Administration – New York Branch)

Right Later in the afternoon, the first lists of survivors are posted. (National Archives and Records Administration – New York Branch)

Below right As additional lists of survivors are posted, and as more visitors clamour for information, confusion reigns. (*New York World*)

Below By day's end, mourning is evident as White Star's company pennant atop their London office is lowered to half-mast. (*Daily Graphic*)

6.30pm, New York, NY: According to the White Star Line's office, Captain Haddock's message is not received at New York until 6.16pm. Mr P.A.S. Franklin immediately issues a public statement to waiting reporters that finally confirms *Titanic*'s disastrous loss.

But New York City is not the only place where confusion reigns. Even at the highest diplomatic levels, any news of the liner and her passengers is eagerly sought, and woefully inaccurate.

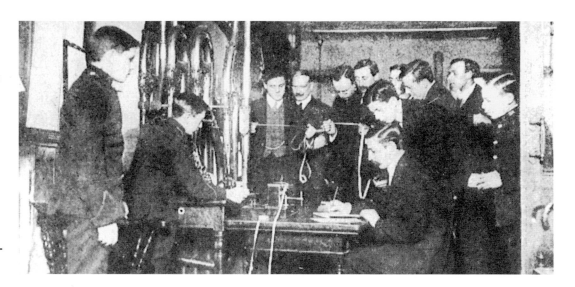

Tuesday, 16 April 1912

IN LONDON, THE frustrations of the Canadian High Commissioner, Lord Strathcona, are evident in his efforts to clarify the situation by cable with Canada's Prime Minister, the Hon Robert Borden. (The phraseology is per the original source):

'... Three cable messages dispatched to you on the 16th instant:

1   "White Star Company cannot furnish list of Canadian passengers *Titanic*. So far we have been able to gather up to present following comprises all Canadians on board, but there may be others: McCaffrey of Vancouver, Hugo Ross, Winnipeg, Major Peuchen,

Top In the telegraph room at Reuters' London office, bulletins concerning *Titanic*'s disaster are received constantly. (*Daily Mail*)

Middle As in New York, anxious enquiries are made at the White Star Line's London office. (*Daily Graphic*)

Right Throughout the day, requests for information continue at White Star's Cockspur Street office. (*Illustrated London News*)

Toronto, Mr and Mrs H.J. Allison, Miss and Master Allison and Maid, Montreal, Mr and Mrs Mark Fortune, three Misses Fortune and Mr Charles Fortune, Winnipeg, H. Hays and Miss Hays and maid, Thornton Davidson, Montreal, Markland Morrison, Montreal."

2 "Following Additional Names: Canadian passengers on *Titanic*: Elsie Bowerman, Montreal, Mr and Mrs Edward G. and Miss Harriet Crosby."

3 "Payne Hays private secretary also on *Titanic*.'"

Later in the week, in a confirming cable, Lord Strathcona can almost be seen holding up his hands in a shrug of disbelief:

'As indicated in the message first quoted, the White Star Line were unable to furnish me with the names of Canadian passengers, the documents containing this information being on the vessel. In these circumstances the information was collected from such sources as available, and one or two slight errors have arisen, it being now uncertain whether the Allison family were Canadians and I am also informed that the Miss Hays whose name was given is not a relative of Mr Charles M. Hays.'

Top At Southampton, home to many of *Titanic*'s crew, the first news of lost and saved is posted on 16 April outside White Star's Canute Road offices. (*Daily Sketch*)

Middle The first lists are short and far from accurate. (*Southampton and District Pictorial*)

Left Anxious faces quickly scan each supplemental list as it is posted. (*Daily Mirror*)

Far left As increasingly powerful marine and land wireless stations pick up *Carpathia*'s weak signals, the lists of lost and saved become longer and more complete, as seen here at Southampton. (*Daily Mirror*)

Middle left Southampton's Canute Road continues to be crowded with the crew's family and friends, eager for more news. (*Southampton and District Pictorial*)

Bottom left Even with more reliable information received by wireless, crowds outside London's Oceanic House have scarcely diminished by 18 April. (Private collection)

Left By 19 April crowds are still besieging White Star's London offices. (Private collection)

Below left As wireless stations continue to relay information to the public, newspapers at last can offer detailed and accurate facts. (Authors' collection)

ON BOARD *CARPATHIA*

MEANWHILE, INTERCEPTED while cruising off Nantucket, about 500 miles from *Carpathia*, the US Navy scout cruiser *Chester* (wireless call letters 'NDG') is dispatched by orders of the Navy Department to proceed to the sinking site and stand by to offer whatever assistance is needed.

Chester's wireless operators try to assist by re-transmitting signals from *Carpathia*'s weaker station to land stations via the US Navy scout cruiser *Salem* ('NRZ'), which has been ordered to stand by the Nantucket Light Vessel.

Early in the morning of 16 April, the US Navy's scout cruiser *Chester* contacts *Carpathia* and tries to assist in transmitting lists of survivors' names. (Authors' collection)

Carpathia's wireless operator, Harold Cottam, later complains that the operators on the Navy vessels had been incompetent; that they had constantly interrupted his signals; that they frequently had requested he repeat his messages; and that their signals to him were broken, garbled and painstakingly slow.

Salem and *Chester* withdrew on 18 April.

The following times, for 16 April 1912, continue to be New York time (EST).

4.00am: During the night, *Titanic* seaman William H. Lyons dies from the effects of exposure. Once again *Carpathia*'s engines are stopped. In the fog-shrouded loneliness of pre-dawn darkness, the young man's body is consigned to its final resting place.

A strong wind and heavy sea develop during the morning.

2.30pm: A meeting of uninjured passengers takes place in *Carpathia*'s

William H. Lyons. (Authors' collection)

main saloon. Mr Samuel Goldenberg is elected chairman, and Mr Isaac Gerald Frauenthal is elected chairman of the committee on subscriptions. Resolutions are passed expressing thanks to *Carpathia*'s officers, surgeons, crew and passengers. Mr Frauenthal appoints his committee to raise funds aboard *Carpathia* for relief of destitute survivors. Before the liner docks nearly $15,000 (£3,000) is raised.

A committee consisting of Mrs J.J. Brown, Mrs William Bucknell and Mrs George Stone is appointed to look after the immediate needs of the destitute.

11.00pm: A message from *Carpathia*, relayed via Halifax, states that the liner is about 596 miles from Ambrose Channel.

Wednesday, 17 April 1912

6.10am: *Carpathia* establishes wireless contact with the Cunard liner *Franconia* ('MEA'), eastbound, Boston to Liverpool, and is also in communication with the Sable Island land station ('MSD'). *Carpathia* is 498 miles east of Ambrose Channel.

7.00am: During the day, *Carpathia* is in wireless contact with the tug *Mary F. Scully* ('JB'), chartered by the newspaper, the *Boston Globe*, with wireless operator Jack Binns (of *Republic* fame) aboard. In the exchange of signals, rumours are dispelled and survivor lists verified.

Top *Franconia*. (Authors' collection)

Middle Young Gurshon ('Gus') Cohen naps in a *Carpathia* deckchair en route to New York. (*New York Journal*)

Right With pride of accomplishment, some members of *Carpathia*'s crew pose on the liner's forward deck. (Authors' collection)

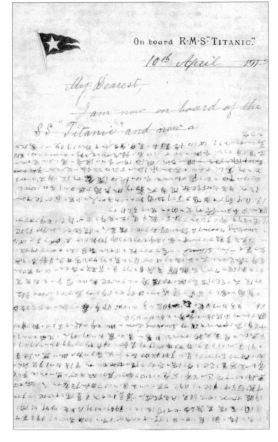

Top left For some, the tragedy has already begun to recede from memory. Sir Cosmo and Lady Lucy Duff-Gordon ask the crew of their lifeboat, number 1, to autograph a life jacket. (*Daily Sketch*)

Above left As *Carpathia* forges westward, Japanese government railway official Masafumi Hosono begins to write one of the earliest survivor accounts of the tragedy. (Courtesy of the Hosono family)

Above He writes on a piece of stationery on which he had begun a letter to his wife while on board *Titanic*, carried in his pocket into a lifeboat. (Courtesy of the Hosono family)

Left On 17 April Mr Hosono writes that *Carpathia*'s smoking room 'was so filled with people that no space to sleep was available to me. As a last resort, I seated myself on a chair and spent the whole night in a half sleep. This was indeed a trying voyage.' (Authors' collection)

As *Carpathia* proceeds towards New York, her radio signals, though still weak, continue to transmit lists of survivors' names and, now, their personal messages. At New York, the Wanamaker department store's wireless station (call letters 'MHI'), among the first to receive news of *Titanic*'s danger, remains on the air to receive messages, as explained in this 17 April newspaper notice. (*New York Evening Mail*)

END OF VOYAGE

Thursday, 18 April 1912

6.00pm: Approaching New York, *Carpathia* passes the Ambrose Light Vessel.

7.00pm: Off Staten Island, the liner slows to take aboard Dr Joseph J. O'Connel, the port physician, who arrives aboard the quarantine vessel *Governor Flower*.

7.45pm: *Carpathia* draws slowly past the Battery at Manhattan's southern tip, where thousands of spectators stand silently in a heavy rain.

8.40pm: Moving slowly up the North River to a spot in the vicinity of Pier 60 at the foot of West 20th Street, *Carpathia* wheels around to port and comes to a stop in mid-river. *Titanic*'s lifeboats are lowered to the water using *Carpathia*'s davits, and are taken in tow

Above At about 4.00pm *Carpathia* passes Fire Island, about 50 miles east of New York Harbor. (*Harper's*)

Right Even as *Carpathia* nears her dock, a newspaper advertisement exploits the situation – half sympathetically, half commercially. (*Philadelphia Inquirer*)

by Merritt & Chapman's tug *Champion*. In solemn file the boats are conveyed to the space between Piers 58 and 59. *Carpathia* moves slowly, almost drifting, down river to her own pier, 54, at the foot of West 14th Street.

9.30pm: After docking and tying up on the north side of Pier 54, *Carpathia* lowers her gangways. Aboard are 743 of her own passengers, 326 officers and crew and 712 survivors of *Titanic*'s tragic loss.

The pier is packed with reporters, officials and survivors' friends and relatives. First up the gangway is Captain David J. Roberts, the Cunard Line's marine superintendent at New York, followed moments later by Mr P.A.S. Franklin, American vice-president of the International Mercantile Marine Company, *Titanic*'s parent company. On board, Franklin goes at once to the surgeon's cabin, where he confers with J. Bruce Ismay.

9.35pm: *Titanic*'s First and Second Class survivors begin to disembark. From the watchers on the pier emerges the sound of a low moan, punctuated by outbursts of sobbing. Most of the 317 passengers are met by friends and family members.

9.45pm: Pressing past the disembarking survivors is Senator William Alden Smith, who arrived at Pennsylvania Station from Washington at 9.00pm, and his party of five (which includes three United States marshals, Senator Smith's secretary, and Senator Francis Newlands, a member of the hastily formed Senatorial investigative committee).

Pushing up the gangway, Senator Smith asks for directions to Ismay's cabin and is escorted there by two of *Carpathia*'s officers. Knocking loudly and entering the cabin, Smith is confronted by Phillip Franklin, who has arrived only moments before. Senators Smith and Newlands confer privately with Franklin and Ismay. Their interview is apparently amicable; the senators depart with promises of full cooperation

Top *Titanic*'s lifeboats are lowered from *Carpathia*. (*Popular Mechanics*)

Middle Before being towed by the tug *Champion*, the boats drift aimlessly in the North River. (*Harper's*)

Right *Titanic*'s boats are towed toward shore. (*Philadelphia Inquirer*)

Passengers aboard *Carpathia* appear on deck as the liner nears her pier. (*Harper's*)

Her rescue mission completed, *Carpathia* docks at her own pier. (*Philadelphia Bulletin*)

Police attempt to get the crowd cleared from 13th Avenue across from Pier 54. (*Harper's*)

At the pier, pedestrians and automobiles vie for space in which to await the disembarkation of *Titanic*'s passengers. (*Harper's*)

All eyes are fixed as the first survivors leave the pier. (Private collection)

A woman identified as May Futrelle is escorted to a cab by Robert Norton, a reporter for the *Boston Post*. (*Harper's*)

from IMM and White Star during their forthcoming inquiry.

11.00pm: Shortly before the hour the 174 Third Class survivors begin to emerge from the aft gangway. Instead of supportive crowds of well-wishers, many are met by representatives of various relief agencies.

11.30pm: Last to leave *Carpathia*, also by way of the aft gangway, are the 210 survivors of *Titanic*'s crew. At Pier 54's far western end they board the tender *George Starr* and are taken upriver to Pier 60, where they board the Red Star liner *Lapland*. Here they are fed and assigned bunks in the ship's Third Class area. Surviving officers are placed in Second Class cabins.

During the night of 18/19 April, *Titanic*'s lifeboats float at the bulkhead between Piers 58 and 59. Men employed by the White Star Line remove the boats' nameplates, markings and sailing equipment, but not before some unauthorised pilferage occurs.

Owing to the Death of

Mr. and Mrs. Isidor Straus

This Store Will be Closed

Friday and Saturday

Abraham & Straus

Brooklyn, N. Y.

Owing to the death of
Mr. and Mrs. Isidor Straus
this store will be closed
Friday and Saturday

R. H. Macy & Co.

HERALD SQUARE
Broadway, 34th to 35th Street.
NEW YORK.

Top One of the few photographs of several *Titanic* Third Class passengers. (*New York Evening Journal*)

Middle left During 18/19 April *Titanic*'s lifeboats float at the bulkhead between Pier 58 and Pier 59. (*New York World*)

Middle right Officials move to protect the 13 boats from souvenir hunters. (Authors' collection)

Left Apparently running for three consecutive evenings are notices that Macy's and Abraham & Straus will be closed on Friday and Saturday, 19 and 20 April, to honour the memory of Isidor and Ida Straus. (*New York Evening Mail*)

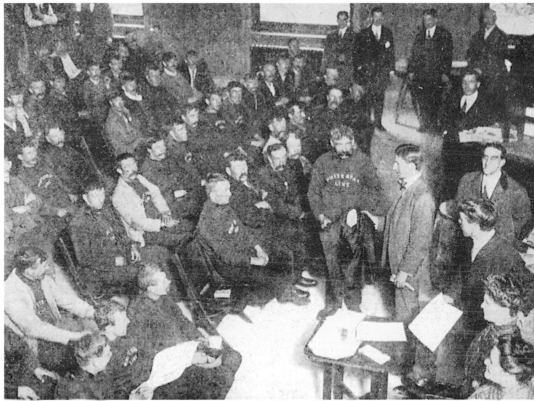

Top left During the morning of 19 April members of *Titanic*'s crew visit the Institute of the Seaman's Friend at 507 West Street near Pier 54. (Authors' collection')

Top right Later that day, the Institute provides the destitute men, whose pay stopped the moment *Titanic* sank, with replacement clothing. (*Daily Mail*)

Right Cunard Line immediately begin to restock *Carpathia* for a resumption of her interrupted voyage to the Mediterranean. (*Popular Mechanics*)

Friday, 19 April 1912

DURING THE EVENING *Titanic*'s lifeboats are hauled up to the second-floor loft of Pier 59.

Saturday, 20 April 1912

4.00pm: *Carpathia* departs New York to continue her interrupted voyage to Gibraltar and the Mediterranean. While at New York between 18 and 20 April, 12 First and four Second Class passengers have left the ship, while four First and four Second Class passengers have come aboard. When *Carpathia* sails she has aboard 735 passengers (120 First, 50 Second, 565 Third), six officers and 320 crew. During the voyage Captain Rostron writes of his rescue of *Titanic*'s survivors in a parchment for the Modern Historic Records Association. His declaration of '705 souls' saved is generally regarded as an accurate count of the disaster's survivors.

Top Just before their departure aboard *Lapland*, *Titanic*'s crew pose for a photograph on the steps of the Institute of the Seaman's Friend. (Authors' collection)

Middle Provisioned and refuelled, *Carpathia* backs away from her New York pier. (Library of Congress)

Left Tugs in attendance, the gallant liner resumes her interrupted voyage. (Library of Congress)

The conclusion of Captain Rostron's account: 'Saved ... Total. 705 souls'. Dated 'At Sea, 27 April 1912'. (Modern Historic Records Association)

We steamed 56 miles round the ice field & passed many bergs after leaving vicinity of disaster, had rather a trying voyage back, having very disagreeable weather with fog ch. right up to our arrival in Dock. New York.

We arrived in New York & docked 9.10 p.m. Thursday the 18th of April 1912.

Saved. 1st Class passengers. 202.
2nd . 115.
3rd . 178
Officers. 4
Crew. 206. TOTAL. 705 SOULS
Boats. 13.

A.H. Rostron.
Commander R.N.R.
Commanding R.M.S. "Carpathia".

The drama of *Titanic*'s loss and *Carpathia*'s rescue of survivors appears as two prosaic lines in a 1913 shipping report. (Frank O. Braynard collection)

TRANS-ATLANTIC PASSENGER MOVEMENT, 1912.

Table XXIII. CUNARD LINE.
NEW YORK—LIVERPOOL.

N.Y. Arrival	Westbound I	II	III	STEAMER	N.Y. Departure	I	Eastbound II	III	Dept.
Jan. 2	59	74	185	....Saxonia	Jan. 6	19	49	101	7
" 4	335	226	217	....Lusitania	" 10	377	222	427	7
				....Ivernia	" 13	18	14	89	6
" 15	84	233	299	....Franconia					
" 21	95	124	216	....Carmania	" 27	160	115	249	11
" 29	160	285	394	....Laconia					
Feb. 5	31	116	317	....Cameronia ...					
" 10	65	246	285	....Campania	Feb. 14	29	84	200	9
" 18	70	372	279	....Carmania					
" 24	311	428	900	....Lusitania	" 28	316	160	387	14
Mar. 2	83	275	540	....Campania	Mar. 6	91	117	324	3
" 8	245	275	933	....Mauretania ...	" 13	245	130	384	5
" 15	362	328	1076	....Lusitania	" 20	287	174	634	5
" 24	93	374	618	....Campania	" 27	61	115	289	8
" 29	339	325	1032	....Mauretania ..	Apr. 3	305	154	490	13
Apr. 7	175	298	1623	....Caronia	" 10	117	128	451	1
" 14	96	366	933	....Carmania	" 17	102	151	361	31
18	201	118	179	{ Carpathia ..					
		207 crew		{ ex Titanic.					
" 19	238	296	942	....Mauretania ...	" 24	465	291	677	25
" 28	96	368	1004	....Caronia	May 4	197	212	364	9
May 3	347	262	1056	....Lusitania	" 8	401	326	896	3
" 12	141	348	995	....Carmania	" 18	196	279	590	9

EIGHT

AFTERMATH

THE DAYS AND WEEKS following *Titanic*'s loss saw several separate series of events occur on both sides of the Atlantic. One involved *Titanic*'s human complement, lost and saved: burials of victims at sea, and burials ashore; repatriation of surviving passengers and crew; and, by means of services and memorials the world over, remembrance of those lost. Another involved the United States Senate's efforts to obtain answers necessary before framing legislation to protect the travelling public from similar future disasters. Finally, with the luxury of time – and the opportunity to learn from the American investigation's findings and omissions – came the British Government's searching Inquiry into the disaster. The dates in this chapter are arranged for convenience and clarity into three separate 'chronologies' reflecting each of these series, although in reality they occurred simultaneously; recovery of bodies occupied 17 April to 11 June, the final burial of a *Titanic* victim taking place on 12 June; the American Inquiry lasted from 19 April to 4 May, the report being read to the Senate on 28 May; and the British Inquiry lasted from 2 May to 8 July, the report being published on 30 July.

THE HUMAN COST

Wednesday, 17 April 1912

12.15pm, Halifax, Nova Scotia: The Commercial Cable Company's cable ship *Mackay-Bennett* departs from Halifax in search of *Titanic*'s victims, having been chartered by the White Star Line. The search is conducted in the vicinity of 42°N, 49°20'W.

Mackay-Bennett. (Authors' collection)

Friday, 19 April 1912

Noon, London, England: A solemn memorial service for *Titanic*'s dead is conducted at St Paul's Cathedral. The service is attended by almost 10,000 mourners.

Top right Morticians aboard *Mackay-Bennett* are from the Halifax firm of John Snow, Undertakers. (Nova Scotia Archives)

Middle Crowds outside St Paul's Cathedral, London, for the memorial service. (*Lloyds Deathless Story*)

Below The programme for the service. (Bob Forrest collection)

Below right *Lapland* leaves New York. (*Boston Post*)

ST. PAUL'S CATHEDRAL.

FRIDAY, 19TH APRIL, 1912,
AT 12 NOON.

Memorial Service

FOR

THOSE WHO PERISHED THROUGH THE
FOUNDERING OF THE SS. "TITANIC"
ON
MONDAY, APRIL 15TH, 1912.

Early morning, New York, NY: During the early morning hours, 29 of *Titanic*'s crew who are to remain behind to testify at the American hearings are removed from the *Lapland* and taken to the White Star Liner *Celtic*, moored at Pier 60, where they are housed during the New York phase of the Inquiry.

10.00am: The Red Star liner *Lapland* departs from Pier 61 for England. Aboard are 172 survivors of *Titanic*'s crew: 152 men and 20 women. *Lapland* also carries 1,927 sacks of mail originally intended for *Titanic*. At Sandy Hook, New Jersey (the outer limit of New York Harbor), *Lapland* is held up as five crewmen, including quartermaster Robert Hichens, are removed aboard the tug *R.J. Barrett* by order of Senator Smith, who wishes to question them further on newly discovered evidence.

Top On 21 April a recovery team from *Mackay-Bennett* sights and examines *Titanic*'s overturned collapsible lifeboat B. Several efforts to retrieve the boat are unsuccessful; it is left adrift. (National Archives and Records Administration – New York Branch)

Middle A log is carefully maintained of all bodies recovered by the *Mackay-Bennett*. Each page represents a single body. On 30 April a page records the recovery of John Jacob Astor's body, number 124. (Nova Scotia Archives)

Left The handwritten records are later published in printed form. (Nova Scotia Archives)

NO. 124.   MALE.   ESTIMATED AGE, 50.   LIGHT HAIR AND MOUSTACHE.

CLOTHING—Blue serge suit; blue handkerchief with "A. V."; belt with gold buckle; brown boots with red rubber soles; brown flannel shirt; "J. J. A." on back of collar.

EFFECTS—Gold watch; cuff links, gold with diamond; diamond ring with three stones; £225 in English notes; $2440 in notes; £5 in gold; 7s. in silver; 5 ten franc pieces; gold pencil; pocketbook.

FIRST CLASS.   NAME—J. J. ASTOR.

Monday, 22 April 1912

11.45pm, Halifax, Nova Scotia: The Anglo-American Telegraph Company's cable ship *Minia* departs in search of additional *Titanic* victims.

Top *Minia*. (Courtesy of the Mariners Museum, Newport News, Va)

Middle Prior to leaving Halifax to relieve the *Mackay-Bennett*, already on site, a *Minia* officer supervises the loading of coffins aboard the ship. (*Daily Mirror*)

Bottom The crew from *Minia* retrieve another victim's body; the photograph is taken by a crew member of *Mackay-Bennett*, soon to depart for Halifax. (Nova Scotia Archives)

Below As *Titanic* was sinking, Edith Corse Evans gave up her lifeboat to an older woman with children. On Monday 22 April at New York City's Grace Episcopal Church, a memorial service is held for this heroic lady. Later a memorial plaque is installed in the church. (Authors' collection)

April 22, 1912.
1.5 PM.

A. G. Jones, White Star - Dominion Line,
~~Montreal~~XX~~Canada~~XX Halifax, N.S.

We have arranged with Western Union people send down cable ship
"Minia" to assist Mackay Bennett in recovery of bodies. Please immediately
make same arrangements for caskets etc for Minia as were made for
Mackay Bennett. Most urgent Minia proceed to sea at earliest ~~XXXXX~~
moment. Advise us immediately when she expects to sail. Mackay Bennett
wires she has recovered 50 bodies and will probably be returning to
Halifax promptly make all necessary arrangements ahead for her reception.
                                        P.A.S.Franklin.

                Franklin

During her voyage to recover *Titanic*'s victims, *Mackay-Bennett* is in constant communication with White Star's Halifax agents and New York office. The horror and drama of the first days' searches are clearly seen in these telegrams from the *Mackay-Bennett* to White Star's New York office. (All © 1999 John P. Eaton and Charles A. Haas)

At an early time it is already decided that a second recovery vessel will be needed.

1 LCL 7   C S MACKAY-BENNETT VIA S S LACONIA AND CAPERACE 22

        ISMAY WHITE STAR LINE CARE COMMERCIAL CABLE COMPANY

                        NEWYORK.

A CAREFUL RECORD HAS BEEN MADE OF ALL PAPERS MONEYS AND
VALUABLES FOUND ON BODIES WOULD IT NOT BE BETTER TO
BURY ALL BODIES AT SEA UNLESS SPECIALLY REQUESTED BY
RELATIVES TO PRESERVE THEM
                        MACKAY BENNETT.

Mackay-Bennett's crew is overwhelmed by the scope of its recovery work and wonders whether burials at sea would be best.

16. Dbl.—7647
    LCL 3 C S MACKAY BENNETT VIA S S ROYAL GEORGE   APR 23 1912
                        VIA CAPERACE NFLD
    ISMAY WHITE STAR LINE CARE COMMERCIAL CABLE CO
                        NEWYORK.
    FOLLOWING IDENTIFIED TODAY MONDAY STOP MRS MACK MRS N
    MCNAMEE STOP CATAVELAS VASSILIOS STOP W VEAR STOP MARY
    MANAGAN STOP WILLIAM SAGE STOP JAMES FARREL STOP HENRY
    D HANSEN STOP JAMES KELLY STOP MAURETZ ADAHL STOP REG
    HALE AND W D DOUGLAS STOP DOUGLAS HAS BEEN EMBALMED STOP
    ABOVE ALL PASSENGERS HAVE ALSO IDENTIFIED J R RICE ASST
    PURSER STOP G HINCKLEY STOP HOSPITAL ATTENDANT STOP AND
    W BUTT OF CREW TOTAL BODIES TO DATE SEVENTY SEVEN.
                        MACKAY BENNETT

To assist in answering insistent queries, *Mackay-Bennett* telegraphs the identified dead to New York via the *Royal George*.

POSTAL TELEGRAPH – COMMERCIAL CABLES
TELEGRAM

Wireless, RUSH.

Apl. 23, 1912.   8.35 AM.

Commander, cable ship "Mackey-Bennett.

"Titanic" foundered 41.15 north, 50.14 west. Absolutely essential you should bring to port all bodies you can possibly accommodate. Your first list identifications shows George Widen. Can you possibly confirm this as George D. Widener. Wire us when you propose leave scene for Halifax.

Franklin.

White Star responds to *Mackay-Bennett*'s 22 April cable and requests that as many bodies as possible be brought to shore.

A. G. Jones & Co.,
    White Star-Dominion Line,
    Halifax, N.S.

Apl. 24, 1912.   10 AM.

Liverpool Managers cable as follows begins ODVAXUFHIV ROVRQUKXIR AHZYKRABFK HYIWOBIHTA CKMPAAKFIM RISCOSIDVUD RAJKO GRAVES WISAZHIPFR TUGJR. ENDS. Bentley Code used.

Franklin.

Translation: Liverpool Managers cable as follows begins: "Please take care that all bodies identified but not claimed are buried in separate graves with head stones". Ends. Bentley Code used.

Early in the recovery process, White Star's Liverpool headquarters issues instructions in a coded message regarding the unclaimed dead.

Form 1864

THE WESTERN UNION TELEGRAPH COMPANY
INCORPORATED
25,000 OFFICES IN AMERICA.   CABLE SERVICE TO ALL THE WORLD

This Company TRANSMITS and DELIVERS messages only on conditions limiting its liability, which have been assented to by the sender of the following message. Errors can be guarded against only by repeating a message back to the sending station for comparison, and the Company will not hold itself liable for errors or delays in transmission or delivery of Unrepeated Messages, beyond the amount of tolls paid thereon, nor in any case beyond the sum of Fifty Dollars, at which, unless otherwise stated below, this message has been valued by the sender thereof, nor in any case where the claim is not presented in writing within sixty days after the message is filed with the Company for transmission. This is an UNREPEATED MESSAGE, and is delivered by request of the sender, under the conditions named above.

THEO. N. VAIL, PRESIDENT   BELVIDERE BROOKS, GENERAL MANAGER

RECEIVED AT   3 Co CH 12 Rush X
                 Halifax NS 24

A. S. Franklin,

Have all preliminaries well in hand writing particulars   unless instructed to Pierre

P. V. G. Mitchell

White Star passenger manager Percy Van Gelder Mitchell assures IMM vice president P.A.S. Franklin that preparations are complete for *Mackay-Bennett*'s arrival at Halifax.

CL 5 C S MACKAY BENNETT   VIA CAPERACE NFLD   APL 25TH 12
ISMAY WHITE STAR LINE CARE COMMERCIAL CABLE CO NY.

BODIES ARE NUMEROUS IN LAT 47.35 N 48.37 W EXTENDING MANY
MILES EAST AND WEST MAILSHIPS SHOULD GIVE THIS A WIDE
BERTH STOP MEDICAL OPINION IS THAT DEATH HAS BEEN
PRACTICALLY INSTANTANEOUS IN ALL CASES OWING TO PRESSURE
WHEN BODIES DRAWN DOWN IN VORTEX.

MACKAY-BENNETT.

2.20AM

Recovery becomes almost impossible as bodies are dispersed by wind and currents.

LCL 3   C S   MACKAY-BENNETT VIA CAPERACE NFLD   APL 25TH 12
ISMAY WHITE STAR LINE CARE COMMERCIAL CABLE CO NY

DRIFTING IN DENSE FOG SINCE NOON YESTERDAY TOTAL PICKED
UP TWO HUNDRED AND FIVE WE BROUGHT AWAY ALL EMBALMING
FLUIDS TO BE HAD IN HALIFAX ENOUGH FOR SEVENTY [STOP] WITH
A WEEKS FINE WEATHER I THINK WE WOULD PRETTY WELL CLEAN
UP THE RELICS OF THE DISASTER IT IS MY OPINION THAT
THE MAJORITY WILL NEVER COME TO THE SURFACE.
MACKAY-BENNETT.
2.30AM

The problems are exacerbated by fog and depleted supplies.

SS. MACKAY-BENNETT, Via Cape Race,NF, 26th.   APR 27 1912
    ISMAY- care Commercial Cable Co., New York.
Noon picked up fourteen more bodies today. Now leaving for Halifax.
Minia now working on position.
                    MACKAY-BENNETT.

As *Mackay-Bennett* makes her final recoveries and prepares to return to Halifax, *Minia* is already at work. (Images © 1999 John P. Eaton and Charles A. Haas)

Sunday, 28 April 1912

7.45am, Plymouth, England: *Lapland* arrives carrying 167 members of *Titanic*'s crew. The liner anchors at Cawsand Bay, some distance from the docks, and the survivors are ferried ashore aboard the tender *Sir Richard Grenville*.

6.00pm: After questioning by Board of Trade authorities and receiving subpoenas to appear at further hearings, some 85 seamen and firemen depart on a special train for Southampton, where they arrive shortly after 10.00pm.

Top *Lapland* arrives at Plymouth. (*Daily Sketch*)

Middle A high dockyard gate separates some of *Titanic*'s crew from members of the public in search of news. (Authors' collection)

Bottom Rows of beds awaiting *Titanic*'s crew at Plymouth prove unnecessary as crew members are not detained overnight for questioning. (*Illustrated London News*)

Below *Titanic* crewmen arrive at Southampton. (Private collection)

BENEFIT PERFORMANCE
FOR THE FAMILIES OF THE VICTIMS
of the
"TITANIC" DISASTER

The Twenty-Ninth of April, 1912
METROPOLITAN OPERA HOUSE
NEW YORK

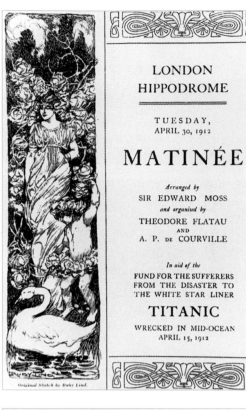

LONDON
HIPPODROME

TUESDAY,
APRIL 30, 1912

MATINÉE

Arranged by
SIR EDWARD MOSS
and organised by
THEODORE FLATAU
AND
A. P. DE COURVILLE

In aid of the
FUND FOR THE SUFFERERS
FROM THE DISASTER TO
THE WHITE STAR LINER
TITANIC
WRECKED IN MID-OCEAN
APRIL 15, 1912

Original Sketch by Ruby Lind.

Monday, 29 April 1912

A MEMORIAL BENEFIT concert is held at the Metropolitan Opera House, New York. Among the distinguished performers is renowned tenor Enrico Caruso. Meanwhile, in London, England, large benefit matinees are also held at several theatres around this date, including the London Hippodrome (30 April) and the Coliseum (1 May). **9.20pm**, Southampton, England: After interrogation at Plymouth, 86 stewards and stewardesses, Southampton survivors of *Titanic*'s crew, arrive home aboard a special train.

Titanic benefits are held at New York's Metropolitan Opera House, the London Hippodrome, and Southampton's own Hippodrome. Elsewhere other theatres great and small contribute their facilities to disaster fundraising. (Authors' collection/Bob Forrest collection/*Southampton and District Pictorial*)

Theatrical and Enterta

THE NEW Telegraph Grand Theatre
GRAND THEATRE.
West Marlands, Southampton.

Sole Lessees: Exors. of the late FREDK. MOUILLOT
Resident Manager - - Mr. ARTHUR WESTON

Free List Entirely Suspended!

For Week commencing April 22nd.
Matinee, Saturday, at 2.30.

Under the Patronage of the Mayor and
Corporation.

MR. ARTHUR HARDY presents:—

Lady Beerbohm Tree,
Mr. Kenneth Douglas,
And the Entire Original
LONDON COMPANY,
From the Queen's Theatre,
IN
THE CHALK LINE.

TITANIC DISASTER.

MR. HARDY and the MANAGEMENT of the GRAND THEATRE will hand over 25 per cent. of the Gross Takings for the Week to the MAYOR'S FUND,—

In aid of the Widows, Orphans, and Dependents of the Crew.

Public patronage is earnestly requested.

DRESS CIRCLE 3/6 & 3/-. STALLS 2/- (doors 2/6).
Early Door, 7/6. Ordinary Door, 7.15.

Seats once booked cannot be exchanged, and under no circumstances can Money be returned.

MONDAY, 29th APRIL, for Six Nights at 7.30,
MATINEE, Saturday at 2.30,
The Playhouse Theatre Comedy,
"DAD."
By arrangement with CYRIL MAUDE.

HIPPODROME
SOUTHAMPTON.

Proprietors - The South of England Hippodromes, Ltd.
Managing Director - Mr. WALTER DE FRECE
Resident Manager - Mr. H. YARDLEY

PRELIMINARY NOTICE.

A Special =
Matinee

WILL BE GIVEN ON

WEDNESDAY, MAY 1st,

IN AID OF

THE MAYOR'S FUND

To relieve the sufferings of the Widows and Children caused through the terrible catastrophe which has overtaken the "Titanic."

The following Gentlemen have kindly consented to act as a Committee:—

His Worship the Mayor; Sir Geo. A. E. Hussey; Col. Candy; Vascon, Sellors, Esq.; Consul for Brazil; Dr. Russell Bencraft; Capt. Plunkett, Royal Mail; P. V. Bowyer, Esq., Chairman of Guardians; Mr. Alderman Sharp; Mr. Alderman W. Bagshaw; Mr. Alderman Ensor; Mr. Councillor Hair; F. E. Allen, Esq.; W. Bulpitt, Esq.; Archie Ede, Esq.; A. Foster, Esq.; Walter de Frece, Esq.; George Gear, Esq.; A. G. Grainger, Esq.; W. Green, Esq.; F. A. K. Housell, Esq.; J. Laidman, Esq.; J. S. Medd, Esq.; A. E. Plumb, Esq.; W. Saunders, Esq.; W. Vincent, Esq.; H. Yardley, Esq. From whom Tickets May be Obtained.

For List of Artistes who have kindly consented to appear, see Special Bills.

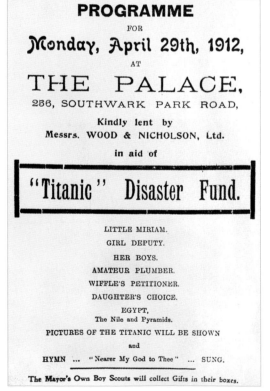

PROGRAMME
FOR
Monday, April 29th, 1912,
AT
THE PALACE,
256, SOUTHWARK PARK ROAD,

Kindly lent by
Messrs. WOOD & NICHOLSON, Ltd.

in aid of

"Titanic" Disaster Fund.

LITTLE MIRIAM.
GIRL DEPUTY.
HER BOYS.
AMATEUR PLUMBER.
WIFFLE'S PETITIONER.
DAUGHTER'S CHOICE.
EGYPT,
The Nile and Pyramids.
PICTURES OF THE TITANIC WILL BE SHOWN
and
HYMN ... "Nearer My God to Thee" ... SUNG.

The Mayor's Own Boy Scouts will collect Gifts in their boxes.

Above Individuals as well as groups help to collect money for the ever-increasing *Titanic* Relief Fund. Here someone makes a public contribution to the Lord Mayor's Fund, London. (*Daily Graphic*)

Above right At a large rally held at *Titanic*'s home port of Southampton, a group of nurses prepare to enter the crowds in search of relief money. (Authors' collection)

Right A second group of crew survivors arrives at Southampton from Plymouth aboard a special train. (Private collection)

Left London's 8th Westminster Boy Scouts proudly prepare to solicit public contributions. (*Daily Telegraph*)

Below right *Mackay-Bennett* returns to Halifax with *Titanic*'s victims aboard. (Russ Lownds collection)

Tuesday, 30 April 1912

9.30am, Halifax, Nova Scotia: *Mackay-Bennett* returns, having recovered 306 bodies, 116 of which have been buried at sea.

Thursday, 2 May 1912

BRUCE ISMAY, OFFICERS Lightoller, Pitman, Lowe and Boxhall, and 30 other survivors of the *Titanic* disaster sail for Liverpool from New York aboard the *Adriatic*.

Friday, 3 May 1912

THE FIRST OF *TITANIC*'S dead are buried in Fairview Lawn, Mount Olivet and Baron de Hirsch cemeteries, Halifax, Nova Scotia. At Sorel, Quebec, the Canadian Government's Department of Fisheries steamship *Montmagny* is dispatched to Halifax to take on personnel and supplies in order to join in the search for *Titanic*'s victims.

Titanic victims' graves at Fairview Lawn (top), Mount Olivet (middle) and Baron de Hirsch (bottom) cemeteries at Halifax, Nova Scotia. (Authors' collection)

J. Bruce Ismay. (Private collection)

Monday, 6 May 1912

AFTER ARRIVING AT quarantine outside Halifax Harbour around 2.00am and waiting until daylight, *Minia* sails on to the naval dockyard, where she berths at about 7.00am at Pier 4. Of the 17 bodies recovered during her cruise, 15 are brought to port for burial. Later in the morning *Montmagny* departs Halifax on her search mission. *Celtic* docks at Liverpool, England, with the remaining members of *Titanic*'s crew who have been detained at the American Inquiry.

Saturday, 11 May 1912

7.30am, Liverpool, England: The White Star liner *Adriatic* docks at the Princes Landing Stage. Disembarking are J. Bruce Ismay and *Titanic*'s four surviving officers, Lightoller (second), Pitman (third), Boxhall (fourth) and Lowe (fifth). Accompanied by Mrs Ismay, who had boarded the inbound *Adriatic* at Queenstown, Bruce Ismay is met by a large crowd of well-wishers, who 'waved hats and handkerchiefs and loudly cheered the White Star chairman'.

Top *Montmagny*. (Canadian Ministry of Transport)

Middle Having earlier joined her husband at Queenstown, Florence Ismay joins Bruce Ismay (centre) in descending *Adriatic*'s gangway on 11 May. (*Daily Graphic*)

Right Among the other survivors arriving aboard *Adriatic* are third officer Herbert Pitman and second officer Charles Lightoller. (*Daily Graphic*)

Above left Carnegie Hall is the venue for a memorial service to Isidor and Ida Straus. (*New York Evening Journal*)

Above Ida and Isidor Straus are remembered in other ways, as this sheet music cover shows. (Authors' collection)

Left and below Collapsible A is discovered still afloat, and is brought back to New York. (*Daily Sketch/Southampton and District Pictorial*)

Sunday, 12 May 1912

NEW YORK CITY'S mayor William J. Gaynor and philanthropist Andrew Carnegie are among the speakers at a memorial service for Isidor Straus and his wife Ida, held at Carnegie Hall. Every seat in the large hall is filled. Thousands, unable to squeeze inside, stand outside in the rain and fill West 57th Street to pay tribute to the Strauses' memory.

Monday, 13 May 1912

MONTMAGNY RETURNS TO Louisburg, Nova Scotia, with four bodies, which are shipped to Halifax via the Sydney & Louisburg and Canadian National Railway. The ship re-bunkers and takes aboard more supplies for another trip to the disaster area. At sea, at 47°01'N, 30°56'W, *Titanic*'s collapsible boat A, cast adrift with its sea cocks open on 15 April by fifth officer Lowe, is found still afloat by White Star's *Oceanic* during a westbound crossing from Liverpool to New York. The three bodies that were in the boat when it was set adrift are still on board: First Class passenger Thompson Beattie and a fireman and a seaman, both unidentified. Under the supervision of *Oceanic*'s surgeon, Dr Riversdale Sampson French, the bodies are examined for identification, then wrapped in canvas, weighted and committed to the deep, the burial service being read by Dr French. The collapsible is taken aboard *Oceanic* and brought to New York, where, on 16 May, it is placed with the remaining boats in Pier 59's second-floor loft.

Tuesday, 14 May 1912

THIS IS THE PLANNED release date in New York of the film *Saved From The Titanic*. Produced by the Eclair Film Company of Fort Lee, New Jersey, the film features the company's star, Miss Dorothy Gibson, herself a *Titanic* survivor. The Royal Opera House at Covent Garden, London, England, hosts a memorial benefit concert for the Titanic Relief Fund. The Canadian Government's vessel *Montmagny* departs from Louisburg, Nova Scotia, for the disaster site. The vessel cruises back and forth seeking additional bodies, but the search is fruitless. *Montmagny* finally leaves the area at 11.00pm on Sunday, 19 May.

The cover and title page of the Covent Garden Opera House benefit programme. (Authors' collection)

Thursday, 16 May 1912

THE BOWRING BROTHERS' steamer *Algerine* departs from St John's, Newfoundland, on a search for *Titanic* victims. Only one is found, steward James McGrady. His remains are brought to St John's and transshipped to Halifax aboard the steamer *Florizel*, arriving on 11 June at Nova Scotia's capital. Meanwhile, in New York, a mystery that began with Michel Navratil kidnapping his two sons from his own family home in Nice, France, is solved with the reunion of the '*Titanic* Orphans' with their mother, Mme Marcelle Navratil, in the Manhattan home of Miss Margaret Hays at 304 West 83rd Street.

Dorothy Gibson, star of *Saved From the Titanic*. (Library of Congress)

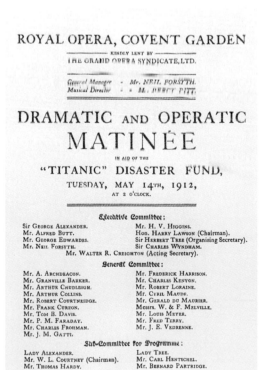

ROYAL OPERA, COVENT GARDEN

KINDLY LENT BY
THE GRAND OPERA SYNDICATE, LTD.

General Manager - Mr. NEIL FORSYTH.
Musical Director - Mr. PERCY PITT.

DRAMATIC AND OPERATIC
MATINÉE
IN AID OF THE
"TITANIC" DISASTER FUND,
TUESDAY, MAY 14TH, 1912,
AT 2 O'CLOCK.

Executive Committee:

Sir George Alexander.
Mr. Alfred Butt.
Mr. George Edwardes.
Mr. Neil Forsyth.
Mr. H. V. Higgins.
Hon. Harry Lawson (Chairman).
Sir Herbert Tree (Organising Secretary).
Sir Charles Wyndham.
Mr. Walter R. Creighton (Acting Secretary).

General Committee:

Mr. A. Archdeacon.
Mr. Granville Barker.
Mr. Arthur Chudleigh.
Mr. Arthur Collins.
Mr. Robert Courtneidge.
Mr. Frank Curzon.
Mr. Tom B. Davis.
Mr. P. M. Faraday.
Mr. Charles Frohman.
Mr. J. M. Gatti.
Mr. Frederick Harrison.
Mr. Charles Kenyon.
Mr. Robert Loraine.
Mr. Cyril Maude.
Mr. Gerald du Maurier.
Messrs. W. & F. Melville.
Mr. Louis Meyer.
Mr. Fred Terry.
Mr. J. E. Vedrenne.

Sub-Committee for Programme:

Lady Alexander.
Mr. W. L. Courtney (Chairman).
Mr. Thomas Hardy.
Lady Tree.
Mr. Carl Hentschel.
Mr. Bernard Partridge.

Mme Marcelle Navratil is reunited with her children Michel (left) and Edmond in New York City. (Authors' collection)

After purchasing a ticket through Thomas Cook at Monte Carlo, Monsieur Navratil had taken the boys – Michel, aged 4, and Edmond, aged 2 – first to London, then to Southampton, where they had boarded *Titanic* on her maiden voyage.

During the doomed liner's evacuation, Navratil had placed the boys in collapsible boat 'D' while he stayed behind and perished.

Aboard *Carpathia* the boys had been 'adopted' by Miss Hays, who spoke French and could communicate somewhat with the older boy, Michel. At New York Miss Hays had taken the boys to her home, clothed and comforted them, and had initiated the effort to discover the boys' mother.

Through the cooperation of the Consul-General at New York and the British Consul in Nice, Marcelle Navratil is located, and, with the White Star Line's help, is transported to New York aboard *Oceanic*. Upon her arrival, he goes immediately to Miss Hays's residence, where a joyful reunion takes place. The family returns to France aboard *Oceanic*, departing from New York on Saturday, 18 May.

Top *Algerine* at St John's, Newfoundland, 1903. (J.D. Somborger Collection, Canadian Museum of History)

Middle Harold Bride (centre) returns aboard *Baltic*. (*Daily Sketch*)

Left The flower-covered casket of bandmaster Wallace Hartley is borne from the funeral service conducted in Bethel Chapel, Primet Bridge, Colne, Lancashire. (*Daily Graphic*)

Saturday, 18 May 1912

HAROLD BRIDE, *TITANIC*'S surviving junior telegraphist, arrives back in Liverpool, England, aboard the White Star liner *Baltic*. Meanwhile, in Colne, Lancashire, *Titanic*'s orchestra leader, Wallace Hartley, is buried. A crowd estimated at 30,000 attends the emotion-filled ceremony and burial service. A special thanksgiving service is held the next day at the Shortlands (Kent) Congregational Church that is attended by Mr Bride and his family. During the service the hymn 'Nearer my God to Thee' is sung in the Arthur Sullivan setting.

Above right A large crowd outside awaits the passage of the funeral cortege. (Arnold Watson collection)

Below Hartley's hearse is followed by a crowd estimated at 30,000 mourners (*Daily Graphic*)

Right A handsome stone marks Wallace Hartley's burial place at Colne's Public Cemetery. (Arnold Watson collection)

Far right Later, the citizens of Colne erect a handsome memorial statue to Hartley in Albert Road. (Arnold Watson collection)

SOUVENIR
PROGRAMME
OF THE GRAND
Memorial Concert
IN AID OF
Heroic Band of the

"S. S. TITANIC."
AT THE
ROYAL ALBERT HALL
Friday May 24th, 1912.

ROYAL ALBERT HALL.
Manager - HILTON CARTER.

Under the Auspices of the Orchestral Association.

THE "TITANIC" BAND
MEMORIAL CONCERT
FRIDAY, 24th MAY, 1912 (Empire Day) at 3 p.m.

THE PHILHARMONIC ORCHESTRA.
THE QUEEN'S HALL ORCHESTRA.
THE LONDON SYMPHONY ORCHESTRA.
THE NEW SYMPHONY ORCHESTRA.
THE BEECHAM SYMPHONY ORCHESTRA.
THE ROYAL OPERA ORCHESTRA.
THE LONDON OPERA HOUSE ORCHESTRA.
(By kind permission of their respective Managements).

Conductors.
SIR EDWARD ELGAR, O.M.
(Conductor of the London Symphony Orchestra).
SIR HENRY J. WOOD
Conductor of the Queen's Hall Orchestra).
Mr. LANDON RONALD
(Conductor of the New Symphony Orchestra).
Mr. THOMAS BEECHAM
(Conductor of the Beecham Symphony Orchestra).
Mr. PERCY PITT
(Musical Director of the Royal Opera House).
M. FRITZ ERNALDY
(Conductor of the London Opera House).
and
Herr MENGELBERG
Vocalist:
Madame ADA CROSSLEY.

The Albert Hall Memorial Concert for *Titanic*'s bandsmen. (Bob Forrest collection/*Daily Sketch*)

Denver socialite Margaret Tobin Brown presents Captain Arthur Rostron with a silver loving cup from *Titanic*'s rescued passengers. (Private collection)

Friday, 24 May 1912

A BENEFIT MUSICAL concert for *Titanic*'s musicians is held at the Albert Hall, London, England. The circular auditorium is filled to capacity, with nearly 10,000 in attendance. An ensemble of 500 musicians from London's symphonic and concert orchestras performs under the leadership of several prominent conductors. At the concert's end the entire audience rises and sings with deep feeling Dyke's setting of 'Nearer My God to Thee', under the leadership of Sir Henry Wood.

Wednesday, 29 May 1912

CARPATHIA ARRIVES AT New York on her first return visit following her rescue of *Titanic*'s survivors. After the passengers have disembarked, a survivors' committee, headed by Margaret 'Molly' Brown, boards the liner and presents Captain Rostron with a loving cup. Gold medals are given to

One of the medals presented *to Carpathia*'s crew. (Authors' collection)

Carpathia's senior officers, silver medals to the junior officers and department heads, and bronze medals to members of the general crew.

Tuesday, 4 June 1912

SOUTHAMPTON'S JUDGE GYE makes the first distribution of payments for claims by dependants of lost members of *Titanic*'s crew. Liability is not disputed by the White Star company; they had already paid to the court's registrar the full amount of the claims. The maximum amount is £300 ($1,500) for stewards; £294 ($1,470) for leading firemen and greasers; £237 ($1,185) for firemen; and £223 ($1,115) for trimmers.

Saturday, 8 June 1912

THE FREIGHTER *ILFORD*, eastbound from Galveston, Texas, to Hamburg, Germany, recovers the drifting body of *Titanic* steward W.F. Cheverton at 40°06'N, 52°51'W. The body is recommitted to the sea.

Wednesday, 12 June 1912

THE FINAL BURIAL at Halifax, Nova Scotia, of a *Titanic* victim takes place; it is body 330, steward James McGrady.

Wednesday, 3 July 1912

IN LONDON, ENGLAND, at the High Court of Justice, King's Bench Division, Case 1912 R No. 1111 between Thomas Ryan, Plaintiff, and The Oceanic Steam Navigation Company Limited, Defendant, is begun with the Statement of claim filed by Mr Thomas Scanlan representing the Plaintiff. Mr Thomas Ryan, father of Third Class passenger Patrick Ryan, who was lost in the disaster, states in his Particulars of Negligence that the Defendant's servants:

SUMMARY OF TITANIC BODY RECOVERIES

A total of 328 'numbered' bodies were recovered by *Mackay-Bennett*, *Minia*, *Montmagny* and *Algerine*. Of these, 119 were buried at sea, and 209 were returned to Halifax.

- *Mackay-Bennett* recovered bodies 1 to 306; 116 were buried at sea and 190 brought back to Halifax.
- *Minia* recovered bodies 307 to 323; two were buried at sea, 16 brought to Halifax. (The numbers 324 and 325 are not accounted for.)
- *Montmagny* recovered bodies 326 to 329; one was buried at sea, the remaining three being brought to Halifax.
- *Algerine* recovered body number 330, which was brought to Halifax aboard *Florizel*.

Of the 209 bodies returned to Halifax, 150 were buried in the city's Fairview, Mount Olivet or Baron de Hirsch cemeteries. An additional 59 were claimed and shipped to other locations for interment.

Regardless of disposition, of the 328 bodies recovered, 124 remained unidentified.

In addition to the 328 numbered bodies, there were:

- buried at sea from *Carpathia*
  15 April   4
  16 April   1
- buried at sea from *Oceanic*
  13 May   3
- buried at sea from *Ottawa*
  6 June   1
- buried at sea from *Ilford*
  8 June   1

Thus, of the 2,225 aboard *Titanic*, apart from the 712 survivors, only 338 bodies are accounted for in some way.

- navigated *Titanic* at excessive and improper speed in view of the conditions then prevailing: exceptional darkness; haze; the absence of wind and movements of the sea; knowing the presence of ice;

- failed to alter course or diminish their speed and failed to provide a sufficient and proper lookout and to provide the lookout with binoculars;

- failed to provide adequate lifeboat accommodation having regard to the number of passengers and crew she was then carrying;

- and that the Defendants failed to have the said crew sufficiently drilled and organised for the work of manning, filling and launching such lifeboats as were provided.

Friday 26 July 1912

THE PLAINTIFF'S SOLICITOR files a Statement of Further Particulars of Plaintiff's Claim in which appears a description of ice warning received by *Titanic*; the alleged negligence of lookouts and lifeboat crews is also reinforced.

Top left Col Archibald Gracie, photographed wearing the clothing worn at the time of his rescue. (*Chicago Record-Herald*)

Top right While writing his book, *The Truth About the Titanic*, based primarily on correspondence with many of the disaster's survivors, Col Gracie lived in this Washington, DC, home. (Authors' collection)

Right The programme for the Century Theatre Memorial. (Authors' collection)

GREATER THAN SELF. STRONGER THAN FATE.
HEROIC SOULS ASK OF US NO TRIBUTE BUT REMEMBRANCE

Century Theatre

NEW YORK

(BY COURTESY OF MR GEORGE C. TYLER)

Friday, December 6th, 1912, at 1:30 p. m.

BENEFIT PERFORMANCE

IN AID OF THE

Woman's Titanic Memorial

UNDER THE AUSPICES OF THE COMBINED THEATRICAL MANAGERS OF GREATER NEW YORK

Under the Direction of . . . . DANIEL FROHMAN
President of the Actors Fund of America

Miss ALICE FISCHER . . . . Assistant Director
Mrs. JOHN HAYS HAMMOND . . . Chairman of the Women's Executive Committee

Program

OVERTURE . . . . . "Up and Down Broadway"
PLAYED BY FRANK R. WHITE ON THE INSTRUMENT CALLED THE "WURLITZER HOPE-JONES UNIT ORCHESTRA." (INVENTED BY R. HOPE-JONES.)

"**Joy and Gloom**"
A Comedy Sketch

ED. WYNNE (the boy with the funny hat)
EDMOND RUSSON (English comedian)
By courtesy of B. F. Keith

Program continued on second page following

Friday, 29 November 1912

A DENIAL OF ALL CLAIMS appears in a statement by Hill, Dickinson & Co. of Liverpool, solicitor for the defendants, including a refusal to admit that the said Patrick Ryan was even aboard *Titanic*. The case comes to court on 20 June 1913.

Wednesday, 4 December 1912

THE DEATH OCCURS in New York at the age of 53 of Colonel Archibald Gracie. Col and Mrs Gracie had been visiting New York from Washington, DC, where they had a home at 1527 16th Street, NW.

Col Gracie interviewed and corresponded with many fellow survivors and incorporated their responses into his own detailed narrative of *Titanic*'s disastrous voyage.

His death less than eight months after the sinking is ascribed by his family to the 'far-reaching effects of his *Titanic* experience,' and also to 'the relentless energy with which he pursued his investigation of the disaster'. His book, *The Truth About the Titanic*, is the most detailed account of the disaster by a survivor.

Gracie is buried at New York City's Woodlawn Cemetery wearing, at his request, the same clothing he wore when he jumped into the water from the sinking liner.

Friday, 6 December 1912

NEW YORK'S CENTURY Theatre hosts a benefit concert for the Titanic Relief Fund.

THE AMERICAN INQUIRY

Wednesday, 17 April 1912

EARLY IN THIS DAY'S session of the United States Senate, Washington, DC, William Alden Smith of Michigan, a member of the standing Committee on Commerce, United States Senate, submits a resolution for the creation of a subcommittee to investigate the loss of the *Titanic* as well as to determine what safety regulations might be necessary to preclude recurrences of similar disasters. The resolution is accepted by unanimous consent, and the Commerce Committee's chairman, Senator Knute Nelson, instantly names Smith chairman of the investigative subcommittee.

The subcommitee is composed of an equal number of Republicans and Democrats, and each party is represented by a liberal, a moderate and a conservative member. The membership of the subcommittee is as follows:

William Alden Smith, Michigan, Chairman
George C. Perkins, California
Jonathan Bourne Jr, Oregon
Theodore E. Burton, Ohio
Furnifold M. Simmons, North Carolina
Francis G. Newlands, Nevada
Duncan U. Fletcher, Florida

The investigative body bears the imposing official title of 'Subcommittee of the Committee on Commerce, United States Senate, Sixty-second Congress, Second Session, Pursuant to Senate Resolution 283, Directing the Committee on Commerce to Investigate the Causes Leading to the Wreck of the White Star Liner "Titanic"'.

To interview witnesses with what is first thought to be 'as little trouble as possible', Senator Smith and his subcommittee convene at New York City's Waldorf-Astoria Hotel, where hearings are conducted for the first two days.

Senator William Alden Smith, Michigan. (US Senate Historical Office, Library of Congress)

Senator George C. Perkins, California. (US Senate Historical Office, Library of Congress)

Senator Jonathan Bourne Jr, Oregon. (US Senate Historical Office, Library of Congress)

Senator Theodore E. Burton, Ohio. (US Senate Historical Office, Library of Congress)

Senator Furnifold M. Simmons, North Carolina. (US Senate Historical Office, Library of Congress)

Senator Francis G. Newlands, Nevada. (US Senate Historical Office, Library of Congress)

Senator Duncan U. Fletcher, Florida. (US Senate Historical Office, Library of Congress)

Friday, 19 April 1912

10.30am to 10.30pm, New York, NY: The hearings' first witness is Joseph Bruce Ismay, managing director of the White Star Line. He is followed by the *Carpathia*'s captain, Arthur Henry Rostron.

Also heard during the first day are Guglielmo Marconi; Harold Thomas Cottam, *Carpathia*'s wireless operator; Alfred Crawford, a bedroom steward aboard *Titanic*; and Charles Herbert Lightoller (ex-second officer, RMS *Titanic*).

Saturday, 20 April 1912

10.50am to 3.30pm, New York, NY: The second day of hearings, and the last at New York, sees Harold Cottam, *Carpathia*'s wireless operator recalled. *Titanic*'s surviving wireless operator, Harold S. Bride, also gives testimony, as does Herbert John Pitman, ex-third officer, *Titanic*. It is soon realised that the investigation's scope – including as it does *Titanic*'s surviving officers and crew, White Star Line officials and others who can shed light on the disaster – and its more extensive agenda will take longer to complete than originally planned.

Top The East Room in New York's Waldorf-Astoria is crowded with press, visitors, senators and witnesses. (*New York Sun*)

Middle During the inquiry's first day, a weary Bruce Ismay is persistently questioned by Senator William Alden Smith. (Authors' collection)

Right Also questioned are Harold Bride, *Titanic*'s surviving telegraphist (right), and wireless's inventor Guglielmo Marconi (left). (*Philadelphia Inquirer*)

After two days of hearings at New York, Senator Smith returns to Washington. There, in the ornate Senate Caucus Room and, later, the Committee on Territories Room, testimony from significant witnesses is heard over the next ten days; affidavits, memoranda and letters are entered into evidence, and several *Titanic* passengers are interrogated.

Sunday, 21 April 1912

THIS SUNDAY IS A travel day, as the hearings with its witnesses and investigative senators go by train from New York to Washington.

APRIL 21, 1912.

STEAMSHIP
DED CALL FOR AID

d from first page.

at relayed by the Titanic for the Amer-
accident he returned to his quarters
not serious. He then relieved Phillips,
nt, and in a short time Captain Smith
or assistance," whereupon Phillips put
Q D."

d the assistance and Phillips proceeded
ic and to ask that of the Frankfurt, to
mmediately thereafter the Carpathia

The Compagnie Generale Transatlantique takes this opportunity to advise
the travelling public that all steamers of
their fleet are already under instructions
from the Home Office in Paris to follow,
both eastbound and westbound, the most
southerly course, in order to avoid any
possibility of danger due to the presence
of ice-fields already reported.

APRIL 21, 1912.

TIME TABLES. | TIME TABLES. | TIME TABLES.

CUNARD
The Fastest Steamers in the World
Mauretania
Lusitania

APRIL 24 | June 12 | Aug. 21
May 22 | July 3 | Sept. 11
1 A.M. | July 24 | Oct. 2
May 8 | June 19 | Aug. 28
May 29 | July 10 | Sept. 18
1 A.M. | Aug. 7 | Oct. 9

Caronia   Campania   Carmania
May 4, 10 A.M. June 29 | May 15, 1 A.M. June 26 | May 18, 10 A.M. July 13
June 1 10 A.M July 31 | June 5 1 A M July 17 | June 15 10 A M Aug 10

THE LIFE BOAT
CAPACITY OF THE
HAMBURG-AMERI-
CAN LINE STEAM-
ERS WILL HERE-
AFTER BE AMPLE
TO PROVIDE FOR
EVERY PERSON
ON BOARD.

Emil L. Boas,
Resident Director and General Manager.
HAMBURG   AMERICAN

Top left Harold Cottam. (*Daily Sketch*)

Top middle As he testifies, telegraphist Harold Bride's face shows clearly the stress of his last six days. (*Portland* [Oregon] *Journal*)

Top right Former *Titanic* third officer Herbert J. Pitnam. (*Daily Sketch*)

Left and middle left The Senate hearings' serious tone is reflected by shipping companies' advisories appearing on 21 April 1912 in the *New York Times*. (*New York Times*)

Previous page 'Pride and Splendour', *Titanic* as her well-wishers would have liked her to be remembered. (E.D. Walker)

Right *Titanic* departs Belfast at the start of sea trials, 2 April 1912, her future seemingly assured as the most glamorous and technically advanced ship afloat. (E.D. Walker)

Titanic leaving Southampton where passengers and crew had boarded. (E.D. Walker)

Shortly after departure, heading for her next port of call, across the English Channel at Cherbourg. (Simon Fisher)

Anchored in the roadstead at Cherbourg. (Simon Fisher)

Before heading for Queenstown, and the passengers' first night afloat. (E.D. Walker)

Opposite 'Queen of the Seas'. Who would have guessed from Ted Walker's painting (**top**) that this regal ship would meet such a terrible end painfully depicted in Simon Fisher's 'Titanic Breaking Up' (**bottom**)?

Titanic's starboard bridge wing was flattened during the sinking. The two circular electrical controls (upper left) are labelled 'Speed' and 'Time', and regulated the length and frequency of fog signals sounded by the ship's whistles. (Authors' photo © 1996 RMS Titanic, Inc.)

This authors' photograph taken in 1996 shows the grating against which second officer Charles Lightoller reported being pinned as *Titanic* sank. A bubble of air from below hurled him free. (Authors' photo © 1996 RMS Titanic, Inc.)

The wooden frame of the Marconi room's skylight lies displaced on the roof after an intrusion by a Russian submarine in 1995. 'Rusticles' have begun to engulf the wireless room's interior. (Authors' photo © 1996 RMS Titanic, Inc.)

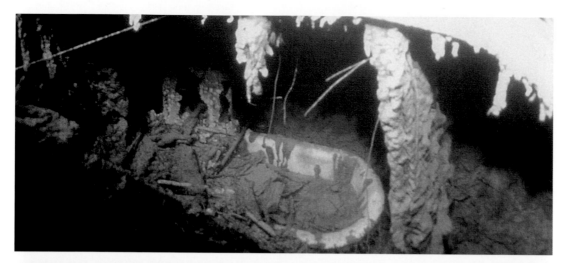

Abaft the officers' quarters on the boat deck's port side, between First Class cabins 'X' and 'Y', the outer wall has fallen, exposing the partially buried bathtub that served passengers in this part of the ship. (© 1996 RMS Titanic, Inc.)

The forward expansion joint has split wide open from the boat deck downward, permitting glimpses of the ship's interior. (© 1996 RMS Titanic, Inc.)

Little remains today of *Titanic*'s opulent wood decor. This piece of oak from *Olympic*'s grand staircase hints at what was once a piece of moulding directly beneath the glass dome. (Authors' collection)

Once thought to be 'richly carpeted', the floor covering of *Titanic*'s First Class dining saloon was described in *The Shipbuilder*'s special *Olympic-Titanic* issue as 'linoleum tiles of a unique pattern'. (Authors' collection)

Recovery from the debris field of a section of flooring confirms the design, formed of separate inlaid pieces for each colour. (Authors' photo © 1998 RMS Titanic, Inc.)

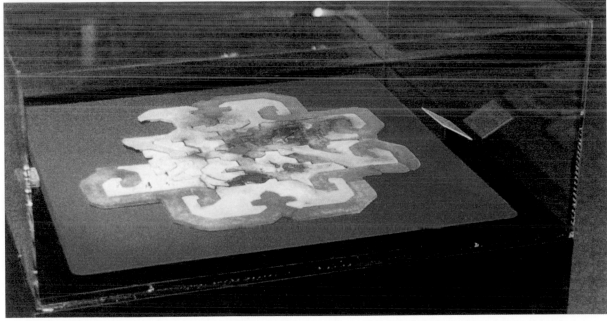

Left A plate from the à la carte restaurant features gold trim and a cobalt blue band. (© RMS Titanic, Inc.)

Right This gilded electroplate chandelier base originally held ten light bulbs and graced a corridor or public room in First Class. (© RMS Titanic, Inc.)

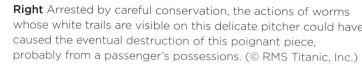

Above Not part of *Titanic*'s dinner service, this colourful plate was probably from the ship's cargo. (© RMS Titanic, Inc.)

Right Arrested by careful conservation, the actions of worms whose white trails are visible on this delicate pitcher could have caused the eventual destruction of this poignant piece, probably from a passenger's possessions. (© RMS Titanic, Inc.)

Items recovered from *Titanic*'s debris field range in size and function from massive to delicate and personal. Among the latter is this exquisite perfume bottle, still bearing traces of its original contents on its interior surfaces. (© RMS Titanic, Inc.)

Perhaps a souvenir or a gift for a friend in America, this ceramic watering sprinkler may have belonged to Mrs Elizabeth Nye, the only *Titanic* passenger known to have lived in Folkestone. (© RMS Titanic, Inc.)

A committee headed by wealthy Denver socialite Molly Brown presented members of *Carpathia*'s crew with medals in gratitude. Six officers received gold medals, junior officers received silver versions, and crew received bronze ones. (Authors' collection)

TITANIC'S FLAGS

Left On 25 March 1912, *Titanic*'s signal letters (top to bottom) H V M P are assigned by the Registrar General of the General Register and Record Office of Shipping and Seamen.

Above In 1912 this red and white pennant, the company's house flag, was the sole remnant of the original White Star Line of Australian packets, purchased in 1867 by Thomas H. Ismay.

Above right The 46-star American flag from early 1912 was flown by *Titanic*. (See Appendix 1.)

Below The Red Ensign, in general the rightful flag of ships in Britain's merchant service, is sometimes referred to as the 'Red Duster'.

Below right The Blue Ensign generally is the distinguishing flag of the Royal Naval Reserve. 'It is worn under Admiralty warrant in merchant ships commanded by a retired officer of the Royal Navy or an Officer of the Royal Naval Reserve, provided the crew includes ten Officers or men of the naval reserve.' *Titanic*'s commander, Captain Edward J. Smith, held the Admiralty's Blue Ensign. Warrant No. 690.

(All authors' collection)

During the 1998 Research and Recovery Expedition breathtaking underwater views of *Titanic* were obtained by the Remote Operated Vehicle *Magellan*. These enabled the expedition's naval architect and historians to use on-demand wide-angle and telephoto views of *Titanic*'s structure to achieve a better understanding of the liner's sinking, its impact with the ocean floor, and its current condition. (Authors' photo © 1998 RMS Titanic, Inc.)

Inventors Susan and Bill Willard, then of Seneca South Carolina, pose with their miniature robotic vehicle *T-Rex*, which was designed to penetrate deep into *Titanic*'s interior. During the 1998 expedition it underwent extensive underwater testing. (Photo by Claes-Goran Wetterholm, authors' collection © 1998 RMS Titanic, Inc.)

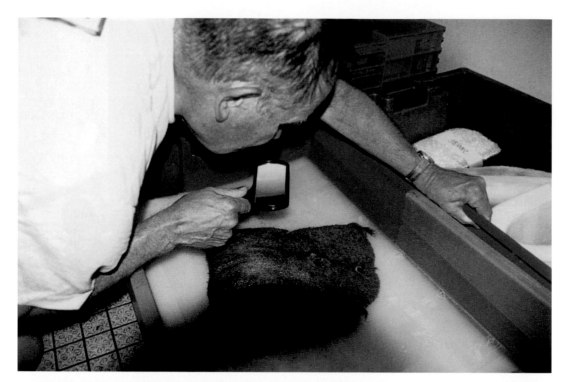

Co-author John Eaton examines a cloth pouch, hand-sewn from a piece of canvas or burlap, recovered from the ocean floor during the 1998 expedition. The authors, as expedition co-historians, tentatively identified it as a 'ditty-bag' or money bag, perhaps of a Third Class passenger. (Authors' photo © 1998 RMS Titanic, Inc.)

A delicate pitcher, still bearing faint traces of flowers on its side, is examined by a trained expedition conservator upon emerging from *Nautile*'s collection basket during the 1998 expedition. (© 1998 RMS Titanic, Inc.)

Opposite Crew of the *Nadir* gently manoeuvre a 1-ton door from *Titanic*'s forward port side on D deck. The door, which had lain in the corrosive sand alongside the wreck, had been brought to the surface using the lift-bag system. The door's glass windows and their brass operating mechanisms gleam in the sunlight, but steel portions are heavily coated in bacterial corrosion as the door is placed in a protective bath aboard *Nadir*. (© 1998 RMS Titanic, Inc.)

Overleaf 'RMS Titanic life-ring', a poignant reminder of a tragedy the world will never forget. (E.D. Walker)

Above left Testifying during the Senate hearings' first day at Washington is *Titanic*'s former fourth officer, Joseph Groves Boxhall. (Authors' collection)

Above Because of crowding and poor acoustics, on the second day of hearings the subcommittee moves from the new Senate Caucus Room to the smaller conference room of the Committee on Territories, whose chairman, Senator William Alden Smith, also heads the *Titanic* investigation. (US Senate Historical Office, Library of Congress)

Monday, 22 April 1912

10.30am to 6.20pm, Washington, DC: Reconvening in the Senate Caucus Room, the subcommittee hears Phillip A.S. Franklin, United States vice president of the International Mercantile Marine Company, parent organisation of the White Star Line.

Also heard is *Titanic*'s ex-fourth officer, Joseph Groves Boxhall. Later, due to excessive public crowding and noise, the committee decides to meet in the conference room of the Committee on Territories, also chaired by Senator Smith.

Tuesday, 23 April 1912

10.00am to 5.40pm, Washington, DC: Frederick Fleet, *Titanic*'s lookout on duty at the time of the collision, is heard; third officer Pitman is recalled and the first testimony by a passenger is given by Major Arthur G. Peuchen of Toronto, Canada, who is questioned at some length by the senators.

Titanic Tragedy Enacted Every Day

In the Awful Catastrophe 1600 Lives Were Lost—the Majority of Them Men

A telegram received by us from the "Insurance Field," Louisville, Kentucky, dated Saturday, states that they have telegraphic information to the effect that the losses to be paid by Life Insurance Companies will be about $1,771,000, which is less than One Thousand Dollars insurance for each life lost. The estimated Accident Insurance losses will be about $2,700,000, and the Marine Insurance losses about $10,000,000.

Without any disposition to criticise those unfortunates who lost their lives on the Titanic, we cannot in justice to the living fail to point out the disposition of Man to insure his possessions and neglect his own valuable life.

The average man carries too little protection, and the time to secure it is when you are able to get it.

Thousands die every day leaving their families with little or no protection.

Three Hundred Dollars a year (Twenty-five Dollars a Month) at age 30, will give to your family $25,000 protection, payable in one lump sum in the event of your death any time during the next twenty years. This is straight life insurance without frills.

We will arrange a loan for you, if you desire it, subject to an agreement, to pay the first two years' premiums on the policy you buy, and your note will not be discounted at bank. Do it now. Putting it off increases the cost.

LOCKYER & RHAWN, *Incorporated*
M. B. LOCKYER   G. W. RHAWN   M. S. ATWOOD, JR.
Land Title Building, Philadelphia
The largest life insurance agency in America, writing life insurance for various companies
W. L. MEGARY   C. W. MARSHALL   A. P. SIMMONDS
City Managers

Outside of the conference room, newspaper advertisements continue to market services by recalling aspects of the *Titanic*'s loss. (*Philadelphia Bulletin*)

First Class passenger Major Arthur G. Peuchen. (*New York American*)

Left Former fifth officer Harold G. Lowe. (*Washington Evening Star*)

Above Former second officer Charles H. Lightoller. (*New York American*)

Below Carpathia's wireless operator Harold T. Cottam is questioned. (*Frankfort* [Indiana] *Independent*)

Wednesday, 24 April 1912

10.00am to 6.20pm, Washington, DC: During the morning session, Frederick Fleet – one of the two lookouts at the time of the collision – is questioned by the senator. Their queries about the ship's missing binoculars are somewhat detailed.

Also during the morning *Titanic*'s former fifth officer, Harold Godfrey Lowe, is questioned on general topics regarding details of *Titanic*, her staffing, and the disaster. Questioned during the afternoon session are former second officer Lightoller (recalled) and Robert Hichens, who had been at the wheel at the time of the collision.

Thursday, 25 April 1912

10.15am to 4.15pm; 4.15pm to 7.45pm; 10.00pm to 11.45pm, Washington, DC: The committee convenes at 10.15am, and only two witnesses are heard during the day's hearings: Harold Thomas Cottam, *Carpathia*'s wireless operator, and Guglielmo Marconi, both recalled. Adjournment is at 4.15pm.

Following the formal adjournment, some 20 of *Titanic*'s former crew are questioned separately by individual members of the committee. These one-on-one sessions continue until 7.45pm. Senator Smith himself questions three crewmen during an evening period that finishes at 11.45pm.

Friday, 26 April 1912

10.55am to 6.00pm, Washington, DC: The hearings do not begin until 10.55am, and during this day's sessions, morning and afternoon, is heard testimony from *Californian*'s captain, her wireless operator and a crew member. Recalled are Frank Oliver Evans, former able seaman aboard *Titanic*, and Phillip A.S. Franklin, IMM's American vice president.

Right Members of *Titanic*'s crew wait to give testimony at the Senate inquiry, Washington, DC. (*New York Times*)

Below Stanley T. Lord, *Californian*'s master. (*Washington Evening Star*)

Below middle *Californian*'s wireless telegraphist, Cyril F Evans. (*New York American*)

Below right Donkeyman Ernest Gill of the *Californian* also testifies on 26 April. (*New York American*)

Saturday, 27 April 1912

10.20am to 6.10pm, Washington, DC: The committee is not yet finished with Mr Franklin or former second officer Lightoller – each is recalled during this day's session.

The morning is occupied with the questioning of Captain James Henry Moore, Master of the *Mount Temple*, who testifies in part about other vessels that were probably in the vicinity of *Titanic* during the night she sank.

Testimony by quartermaster Arthur John Bright and five of *Titanic*'s stewards fills most of the afternoon session. The committee adjourns until Monday morning.

Below *Celtic*. (Authors' collection)

Bottom Bruce Ismay (right) leaves the US Capitol building with P.A.S. Franklin, American vice president of the International Mercantile Marine. (*New York Times*)

Monday, 29 April 1912

10.30am to 7.10pm, Washington, DC: Heard this day are Frederick Sammis, Chief Engineer, Marconi Wireless Telegraph Co. of America, and Hugh Woolner, who had been aboard *Titanic* as a First Class passenger. Recalled are Marconi, Bride, Boxhall and Harold Cottam.

The 34 members of *Titanic*'s crew who have been held at Washington for the completion of the Senate's Inquiry are released by Senator Smith. They immediately leave for New York where they board the waiting *Celtic* and depart at once for Liverpool, where they arrive on 6 May.

Tuesday, 30 April 1912

10.00am to 4.20pm, Washington, DC: Part of the day's hearings relates to whether White Star's New York office had knowledge of *Titanic*'s loss before it was publicly announced. Two witnesses – one being J. Bruce Ismay – appear to testify. At the end of his day's testimony, Mr Ismay is released by Senator Smith. Also heard (one by affidavit) are five *Titanic* passengers.

At the end of the day's session, Senator Smith announces that 'a very important bill will be considered by the full Committee on Commerce tomorrow (a river and harbour bill) and [his *Titanic* committee will] stand adjourned until Friday morning at 10 o'clock'.

Senator Smith takes the opportunity of the three-day hiatus to travel to New York where, over a three-day period, he personally questions a number of witnesses.

Thursday, 2 May 1912

J. BRUCE ISMAY, officers Lightoller, Pitman, Lowe and Boxhall, and 30 other survivors of the *Titanic* disaster sail from New York for Liverpool aboard the *Adriatic*; they arrive on 11 May.

Morning to 4.30pm, New York, NY: Mrs J. Stuart White, a First Class passenger who (conveniently) resides at the Waldorf-Astoria Hotel, is interviewed there by the Senate committee, as is John Bottomley, vice president, general manager and secretary-treasurer of the Marconi Wireless Telegraph Company of America.

Thursday, 2 May–Thursday, 9 May 1912

DISSATISFIED WITH THE responses that witnesses' interrogations have provided, Senator Smith himself conducts additional inquiries in New York.

Friday, 3 May 1912

9.30am to 6.30pm, New York, NY: Four passengers, two from First and two from Third Class, are interviewed by Senator Smith, as are two newspaper employees.

Saturday, 4 May 1912

10.00am to afternoon, New York, NY: Senator Smith interviews Third Class passenger Berk Pickard as well as *Titanic*'s junior wireless operator Harold Bride, a Western Union telegraph window clerk, and a Marconi telegraphic inspector attached to the White Star liner *Baltic*.

Friday, 10 May 1912

SENATOR SMITH RETURNS to Washington and begins to write his formal report.

The hearings occupy another three days at Washington, DC – Thursdays, 9 and 16 May and Friday, 17 May – as well as another day – Saturday, 25 May – at New York.

Telegraph company executives, *Titanic* passengers and United States government officials are interviewed, have their correspondence and reports read into evidence, and offer testimony through affidavits.

Monday, 20 May 1912

THE SUBCOMMITTEE accepts the final report, but on Saturday, 25 May the report is again augmented when Smith returns to New York to interview a former *Titanic* crewman who is in New York as a member of *Olympic*'s crew.

Saturday, 25 May 1912

IN NEW YORK Senator Smith interviews *Olympic*'s captain, Herbert James Haddock, and Frederick Barrett, a former lead fireman on *Titanic*.

Monday, 27 May 1912

SENATOR SMITH'S FORMAL report is not completed until this date, the day before it is to be read and submitted to the entire Senate.

Mrs J. Stuart (Ella) White. (Michael A. Findlay collection)

One of the newspaper reporters interviewed by Senator Smith is John 'Jack' Binns, of *Republic* fame, now a staff member of the *New York American*. (Author's Collection)

Tuesday, 28 May 1912

THE UNITED STATES Senate subcommittee's report on *Titanic*'s loss is read to the full Senate in Washington, DC, and released to the public. The occasion is marked by a speech nearly an hour in length by the subcommittee's chairman, Senator William Alden Smith.

SUMMARY OF THE UNITED STATES SENATE *TITANIC* INQUIRY

THE INVESTIGATION occupies 17 days. Testimony, letters and affidavits filled

```
62D CONGRESS  }           SENATE           { REPORT
  2d Session  }                             { No. 806

            " TITANIC "  DISASTER
                 ─────────

                  REPORT
                   OF THE

       COMMITTEE  ON  COMMERCE
       UNITED  STATES  SENATE

                PURSUANT TO

              S.  RES.  283

       DIRECTING THE COMMITTEE ON COMMERCE TO INVESTI-
       GATE THE CAUSES LEADING TO THE WRECK OF
         THE WHITE STAR LINER "TITANIC"

             TOGETHER WITH SPEECHES
                  THEREON BY

       SENATOR WILLIAM ALDEN SMITH
               OF MICHIGAN

                    AND

        SENATOR ISIDOR RAYNER
               OF MARYLAND

                 ───────

                WASHINGTON
          GOVERNMENT PRINTING OFFICE
                   1912
```

1,145 pages. A total of 83 witnesses are heard in either direct or indirect testimony, including:

- 38 *Titanic* crewmen
- 18 passengers (14 First, one Second and three Third Class)
- 12 witnesses concerning telegraphic and radio 'traffic'.

The committee's suggestions and recommendations include:

- Suggestions regarding structure and lifeboat capacity for vessels licensed to carry passengers from American ports, and further recommendations that all foreign-flag vessels be similarly modified or lose their passenger licences
- Adequate manning of boats, and boat drills for both passengers and crew
- The necessity for the regulation of radiotelegraphy, including 24-hour manning of equipment, action against amateurs' interference, provision of reliable auxiliary power sources, and maintenance of secrecy of all messages
- An end to the firing of Roman candles or rockets on the high seas for the purpose of night-time recognition.

While Smith and his speech are badly received by the British press, American papers are almost unanimous in their acceptance of the report. The Inquiry's total cost is £1,360 ($6,600), including £680 ($3,300) for stenographic services; £227 ($1,100) for train mileage for witnesses; and £453 ($2,200) for housing *Titanic*'s officers and crew.

(Authors' collection)

THE BRITISH INQUIRY

Monday, 22 April 1912

IN LONDON, ENGLAND, pursuing a course not used for many years, Mr Sydney Buxton, President of the Board of Trade, requests the Lord Chancellor, at his discretion and under his authority, to appoint a Wreck Commissioner, who, in turn, would form an absolutely independent Court. The Lord Chancellor gives his assent, and Mr Buxton is pleased to announce to the House of Commons that Lord Mersey will undertake the responsibility.

Sydney Buxton, President of the Board of Trade. (*Illustrated London News*)

Thursday, 2 May 1912

THE BOARD OF TRADE hearings into *Titanic*'s loss are convened in London and the first day of public sessions is held at the Royal Scottish Drill Hall, Buckingham Gate, Westminster. The investigation formally begins with the 'Order for Formal Investigation', as required by the Merchant Shipping Act of 1894. Thus does the Board of Trade somewhat hastily provide itself with the authority to conduct an investigation into *Titanic*'s loss – hastily because it fears that another court or jurisdiction might usurp its authority. As Wreck Commissioner for the investigation, Britain's Lord High Chancellor, Robert, Earl Loreburn, appoints John Charles Bigham, Lord Mersey of Toxteth, President of the Probate, Divorce & Admiralty Division of the High Court, in a warrant dated 23 April 1912.

To assist him in his post, the following names, all experts in maritime and naval fields, particularly in marine

Lord Mersey, Wreck Commissioner. (*Illustrated London News*)

construction and architecture, are submitted to the Home Secretary by Lord Mersey:

Captain Arthur Wellesley Clarke, Trinity [House] Master in Admiralty Court
Prof J. Harvard Biles, Chair of naval Architecture at Glasgow
Rear-Admiral the Hon. Somerset Arthur Gough-Calthorpe
Commander Fitzhugh C.A. Lyon, HM Navy, Retd (an assessor in many previous inquiries)
Mr Edward C. Chaston, senior engineer assessor on the Admiralty's list for appointment to Board of Trade enquiries.

The formidable battery of counsel for the Board of Trade consists of the following:

Sir Rufus Isaacs, KC, the Attorney General
Sir John Simon, KC, the Solicitor-General

The Inquiry is formally instigated. (Crown Copyright material in the Public Record Office, reproduced by permission of the Controller of Her Majesty's Stationery Office; PRO MT9/920 M38984/12, MT9/920 M7534, MT9/920 M7534)

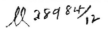

Commander F C. Lyon.
(*Illustrated London News*)

Rear-Admiral S.A. Gough-Calthorpe.
(*Illustrated London News*)

Professor J. Harvard Biles.
(*Illustrated London News*)

Edward C. Chaston. (*Illustrated London News*)

Captain A.W. Clarke.
(*Illustrated London News*)

Attorney General Sir Rufus Isaacs, KC.
(Authors' collection)

White Star's legal representation was headed by Sir Robert Finlay, KC, MP. (*Daily Sketch*)

The Scottish Drill Hall, Buckingham Gate, London SW1. (Authors' collection)

Mr Butler Aspinall, KC
Mr G.T. Rowlatt
Mr Raymond Asquith

The White Star Line's counsel is no less formidable:

The Rt Hon Sir Robert Finlay, KC, MP
Mr Frederick Laing, KC
Mr Maurice Hill, KC
Mr Norman Raeburn (instructed by Messrs Hill, Dickinson & Company)

Eminent members of the legal profession and prominent leaders of the labour movement appear at various times as counsel or as observers during the hearings:

Mr Thomas Scanlan, MP, as counsel on behalf of the National Sailors' and Firemen's Union of Great Britain and Ireland, and as the personal representative of several deceased members of the crew and of survivors who were members of the Union. (Admitted on application; Mr Scanlan was instructed by Mr Smith, solicitor.)

Mr Botterell (instructed by Messrs Botterell & Roche), appearing on behalf of the Chamber of Shipping of the United Kingdom. (Admitted on application.)

Mr Thomas Lewis, appearing on behalf of the British Seafarers' Union. (Admitted on application.)

Mr L.S. Holmes (of Messrs Miller, Taylor & Holmes), appearing on behalf of the Imperial Merchant Service Guild. (Admitted on application.)

Mr Hamar Greenwood, MP (instructed by Messrs Pritchard & Sons), watching the proceedings on behalf of the Allan Line Steamship Company.

Mr Hamar Greenwood, MP (instructed by Messrs William A. Crump & Son), watching the proceedings for the Canadian Pacific Railway Company.

Mr Joseph Cotter, appearing on behalf of the National Union of Stewards (Admitted on application.)

Mr Roche (instructed by Messrs Charles G. Bradshaw & Waterson), appearing on behalf of the Marine Engineers' Association. (Admitted on application.)

Mr A. Clement Edwards, MP, appearing on behalf of the Dockers' Union (Admitted on application.)

Mr W.D. Harbison (instructed by Mr Farrell), appearing on behalf of the Third Class passengers. (Admitted on application.)

Mr C. Robertson Dunlop, watching the proceedings on behalf of the owners and officers of the SS *Californian* (Leyland Line).

Mr H.E. Duke, KC, MP, and Mr Vaughan Williams (instructed by Messrs A.F. & R.W. Tweedie), appearing on behalf of Sir Cosmo and Lady Duff-Gordon. (Admitted on application.)

Mr Frederick Laing, KC, and Mr Alfred Bucknill, appearing on behalf of Messrs Harland & Wolff. (Admitted on application.)

The following description of the British *Titanic* Inquiry is only the briefest of summaries. Readers desiring a more detailed summary are referred to Chapter 18 of the authors' earlier book, *Titanic: Triumph and Tragedy*, 3rd ed. (Haynes Publishing Group, 2011). Copies of the Inquiry's complete minutes of evidence are available through a 1998 reprint published by Britain's National Archives, or via www.titanicinquiry.org.

Each day's session begins at 10.30am.

Thursday, 2 May 1912 (1st day)

AFTER THE READING of the 'Order for Formal Investigation', the Attorney General, Sir Rufus Isaacs, presents a list of 26 questions, the consideration of

Top A large half-model dominates one side of the cavernous hearings room, which suffers from abysmal acoustics. (Authors' collection)

Middle Lord Mersey and his assessors prepare to sift through literally mountains of evidence, the diversity of which is well illustrated by this telegram. (Public Record Office MT9/920 Mll784)

Left During the hearings a large profile section of the liner is hung from the ladies' gallery. (*Daily Sketch*)

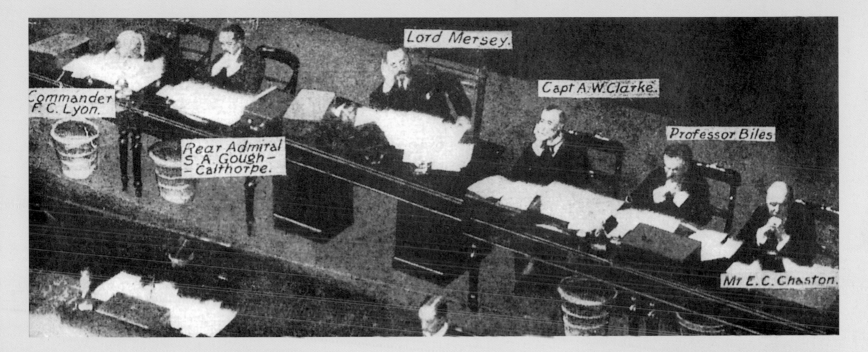

which will constitute the Inquiry's scope, and then orally summarises the questions for Lord Mersey.

Friday, 3 May 1912 (2nd day)

THE INQUIRY'S FIRST two witnesses are heard: lookout Archie Jewell and able seaman Joseph Scarrott.

Top Lord Mersey and his assessors face a capacity throng of spectators, reporters and legal representatives. (*Daily Sketch*)

Right A page from the daily transcript records a verbatim transcript of the proceedings. (Authors' collection)

Middle right *Titanic* lookout Archie Jewell. (*Illustrated London News*)

Far right Able seaman Joseph Scarrott. (*Illustrated London News*)

[Price 1s. 6d.]

In the Wreck Commissioners' Court.

Scottish Hall,
Buckingham Gate,
Thursday, 2nd May, 1912.

PROCEEDINGS

BEFORE

THE RIGHT HON. LORD MERSEY,

WITH

REAR ADMIRAL THE HON. S. A. GOUGH-CALTHORPE, C.V.O., R.N.,
CAPTAIN A. W. CLARKE,
COMMANDER F. C. A. LYON, R.N.R.,
PROFESSOR J. H. BILES, LL.D., D.Sc.,
MR. E. C. CHASTON.

ON A FORMAL INVESTIGATION

ORDERED BY THE BOARD OF TRADE INTO THE

LOSS OF THE S.S. "TITANIC."

[*Transcribed from the Shorthand Notes of W. B. GURNEY & SONS, 26, Abingdon Street, Westminster, S.W.*]

FIRST DAY.

THE RIGHT HON. SIR RUFUS ISAACS, K.C., M.P. (Attorney-General), THE RIGHT HON. SIR J. SIMON, K.C., M.P. (Solicitor-General), MR. BUTLER ASPINALL, K.C., MR. S. A. T. ROWLATT and MR. RAYMOND ASQUITH (instructed by SIR R. ELLIS CUN-LIFFE, Solicitor to the Board of Trade) appeared as Counsel on behalf of the Board of Trade.

THE RIGHT HON. SIR ROBERT FINLAY, K.C., M.P., MR. F. LAING, K.C., MR. MAURICE HILL, K.C., and MR. NORMAN RAEBURN (instructed by Messrs. Hill, Dickinson and Co.) appeared as Counsel on behalf of the White Star Line.

MR. THOMAS SCANLAN, M.P. (instructed by Mr. Smith, Solicitor) appeared as Counsel on behalf of the National Sailors' and Firemen's

Union of Great Britain and Ireland, and of the personal representatives of several deceased members of the crew and of survivors who were members of the Union. Admitted on application —*See below.*

MR. BOTTERELL (instructed by Messrs. Botterell and Roche) appeared on behalf of the Chamber of Shipping of the United Kingdom. Admitted on application—*See below.*

MR. HAMAR GREENWOOD, M.P. (instructed by Messrs. Pritchard and Sons) watched proceedings on behalf of the Allan Line Steamship Company.

MR. HAMAR GREENWOOD, M.P. (instructed by Messrs. William A. Crump and Son) watched proceedings for the Canadian Pacific Railway Company.

Monday, 6 May 1912

LORD MERSEY AND the five assessors visit *Olympic* at Southampton, where they examine *Titanic*'s nearly identical sister and closely observe a boat lowering.

Tuesday, 7 May 1912 (3rd day)

WITNESSES HEARD ON this day are all *Titanic* crew members: George William Beauchamp, fireman, on duty at

The lowering of a lifeboat from *Olympic*, watched by the Inquiry's assessors. (*Daily Graphic*)

number 10 stokehold; Robert Hichens, quartermaster, at the wheel at the time of the collision; William Lucas, able seaman, on duty on the fo'c'sle, port side; and Frederick Barrett, leading stoker, on duty at number 6 stokehold.

Wednesday, 8 May 1912 (4th day)

WITNESSES HEARD ARE again all members of *Titanic*'s crew: Frederick Barrett (recalled); Reginald Robinson Lee, lookout, on duty in the crow's nest; John Poigndestre, able seaman, on duty as 'stand-by'; and James Johnson, night watchman, on duty in the First Class saloon.

Thursday, 9 May 1912 (5th day)

ALL OF THIS DAY'S witnesses are again *Titanic* crew. They include the following: James Johnson (recalled); Thomas Patrick Dillon, trimmer, on duty in the engine room; Thomas Ranger, greaser, in the electric shop, E deck; George Cavell, trimmer, on duty in number 4 section; Alfred Shires, fireman, off watch; and Charles Hendrickson, leading stoker, off watch.

Friday, 10 May 1912 (6th day)

TESTIMONY FROM *TITANIC*'S crew continues. Those heard include the following: Frank Herbert Morris, First Class bath steward, off watch; Frederick Scott, greaser, on duty in the turbine engine room; Charles Joughin, baker, off watch; and Samuel James Rule, bathroom steward, off watch.

Tuesday, 14 May 1912 (7th day)

WITNESSES HEARD TODAY are all from the SS *Californian*: Stanley Lord, Master of the Leyland Line steamship; James Gibson, apprentice; and Herbert Stone, second officer.

A full consideration of the testimony by *Californian*'s witnesses and its implications can be found in the book by the late Leslie Harrison, *A Titanic Myth, the Californian Incident* (William Kimber, London, 1986). Peter Padfield's

Captain Stanley Lord arrives at the hearings. (*Daily Sketch*)

book, *The Titanic and the Californian* (Hodder & Stoughton, London, 1965), and *The Ship That Stood Still*, by Leslie Reade (Patrick Stephens Ltd, 1993), also contain evidence that was not investigated by either Senator Smith or Lord Mersey.

Wednesday, 15 May 1912 (8th day)

ON THIS DAY are heard witnesses from *Californian* and *Mount Temple*: Charles Victor Groves, second officer with duties of third, SS *Californian*; George Frederick Stewart, chief officer, SS *Californian*; Cyril F. Evans, Marconi operator, SS *Californian*; James Henry Moore, Master of the Canadian Pacific Railway's vessel SS *Mount Temple*; and John Durrant, Marconi operator, SS *Mount Temple*.

Top A group of witnesses from the freighter *Californian* outside the Scottish Hall, Buckingham Gate. *Left to right:* G. Glenn, fireman; W. Thomas, greaser; Cyril F. Evans, wireless operator; James Gibson, apprentice; Herbert Stone, second officer; William Ross, able seaman; Charles V. Groves, third officer; and George F. Stewart, first officer. (*Daily Sketch*)

Middle left *Californian*'s second officer, Charles Groves. (*Daily Sketch*)

Middle right John Durrant, *Mount Temple*'s Marconi operator. (GEC-Marconi)

Right Cyril Evans (left) and apprentice James Gibson. (*Daily Sketch*)

Far right James Moore, Master of the *Mount Temple*. (*Daily Sketch*)

Thursday, 16 May 1912 (9th day)

THE DAY'S WITNESSES are from both *Mount Temple* and *Titanic*: John Durrant (briefly recalled); Samuel Rule, *Titanic*, recalled; John Edward Hart, Third Class steward, off watch; Albert Victor Pearcey, Third Class pantryman, off watch; Edward Brown, First Class steward, off watch; Charles Donald Mackay, bathroom steward, off watch; and Joseph Thomas Wheat, assistant Second Class steward, off watch.

Friday, 17 May 1912 (10th day)

WITNESSES HEARD ARE Charles Hendrickson, leading stoker (recalled); George Symons, lookout, off watch; James Taylor, fireman, off watch; James Clayton Barr, Master of Cunard's SS *Caronia*; Albert Edward James

WRECK COMMISSIONER'S OFFICE.

LADIES' GALLERY.

St. Ermin's Hotel,
Caxton Street, S.W.

s.s. "TITANIC" ENQUIRY.

Admit _____

on _____

to the Scottish Hall, Buckingham Gate, S.W.

C. BIGHAM, Secretary.

Top Dressed in their Sunday best, members of *Titanic*'s crew testify on the ninth day of the hearings. Left to right: Joseph Thomas Wheat, Second Class steward; John Hart, Third Class steward; and Albert Pearcey, Third Class pantryman. (*Daily Sketch*)

Middle The lifeboat in which Sir Cosmo Duff-Gordon and his wife left the sinking *Titanic* was in charge of lookout/AB George Symons, seen here testifying during the Inquiry's tenth day. (*Daily Sketch*)

Far left Visitors' passes for the hearings' 11th day are much in demand, as Sir Cosmo Duff-Gordon and Lady Duff-Gordon testify. (*Authors' collection*)

Left Sharing with the public the intensity of the moment, Lord Mersey, his assessors and court stenographers listen with interest. (*Illustrated London News*)

Horswill, able seaman, off watch; and Sir Cosmo Duff-Gordon, First Class passenger aboard *Titanic*.

Monday, 20 May 1912 (11th day)

THOSE TESTIFYING TODAY are Sir Cosmo Duff-Gordon (recalled); Lady Duff-Gordon, First Class passenger; Samuel Collins, fireman; Robert William Pusey, fireman; Mrs Elizabeth Leather, stewardess; Joseph Thomas Wheat (recalled); Mrs Annie Robinson, stewardess; Walter Wynn, quartermaster; and Charles Herbert Lightoller, second officer.

Tuesday, 21 May 1912 (12th day)

THE ENTIRE DAY'S hearings are filled by the testimony of Charles Herbert Lightoller, *Titanic*'s second officer.

Wednesday, 22 May (13th day)

HEARD TODAY ARE three of *Titanic*'s surviving officers: Herbert John Pitman, third officer; Joseph Groves Boxhall, fourth officer (shown in printed

transcripts throughout the hearings as 'Joseph Grove Boxhall'); and Harold Godfrey Lowe, fifth officer. Also heard is George Elliott Turnbull, Deputy Manager, Marconi International Marine Communication Company.

Thursday, 23 May 1912 (14th day)

THE TESTIMONY FROM the Marconi Company's representative and *Titanic*'s

Lady Duff-Gordon also testifies – the only female passenger to give evidence during the hearings. (*Daily Sketch*)

Having already given testimony on the hearings' tenth day, Sir Cosmo Duff-Gordon, recalled, gives further evidence on the following day. (*Daily Mirror*)

surviving officers and wireless operator continues. George Turnbull is recalled, and Harold Bride, *Titanic*'s second wireless operator, is sworn in. Turnbull is again recalled, followed by Bride. Lightoller is also recalled, followed by Boxhall, Pitman and Lowe, all recalled.

Second officer Charles Herbert Lightoller pauses outside the Scottish Drill Hall with his wife Sylvia. (*The Sphere*)

Friday, 24 May 1912 (15th day)

HAROLD THOMAS COTTAM, *Carpathia*'s wireless operator, is called to testify. Also heard are Frederick Fleet, *Titanic* lookout, on duty; George Alfred Hogg, *Titanic* lookout, off watch; George Thomas Rowe, quartermaster, *Titanic*; and Samuel Hemming, lamp-trimmer, *Titanic*.

Tuesday, 4 June 1912 (16th day)

HEARD THIS DAY are Alfred Crawford, First Class bedroom steward; Edward John Buley, able seaman; and Ernest Gill, second donkeyman, SS *Californian*.
  Also giving testimony is Joseph Bruce Ismay, member of the firm Ismay, Imrie & Company, managers of the Oceanic Steam Navigation Co. Ltd, the White Star Line's owner. (Ismay is also president and a voting trustee of the American-owned International

Mercantile Marine Company, which, since 1902, has owned the Oceanic Steam Navigation Co. Ltd.)

Wednesday, 5 June 1912 (17th day)

WHITE STAR management continues its testimony. Ismay is recalled, and also heard is Harold Arthur Sanderson, member of the firm of Messrs Ismay, Imrie & Company and a director of the Oceanic Steam Navigation Co. Ltd.

Thursday, 6 June 1912 (18th day)

MANAGEMENT'S TESTIMONY yields to technical considerations. Sanderson is recalled, and Edward Wilding, naval architect for Harland & Wolff, is heard.

Harland & Wolff naval architect Edward Wilding c. 1923. (© 2016 by John P. Eaton and Charles A. Haas)

Ernest Gill. (*Daily Sketch*)

Recalled from his first day of testimony on 4 June, Joseph Bruce Ismay continues to testify on behalf of White Star's management. (Authors' collection)

Friday, 7 June 1912 (19th day)

HEARD ON THIS day is Paul Maugé, secretary to the à la carte restaurant chef, and Edward Wilding is recalled.

Monday, 10 June 1912 (20th day)

DETAILS OF *TITANIC*'S design and construction are elicited and compared with the structure of *Lusitania*. Edward Wilding is recalled, and also heard are Leonard Peskett, naval architect to the Cunard Company, and the Rt Hon Alexander Montgomery Carlisle, designer of *Olympic* and *Titanic* (retired 30 June 1910), member of Board of Trade's Advisory Committee.

Tuesday, 11 June 1912 (21st day)

PRACTICES AT SEA are elicited from several ships' masters, while regulations under which *Titanic* sailed are also examined. Those heard are: Charles Alfred Bartlett, Marine Superintendent, White Star Line; Bertram Fox Hayes, Master of White Star Line's *Adriatic*; Frederick Passow, Master of American Line's *St Paul*; Francis Spurstow Miller, Assistant Hydrographer at the Admiralty; Benjamin Steel, Marine Superintendent at Southampton for the White Star Line; Stanley Howard Adams, wireless telegrapher, *Mesaba*; and Sir Walter J. Howell, Assistant Secretary to the Board of Trade, Chief of the Marine Department.

Wednesday, 12 June 1912 (22nd day)

THE ENTIRE DAY'S hearings are taken up by the testimony of Sir Walter J. Howell, Chief of the Marine Department, Board of Trade.

Thursday, 13 June 1912 (23rd day)

SIR WALTER J. HOWELL is recalled. Also heard are Sir Alfred Chalmers, Nautical Adviser to the Marine Department of the Board of Trade (retired August 1911), and Alfred Young, successor to Chalmers as Nautical Adviser and Professional Member of the Marine Department, Board of Trade.

Friday, 14 June 1912 (24th day)

TODAY ALFRED YOUNG is recalled, and also giving testimony are Richard Owen Jones, Master of Dominion Line's SS *Canada*; Edward Galton Cannons, captain of steamships for the Atlantic Transport Line; and Francis Carruthers, engineer and ship surveyor to the Board of Trade at Belfast.

Among those testifying on 10 June on the Inquiry's 20th day is the Rt Hon Alexander M. Carlisle, whose evidence includes *Titanic*'s conformance to existing British lifeboat rules. (*Daily Sketch*)

Sir Walter J. Howell. (*Daily Sketch*)

Monday, 17 June 1912 (25th day)

FRANCIS CARRUTHERS is briefly recalled, then William Henry Chantler, ship surveyor in the Marine Department of the Board of Trade at Belfast, is heard, together with Maurice Harvey Clarke, Assistant Emigration Officer under the Board of Trade, stationed at Southampton, and William David Archer, principal ship surveyor to the Board of Trade.

Tuesday, 18 June 1912 (26th day)

HEARD TODAY ARE Alexander Boyle, Engineer Surveyor in Chief to the

Board of Trade; Eber Sharpe, Assistant Emigration Officer in the Marine Department of the Board of Trade, stationed at Queenstown; Joseph Massey Harvey, Principal Examiner of Masters and Mates in the Board of Trade; Sir Norman Hill, Chairman of the Merchant Shipping Advisory Committee, secretary of the Liverpool Steamship Owners' Association and member of the Shipowners' Parliamentary Committee; Guglielmo Marconi, inventor of the Marconi system of wireless telegraphy; Joseph Barlow Ranson, Master of White Star Line's SS *Baltic*; Sir Ernest Shackleton, Arctic explorer; and Dr Riversdale Sampson French, surgeon on the White Star Line vessel SS *Oceanic*.

Wednesday, 19 June 1912 (27th day)

GIVING TESTIMONY TODAY are John Pritchard, late Master of RMS *Mauretania*; Hugh Young, late master for ships of the Anchor Line; William Stewart, master for the Canadian Pacific steamships ; Alexander Fairfull, retired master of the Allan Line; and Andrew Braes, retired master of the Allan Line. Edward Wilding is recalled.

Friday, 21 June 1912 (28th day)

ARTHUR HENRY ROSTRON, Master of Cunard's SS *Carpathia*, gives testimony today, together with Gerhard Christopher Apfeld, Marine Superintendent for the Red Star Line, and Arthur Ernest Tride, Master of Red Star Line's SS *Manitou*.

With the answer by Mr Arthur Ernest Tride to question number 25,622, the end of the Inquiry's witnesses arrives. For the remainder of the 28th day and for the next eight days of hearings (the final two held at Caxton Hall, Westminster), the Commission hears arguments by members of the various counsels.

Above Famed Antarctic explorer Sir Ernest Shackleton gives evidence regarding ice and icebergs. (Royal Geographical Society)

Right On the last day of the Inquiry's public testimony, Arthur Henry Rostron, master of Cunard's SS *Carpathia*, appears as one of the hearings' final witnesses. He receives the acknowledgement and gratitude of Lord Mersey and his Commission. (*The Truth About the Titanic*)

Among those giving testimony on 18 June is distinguished inventor and businessman Guglielmo Marconi. He receives a rare word of thanks from the commissioner. (GEC-Marconi)

Monday, 24 June 1912

DISCUSSION AND deliberation begins among members of the Mersey Commission.

Saturday, 29 June 1912

THE MERSEY COMMISSION meets at the Scottish Drill Hall, site of its original convening, for the last time. The poor acoustics have been a source of constant complaint by the press, the public and the Commission itself.

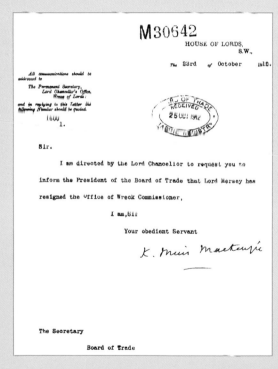

Above Lord Mersey formally resigns as Wreck Commissioner. (Crown Copyright material in the Public Record Office, reproduced by permission of the Controller of Her Majesty's Stationery Office; PRO MT9/920 M30642)

Caxton Hall. (Authors' collection)

Lord Mersey. (*Daily Mirror*)

Monday, 1 July 1912

THE COMMISSION reconvenes at Caxton Hall, Westminster, which has become available.

Wednesday, 3 July 1912 (36th day)

AFTER THE FINAL DAY for hearing arguments, the Commission retires to consider in closed session the evidence that will aid it in reaching answers to the 26 questions posed by the Attorney General at the hearings' outset.

Monday, 8 July 1912

THE PRIVATE DELIBERATIONS by Lord Mersey and his associates conclude.

Tuesday, 30 July 1912

THE MERSEY Commission's findings are published.

Wednesday, 23 October 1912

HIS OFFICIAL FUNCTION fulfilled, Lord Mersey resigns his office as *Titanic*'s Wreck Commissioner. The President of the Board of Trade, Mr Sydney Buxton, is so informed in a note from the Lord Chancellor's office.

SUMMARY OF THE BOARD OF TRADE INVESTIGATION INTO THE LOSS OF THE STEAMSHIP *TITANIC*

THE INQUIRY OCCUPIES 36 days of open hearings and an additional five days of *in camera* deliberations, a total of 41 days. Sessions 1 to 34 are held at the Royal Scottish Drill Hall, and Sessions 35 and 36 at Caxton Hall. Direct testimony consists of answers to 25,622 questions that occupy 959 double-columned pages. A total of 93 witnesses are heard, including:

- 44 *Titanic* officers and crew
- Nine Board of Trade surveyors and examiners
- Two representatives of Harland & Wolff
- Two passengers

A large number of subjects are encompassed in the Commission's findings. Recounted in the briefest form, they are:

- The collision with the iceberg was due to the excessive speed with which the ship was operated
- A proper watch was not kept
- The boats were properly lowered but insufficiently manned
- The liner *Californian* might have reached *Titanic* if she had attempted to do so
- Vigilance was shown in following the ocean track
- Third Class passengers were not discriminated against in the saving of life

The Court exonerates J. Bruce Ismay and Sir Cosmo Duff-Gordon from allegations of improper conduct. It also recommends more watertight compartments for ocean-going ships, the provision of lifeboats for all on board, and better lookout procedures. In conclusion, Lord Mersey severely blames the Board of Trade for its failure to revise the shipping rules of 1894.

Recommendations include the convening of an international conference to consider mutual adoption of regulations regarding safety at sea.

The total cost of the Inquiry was £20,549 5s 10d ($102,746.20). Some typical expenses include the following: hiring of hall and fitting-up expenses £341 7s 1d ($1,706.50); Board of Trade counsel £9,341 21s 0d ($46,709.20); stationery/printing (net) £934 13s 0d ($4,672.60); stenographic services £622 0s 0d ($3,110.00); Rt Hon Lord Mersey £1,050 0s 0d ($5,250.00); and Lord Mersey's secretary (his son) £125 0s 0d ($625.00).

The Inquiry appears to follow this general course:

Titanic's crew: Determining specific events that occurred following the collision and during the loading of the lifeboats. The witnesses are questioned in roughly the same sequence as the boat launchings occurred.

Titanic's officers: A purview of the disaster and the sequence of its components.

Ismay and Sanderson: The White Star Line's organisation and the *Olympic/Titanic* in the overall company picture.

The 'experts' (Wilding, Peskett, etc): How the disaster occurred.

Board of Trade Examiners: Why the disaster occurred.

NINE

THE YEARS PASS

Sunday, 9 March 1913

CHARTERED BY THE Board of Trade, the British vessel *Scotia* departs Dundee, Scotland, on a two-month cruise off Newfoundland Banks to patrol for ice and to make weather observations, together with the United States Coast Guard cutters *Seneca* and *Miami*.

It should be noted that immediately following *Titanic*'s loss in April 1912, the United States Navy sent the cruiser *Birmingham* to patrol the North Atlantic in the region of the disaster, she was relieved in early June by the scout cruiser *Chester*.

Subsequently the International Ice Patrol is established. Financed by the signatories to an international convention (1913–1914), the service is provided by the United States Coast Guard (originally named the United States Revenue Cutter Service). The patrol continues to operate to the present, its only suspension being intervals during the war years. (It is now conducted primarily by the surveillance aircraft and orbiting satellites of the AMVER (Automated Merchant Vessel Report) Service of the United States Coast Guard, with ice reports faxed to all ships so equipped.)

Scotia. (Authors' collection)

Wednesday, 19 March 1913

In London, England, the Mansion House Committee submits its first report regarding the administration and application of a scheme to distribute the proceeds of the 'Titanic Relief Fund'.

As defined by the report:

'The Titanic Relief Fund was raised by public subscription upon the invitation of the Lord Mayor of the City of London for the aid and relief of the widows, orphans and dependent relatives of the persons (whether passengers or crew) who

The Mansion House (left), official residence of the Lord Mayor of London. (Authors' collection)

lost their lives by reason of the foundering in the Atlantic Ocean on the 15th April 1912 of the Steamship *Titanic*.'

The total sum subscribed amounts to £413,121 2s 10d (approximately $2,065,600 at the 1912 exchange rate of £1 = $5). After payments amounting to slightly more than £35,000, mostly for single, lump-sum capital payments to foreign claimants, the residue amounts to £383,754 7s 3d. This amount is invested in railway and government stocks, bonds and debentures to yield an annual return of about 3.2%.

Of the 887 members of *Titanic*'s crew who signed the ship's articles, 673 were lost. Altogether, there are 316 widows of the crew, 592 children and 553 other dependents, a total of 1,461 individuals, to be dealt with, in 654 cases.

As might be expected, a plethora of rules regulates distribution of payments and allowances. Among the most prominent of these:

'The allowance to a widow shall cease upon her re-marriage.

The allowances of children shall cease in the case of males at the age of 16 and in the case of females at age 18. No allowance shall be made to a dependent (other than a widow) over the age of 70 years.

Widows' and children's allowances together can not exceed three-quarters of the deceased's wages.'

(Adjustments are provided for special cases.)

There are seven classes of payments and allowances, classified according to the deceased's earnings (including 'tips'), and payments are made weekly.

There are separate scales for allowances to parents (with or without a widow), and for partial dependents such as brothers, sisters or other relatives.

Allowances are depicted in the chart below. Graduated allowances are made for children. A widow in classes A, B or C will receive 3s 6d extra for one child or 10s 6d for five, making, in all, a weekly allowance of £2 10s 6d maximum. In the lowest class, G (casual stewards), the maximum allowance will be £1 2s 0d for a widow with five children.

The total Titanic Relief Fund of more than £413,000 is distributed over the years to more than 1,400 dependents, and helps many families to survive the first few terrible years after the loss of a family's breadwinner. Many a child is later able to be clothed, fed and educated thanks to financial augmentation provided by the Fund.

According to the 1953 report of the Titanic Relief Fund, 'Inevitably as the years passed, the number of people with a direct claim on the fund diminished. In 1952, 40 years after the disaster, the fund, now administered by the Mansion House National Disasters

Class	No of cases	Earnings of deceased	Description	Weekly allowance
A	13	£250 and over	Leading officers, all departments	£2 0s 0d
B	54	£175–£250	Engineers, senior stewards	£1 12s 6d
C	43	£150–£174	Junior engineers, under stewards	£1 7s 6d
D	177	£100–£149	Engineers, stewards, storekeepers	£1 0s 0d
E	88	£85–£99	Leading firemen, greasers, stewards	17s 6d
F	246	£75–£84	Sailors, firemen, trimmers	15s 0d
G	33	£50–£74	Casual stewards	12s 6d
Total:	654			

Relief Fund, paid out £14,765 to 101 dependents of the Titanic Relief Fund. 'Since 1912,' the report continues, 'the sum of £671,458 has been paid out in grants to dependents – more than one and a half times the amount originally subscribed by the public.'

In December 1952 there is still £157,379 in the fund. In 1954, with the fund's resources standing at £155,083, an increase of 4 shillings a week to widows of men drowned in the disaster is announced; other dependents are granted 2 shillings a week. There are still 94 dependents.

During 1958/59 the fund is converted into annuities for the 64 remaining dependents. The balance of the general fund is then transferred to the Shipwrecked Fishermen & Mariners' Royal Benevolent Society

Today the annuities – instead of the traditional method of grant payment – are administered by the Public Trustee under the direction of the Mansion House Council & Executive Committee. The objective of the latter is that when the last dependent dies, the annuities fund shall be exhausted and also die.

New York's Titanic Memorial Lighthouse. (Authors' collection)

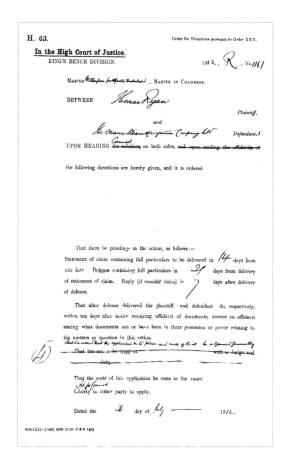

The court action of Ryan v Oceanic Steam Navigation Co. Ltd began with the filing of this full Bill of Particulars on 26 July 1912. It finally reaches court on 20 June 1913. (Public Record Office J54/1548 82953)

Tuesday, 15 April 1913

ON THE DISASTER'S first anniversary, the Titanic Memorial Lighthouse is dedicated in New York. Situated atop the newly completed Seaman's Church Institute on South Street at Manhattan's southern tip, the lighthouse includes a time ball and a beacon.

Friday, 20 June 1913

IN LONDON, ENGLAND, the case of Ryan v Oceanic Steam Navigation Co. Ltd opens before Mr Justice Bailhache and a special jury. The plaintiff is represented by Mr Campbell, KC, and Mr Thomas Scanlan; Mr Duke, KC, Mr Maurice Hill, KC, and Mr Raeburn represent the defendants.

Having opened on 20 June, the trial re-opens on Monday 23 June and continues through the week. Among the witnesses heard are Harold Bride; Charles Herbert Lightoller; wireless operator Stanley Herbert Adams of *Mesaba*; Joseph Scarrott, AB, of *Titanic*; lookout Reginald Lee; Captain E.G. Cumming of the Atlantic Transport Line,

who appears as an expert witness for the defendants, as does Captain Pritchard, formerly of the Cunard Line; and Captain Hayes, commander of White Star's own *Adriatic*.

Thursday, 26 June 1913

AFTER HEARING THE closing statements by counsel for both sides and a summation by Mr Justice Bailhache, the jury retires and after deliberating for an hour and three-quarters returns with the verdict that while the navigation of *Titanic* was not negligent in regard to lookout, it was so in respect of speed. The defendants are assessed damages at £100 and all Court costs.

The Oceanic Steam Navigation Company Limited takes its case to the Court of Appeal.

The decision in the Ryan v Oceanic Steam Navigation Co. Ltd case. (Crown Copyright material in the Public Record Office, reproduced by permission of the Controller of Her Majesty's Stationery Office; PRO J54/1548 82953)

Wednesday, 12 November 1913–Wednesday, 14 January 1914

THE FIRST INTERNATIONAL Conference for the Safety of Life at Sea convenes in London, England, presided over by Lord Mersey, who had headed the Board of Trade's Inquiry into *Titanic*'s loss.

The conference ends on 14 January 1914 with the signatories of the participating nations establishing and authorising the following regulations:

- On passenger-carrying vessels there will be lifeboats for all aboard.
- All ships must slow down and alter their courses when they are near ice.
- Aerial rockets and Roman candles are officially recognised as distress signals only, and are banned for any other use (such as recognition signals).
- All ships are to carry wireless equipment, manned 24 hours a day, and with a reliable source of auxiliary power.
- The United States agrees to continue and expand its ice patrol with the signatory nations' financial support.

Later International Conferences for the Safety of Life at Sea (SOLAS) held in 1929, 1948 and 1960 deal with the ice patrol's continuation; ships' stability, lifeboat equipment, watertight subdivision, fire safety and even precautions for nuclear-powered vessels.

Sunday, 21 December 1913

FOLLOWING *TITANIC*'S LOSS, many memorial monuments are built and dedicated to the individuals and groups who gave their lives in the name of

The Broken Hill memorial. (Arnold Watson collection)

honour. There are few more fitting to this attribute than the monument to *Titanic*'s bandsmen erected in the mining community of Broken Hill, NSW, Australia, and unveiled on this day. Immediately following the disaster, the Amalgamated Miners Association Band started a memorial fund to commemorate the bravery of their fellow musicians. The inscription on the monument reads:

'Erected by the Citizens of Broken Hill as a memorial to the heroic bandsmen of the steamship "Titanic" who, playing to the end, calmly faced certain death whilst women, children, and their fellow-men were being rescued from the wreck of that ill-fated vessel off the coast of Newfoundland on the 15th April 1912.'

This monument serves well to show that the grief over *Titanic*'s loss is felt by all people, great and small, in all lands, near and far.

Monday, 2 February 1914

FOR A WEEK commencing on this date, *The Loss of the Titanic* is presented at 6.50 and 9.00pm at the Palace Theatre in Gateshead, County Durham, England. The 'Loss' is presented in eight tableaux.
There is nothing more than a souvenir postcard to mark the show's existence.

Monday, 9 February 1914

IN THE COURT of Appeal, London, in the case of Ryan v Oceanic Steam Navigation Co. Ltd, Lord Justice Vaughan Williams dismisses the defendant's appeal and lets stand the assessed damages of £100 and all court costs.

Thursday, 26 February 1914

ONCE NAMED *GIGANTIC*, the now renamed *Britannic*, third vessel in the '*Olympic* class', is launched at Harland & Wolff's yards in Belfast.

Britannic is launched at Harland & Wolff. (Authors' collection/*Journal of Commerce*)

Lessons learned from *Titanic*'s loss are incorporated in her design, including an inner skin, higher watertight bulkheads and a unique system of immense motorised 'gantry davits', which, it is claimed, can place lifeboats over either side of the ship even when there is a heavy list.

Wednesday, 22 April 1914

THE ENGINEERS' MEMORIAL is dedicated in the East Park in Southampton, England, by Sir Archibald Denny before a crowd estimated at 100,000. (A metal fence installed across the monument's front is later removed in a scrap metal drive during the First World War, and is never replaced.)

Unveiling the Engineers' Memorial, Southampton. (*Shipping World*)

Unveiling the statue to Captain Smith, Lichfield, England. (Authors' collection)

Saturday, 23 May 1914

LUNA PARK AT Coney Island, Brooklyn, New York, opens its 1914 season with a 'spectacular show' depicting the 'Titanic Disaster' in 'three amazing acts'. The show is so poorly constructed and presented that it lasts barely two weeks.

Monday, 1 June 1914

FOR A WEEK commencing 1 June, at the Public Hall, Runcorn, Cheshire, England, the populace is treated to Charles W. and John R. Poole's 'Gigantic Reproduction Illustrative of the Loss of the Titanic in Eight Tableaux …'

Wednesday, 29 July 1914

A MEMORIAL STATUE to the late Captain Edward John Smith is unveiled by his teenage daughter, Helen Melville Smith, at Lichfield, Staffordshire, England.

Tuesday, 22 June 1915

HEARINGS BEGIN IN New York regarding the request by Oceanic Steam Navigation Company, operator of the White Star Line and *Titanic*'s nominal owner, to limit its liability in the vessel's loss.

Conducted by the United States District Court for the Southern District of New York, the case (docket number 55/279) is presided over by District Court Judge Charles M. Hough. Its function is to apportion the £3,464,785 ($16,804,112) in claims for loss of life and property among the lost liner's salvage, prepaid freight and gross passenger fares' net value of £20,159 ($97,772.02) plus insurance proceeds, unknown at the time of the hearings' opening.

US District Court Judge Charles M. Hough. (Authors' collection)

Tuesday, 27 July 1915

THE STEWARDS' ('below decks') Memorial is dedicated on Southampton Common, England. Made of Portland stone and designed as a drinking fountain, it is moved to the ruins of Holy Rood Church in 1972 following vandalism.

The Stewards' Memorial, Southampton Common, in 1915 ... (Authors' collection)

Tuesday, 9 November 1915

OFF CAPE MATAPAN, Greece (in the vicinity of 36°23'N, 22°29'E), the Leyland freighter *Californian* is torpedoed and sunk by an enemy submarine. One life is lost.

... and in its present site, Holy Rood Church, Southampton. (Authors' collection)

Californian in her early Dominion Line livery. (Private collection)

May 1916

THE 'ENGINE ROOM HEROES' memorial, a tribute to *Titanic*'s engineers, is completed in Liverpool, England. Because of the war there is no formal dedication ceremony of the obelisk, located near the Pier Head.

Left The 'engine room heroes' memorial at Liverpool. (Authors' collection)

Above US District Court Judge Julius M. Mayer. (Authors' collection)

Below His Majesty's Hospital Ship *Britannic*. (Authors' collection)

Friday, 28 July 1916

IN NEW YORK, more than a year after the hearings began on 22 June 1915, United States District Court Judge Julius M. Mayer, who has replaced Judge Hough, signs a decree ending all suits against *Titanic*'s owners and providing pro rata distribution among claimants of £136,701 ($663,000), which represents the salvage and insurance proceeds.

Tuesday, 21 November 1916

OFF PORT ST NIKOLO, Greece (37°42'N, 24°17'E), *Titanic*'s sister vessel *Britannic*, last and greatest of the '*Olympic* class', strikes a mine laid by the German submarine *U-73* in the Aegean Sea while on the outward leg of her sixth voyage on war service as a hospital ship.

Of the 673 ship's crew and 392 hospital staff on board, 21 are lost. The liner sinks in approximately 50 minutes. Among those rescued are fireman John Priest and stewardess Violet Jessop, both of whom had been aboard *Olympic* when it was rammed by HMS *Hawke*, and who had also survived *Titanic*'s sinking.

Wednesday, 17 July 1918

IN THE NORTH ATLANTIC (Cockburn Bank, 124 miles south-west of Fastnet), in the vicinity of 49°39'N, 9°05'W, the Cunard liner *Carpathia* is torpedoed and sunk by German submarine *U-55* with the loss of five crew members.

Monday, 26 January 1920

IN BELFAST, IRELAND, the city's *Titanic* memorial is unveiled. It stands for almost 40 years in Donegall Square North, in the carriageway in front of City Hall. However, because of vehicular traffic problems, the statue is moved in November 1959 to another site within the grounds of City Hall, facing Donegall Square East, between the South African War Memorial and the statue of Sir Edward Harland.

Sunday, 15 April 1923

ON THE DECK of the US Coast Guard cutter *Modoc* in the North Atlantic, vicinity of 41°46'N, 50°14'W, the first memorial service for *Titanic*'s victims is held at the presumed sinking site on the disaster's anniversary. The observance becomes an annual event; it now consists of a wreath dropped at the spot by a patrol aircraft from the International Ice Patrol.

Saturday, 7 June 1924

AT THE AGE OF 77, Viscount William J. Pirrie, former managing director of Harland & Wolff, *Titanic*'s builder, dies of pneumonia in the Panama Canal while cruising aboard the Pacific Steam Navigation Company's liner *Ebro*. Burial takes place at the Belfast City Cemetery on 23 June. (Atop the cemetery monument is a large bronze bust of Lord Pirrie, its eyes fixed on the distantly visible Harland & Wolff shipyard.)

Carpathia. (Authors' collection)

Belfast's *Titanic* memorial. (© 1998 Alan R. Geddes)

The first US Coast Guard *Titanic* memorial service. (US Coast Guard)

Tuesday, 26 May 1931

IN CEREMONIES LED by the widow of former United States President William Howard Taft – who was President in 1912 – the Women's Titanic Memorial is dedicated in Washington, DC. Sculpted by Gertrude Vanderbilt Whitney, whose brother was lost in the sinking of the *Lusitania* in 1915, its inscription reads, 'To the brave men who perished in the wreck of the Titanic, April 15, 1912. They gave their lives that women and children might be saved.'

Top left Lord and Lady Pirrie board the Royal Mail Steam Packet Co's *Arlanza* for the first part of their three-month trip to South America. (*Shipping World*)

Above On the journey's second leg aboard the *Ebro*, northward along South America's west coast, Lord Pirrie contracts pneumonia. He dies while the vessel is traversing the Panama Canal. (Authors' collection)

Top right Pirrie's body is taken to New York, thence to Southampton aboard *Olympic*. His burial at Belfast's City Cemetery occurs on 23 June 1924, the 62nd anniversary of his entry into Harland & Wolff. (Authors' collection)

Monday, 18 November 1929

A SEVERE EARTHQUAKE off North America's north-eastern coast causes a huge slide of mud and debris from the continental shelf into the adjacent ocean depths off the Nova Scotia coast, interrupting cable transmissions between North America and Europe for several days. For many years, plans for locating *Titanic* are influenced by the possibility that the wreck has been destroyed or buried by the slide.

Mrs William Howard Taft. (Authors' collection)

In 1972 the statue is moved to make way for the new Kennedy Center for the Performing Arts. It is subsequently relocated to its present site, Fourth and P Streets SW, adjacent to Fort McNair, on Washington's waterfront.

Thursday, 10 May 1934

IN LONDON, ENGLAND, registration of the Cunard-White Star Line Ltd, a merger of Britain's two largest shipping companies, marks the end of the independent White Star Line, founded on 6 September 1869 by Thomas H. Ismay under the corporate name of Oceanic Steam Navigation Co. Ltd. In a High Court order dated 8 April 1936 White Star's financial affairs are compulsorily ended.

Eliminating the White Star Line by purchase in 1947, the Cunard Steam Ship Company takes over all the activities of the former Cunard-White Star Company on 31 December 1949. The name of White Star disappears from official history.

Friday, 5 April 1935

OLYMPIC DEPARTS FROM New York on 'Number 257 eastbound', her final transatlantic voyage. 'Old Reliable' arrives at Southampton on 12 April. One of the 20th century's most successful liners, *Olympic* sailed more than 1½ million miles in nearly 34 years of service in both peace and war. During the Great War alone, on regular service and as a troop transport, she steamed 184,000 miles and carried without a casualty some 41,000 civilian passengers and 24,000 Canadian and 42,000 American troops, as well as a 12,000-member labour battalion for

PLEASE SEND YOUR CONTRIBUTION WITH THIS COUPON
TO THE

MRS. JOHN HAY
CHAIRMAN
MRS. JOHN HAYS HAMMOND
SECRETARY

WOMAN'S "TITANIC" MEMORIAL
UNION TRUST BUILDING
WASHINGTON, D. C.

EDWARD J. STELLWAGEN
TREASURER
GEORGE X. McLANAHAN
HONORARY COUNSEL

A CONTRIBUTION FROM EVERY WOMAN

For the erection of a Memorial in the Capital of the Nation.

Woman's tribute to those who so bravely sacrificed their lives that others might be saved.

----------------------------1912

Name ....

Address ....

City .... State ....

Amount .... Dollars .... Cents

Remarks ....

....

Above Women's Titanic Memorial contribution pledge slip. (Authors' collection)

Left The Women's Titanic Memorial was moved to its present site in East Potomac Park, adjacent to Washington's Fort McNair, in the early 1970s. (Authors' collection)

Below Following the White Star–Cunard merger, aboard White Star vessels the company's pennant flies above the Cunard flag, while aboard Cunard ships the order is reversed. (Authors' collection)

employment behind the lines on the Western Front.

Olympic was a gallant ship as well: in October 1914 she rescued survivors from the battleship HMS *Audacious*, mined and sunk in the vicinity of Lough Swilly; and on 1 May 1916, while on a trooping voyage, she was attacked by the German submarine *U-103* – evading a torpedo, *Olympic* rammed and sank the submarine.

Refurbished and converted to oil in 1919, at the peak of her career during the 1920s *Olympic* faithfully contributed to White Star's presence on the North Atlantic.

Withdrawn from service in March 1935, she is laid up at Southampton. Sold for scrap in October for £100,000, she is towed to the Thomas Ward scrap yard at Jarrow, Tyneside, where she is dismantled. Her hull, still sound, is towed to Ward's Inverkeithing yard in Scotland for final scrapping on 19 September 1937.

Saturday, 17 October 1936

JOSEPH BRUCE ISMAY, 74, dies at his residence at 15 Hill Street, Mayfair, London, following a stroke. He is cremated and his ashes are buried at Putney Vale Cemetery, Kingston Road, London SW15.

Saturday, 1 June 1940

SAILING FROM RAMSGATE, Kent, England, the 60ft motor yacht *Sundowner*, with owner Charles Herbert Lightoller in command, assists in the evacuation of some of the 338,000 British troops stranded on the beaches of Dunkirk by German Army advances.

Sundowner, the yacht of *Titanic*'s former second officer Charles Lightoller. (Authors' collection)

At the age of 66, Lightoller personally takes aboard his gallant craft a total of 127 troops and brings them safely home across the Channel to Ramsgate while under almost constant harassment by German aircraft.

Monday, 4 November 1940

SIR ARTHUR ROSTRON, KDB, RD, RNR, *Carpathia*'s commander at the time of

Sir Arthur Rostron dies in 1940, aged 71. (*American Magazine*)

Charles Lightoller dies in 1952, aged 78. (Authors' collection)

the *Titanic* survivors' rescue and subsequently Cunard commodore, dies at the age of 71 in Chippenham, Wiltshire, England. Burial takes place on 7 November at Westend, Southampton.

May 1944

AT THE AGE of 61, Harold Godfrey Lowe, *Titanic*'s former fifth officer, dies in Deganwy, Wales.

Monday, 8 December 1952

CHARLES HERBERT LIGHTOLLER, *Titanic*'s former second officer and hero of Dunkirk, dies of pneumonia at the age of 78 at his home at 1 Ducks Walk, Twickenham, Middlesex, England. On 11 December his remains are cremated at nearby Mortlake Crematorium and the ashes scattered in the Garden of Remembrance.

Summer 1953

AN ATTEMPT IS made by a Southampton marine salvage firm, Risdon Beasley Ltd, to locate *Titanic*'s wreck. Between 30 July and 5 August, at a base site of 43°65'N, 52°04'W, high explosives are used to generate a bottom profile 'echo', but the search is unsuccessful.

November 1955

WALTER LORD'S BOOK, *A Night to Remember*, is published in New York. Subsequently translated (at the last count) into 83 foreign languages, the book – on which are based a 1956 live television programme and the 1958 film

Above Author Walter Lord in 1958. During 1998 a renewed interest in *Titanic* propels his book *A Night to Remember* on to the world's bestseller lists for a second time, nearly 45 years after its first publication. (Private collection)

Above Harold Bride, as he appeared during the US Senate Inquiry in 1912. He dies in 1956, aged 66. (*Portland* [Oregon] *Journal*)

Above right Herbert J. Pitman in 1958. He dies in 1961, aged 83. (Authors' collection)

Right Stanley Lord, *Californian*'s Master, dies in 1962, aged 84. (Authors' collection)

of the same name – does more than any other publication to make the public aware of *Titanic*'s awesome story.

Thursday, 7 December 1961

THE DEATH IS RECORDED of Herbert John Pitman, 83, *Titanic*'s former third officer, in Bruton, Somerset, England.

Sunday, 29 April 1956

AT THE AGE OF 66, Harold Sidney Bride, *Titanic*'s junior wireless operator, dies in Glasgow, Scotland.

Thursday, 25 January 1962

STANLEY LORD, LATE master of the Leyland Line freighter *Californian*, dies at the age of 84 in Wallasey, Cheshire, England.

THE CASE OF THE *CALIFORNIAN*

Tuesday, 30 July 1912

THE MERSEY COMMISSION'S findings are made public, and the Inquiry finds that during the night of 14/15 April 1912 the ship *Californian*, westbound from London to Boston and stopped in ice, was between 8 and 10 miles from *Titanic* when the liner hit the iceberg at 11.40pm; that a ship with blazing lights seen from *Californian* at the time was *Titanic*; that eight rockets fired between 12.45 and 1.45am were fired from the liner; and that the ship seen by *Californian* disappeared at 2.20am, the time that *Titanic* sank.

Lord Mersey, who headed the inquiry states:

'The night was clear and the sea was smooth. When she first saw the rockets, the *Californian* could have pushed through the ice to the open water without any serious risk and so have come to the assistance of the *Titanic*.

Had she done so, she might have saved many, if not all, of the lives that were lost.'

Captain Stanley Lord insists that he was 17 to 19 miles from *Titanic*, could not have seen the liner and her rockets, and that he did not know of the disaster because his lone wireless operator had shut down at 11.30pm.

Having appeared at the Inquiry only as a witness, Captain Lord has no recourse to rebuttal of the charges placed against him and his ship after his inquiry testimony.

Saturday, 10 August 1912

CAPTAIN LORD ADDRESSES a letter from Liscard, Cheshire, England, to the Board of Trade's Marine Department in which he makes a strong case on his own behalf and requests assistance in bringing the truth of the situation before the public.

Walter J. Howell, assistant secretary to the Board of Trade, repeatedly denies the request because Lord, appearing at the hearings only as a witness and not as a defendant, is not entitled to a hearing of his case.

Tuesday, 13 August 1912

CAPTAIN STANLEY LORD resigns from the Leyland Line, a company he has served since 1897.

Saturday, 1 February 1913

CAPTAIN LORD IS HIRED by Lawther Latta & Co. (the Nitrate Producers Steam Ship Company Ltd), a British shipping company in the Chilean nitrate trade. He reports for duty on 7 March.

On the night of 14/15 April third officer Charles V. Groves and apprentice James Gibson allegedly viewed the lights of a large passenger steamer from *Californian*'s deck. (Dundee City Archives)

Thursday, 12 July 1928

IN A LETTER to the company on this date, Captain Lord resigns from the Nitrate Producers SS Co. for reasons of health.

November 1955 and July 1958

WITH THE 1955 PUBLICATION of Walter Lord's book *A Night to Remember* and the worldwide screening of the film of the same name a little more than two years later, Stanley Lord's story – and his bitter criticism by the 1912 Board of Trade Inquiry – is once again of public interest. As Captain Lord (no relation to the book's author) says, '... The film gave great prominence to the allegation that *Californian* stood by in close proximity to the sinking *Titanic*.'

Leslie Harrison. (Authors' collection)

Captain Lord now feels it necessary to speak up. Since 1897 he has been a member of the Mercantile Marine Service Association, and in 1958 he walks into the association's Liverpool offices and announces, 'I'm Lord of the *Californian*. I have come to clear my name.'

He enlists the services of the Association's general secretary, Mr Leslie Harrison, who prepares a petition addressed to the President of the Board of Trade containing evidence that would have been presented in 1912 if Captain Lord had been given the opportunity to defend himself.

Thursday, 25 January 1962

CAPTAIN LORD DIES, aged 84.

Friday, 5 February 1965

A PETITION CALLING for a re-opening of the 1912 Inquiry is presented to the President of the Board of Trade.

'I'm Lord of the *Californian*. I have come to clear my name.' (*Washington Evening Star*)

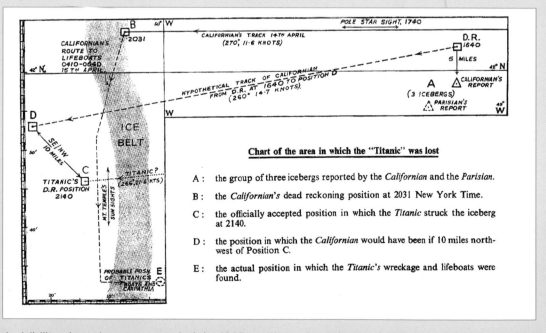

A visibility chart that accompanied the 1965 petition asking that the 1912 Inquiry be re-opened. (Authors' collection)

Monday, 6 September 1965

IN A LETTER TO Leslie Harrison bearing this date, Mr Roy Mason, MP, Minister of State (Shipping), rejects the petition to re-open the case of Stanley Lord.

'... Your petition does not suggest that there is any new and important evidence which would not have been produced at the formal investigation ... [Because of] the time which has elapsed since the original hearing and the death of the great majority of the persons concerned, including Captain Lord, the President does not consider that the Board should ... order a re-hearing.'

Undaunted, Mr Harrison states, 'The Mercantile Marine Service Association will continue its efforts to clear Captain Lord's name.'

Monday, 4 March 1968

A SECOND PETITION, dated February 1968, is submitted by Mr Harrison to the President of the Board of Trade. It contains what is believed to be new evidence based on Harrison's interview with the late Lawrence Beesley regarding the rocket firing times.

Friday, 26 July 1968

MR MASON, MINISTER of State (Shipping), replies to the petition at the behest of the President of the Board of Trade (who has himself consulted with the Attorney General).

'There is no reason to believe that a miscarriage of justice has occurred ... [In] regard to the time that has elapsed and the death of the great majority of the persons concerned the President did not consider that the Board should exercise its discretionary power to order a re-hearing.

The President is advised that the provisions of the Shipping Act of 1894 do not impose upon the Board the obligation of ordering a new hearing, primarily because the evidence submitted is not evidence which could not have been produced at the Inquiry but also because that evidence is not "important" within the meaning of the pertinent Section.'

Mr Harrison says he will now enter legal action to pursue his efforts to clear Captain Lord's name.

1990

REAPPRAISAL OF EVIDENCE in the Captain Stanley Lord case is ordered by the Secretary of State for Transport, The Rt Hon Cecil Parkinson, MP, who makes his decision partly in response to demands for re-examination and also, since the controversy is taking up so much staff time, because it seems more cost-effective to try to resolve it.

Captain Thomas W. Barnett, a retired principal nautical surveyor of the Transport Department, is commissioned to carry out the re-examination for 'a modest fee'. Captain Barnett examines and considers the original Inquiry's 1912 evidence in addition to the facts contained in Mr Leslie Harrison's two petitions to the Board of Trade.

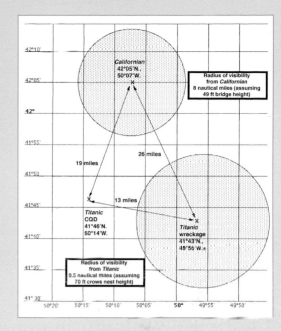

The discovery of the wreck of *Titanic* in 1985 demonstrates that the ship was approximately 13 miles south and east of the traditional 41°46'N, 50°14'W position, requiring a reappraisal of the *Californian* incident. Given visibilities possible from each of the two vessels, it is again argued that *Californian* could not have seen the sinking liner. (© 1999 John P. Eaton and Charles A. Haas)

1991

CAPTAIN BARNETT SUBMITS his report to Captain Peter Marriott, Chief Inspector of Marine Accidents, who does not fully agree with his findings. Marriott asks Captain James de Coverly, Deputy Chief Inspector of Marine Accidents, to carry out further examinations of the evidence.

Thursday, 2 April 1992

LESS THAN TWO WEEKS prior to the 80th anniversary of *Titanic*'s loss, the results of Captain de Coverly's re-examination are issued in a report including both his and Captain Barnett's conclusions, under cover of a submission by Captain Marriott to the Secretary of State. In his submission, Captain Marriott fully endorses the Deputy Chief Inspector's report and conclusions.

Captain de Coverly's conclusions differ on two key points from those of Captain Barnett:

'Capt Barnett finds the two ships were between 5 and 10 miles apart, as believed in 1912, probably nearer 5; but Capt de Coverly finds the distance probably about 18 miles.

Also, Capt Barnett reports the *Titanic* was seen from the *Californian* and kept under observation from 11pm until she sank almost 3½ hours later. Capt de Coverly concludes the ship seen was more probably, another, unidentified, vessel.'

Captain Marriott's report concludes with the following observation:

'Neither party will be entirely satisfied with this Report, but while it does not purport to answer all the questions which have been raised, it does attempt to distinguish the essential circumstances and set out reasoned and realistic interpretations. It is for others if they wish to go further into speculation; it is to be hoped that they will do so rationally and with some regard to the simple fact that there are no villains in this story: just human beings with human characteristics.'

The Marine Accident Investigation Branch's findings are incorporated in a new charting of the ships' positions in 1912. (Authors' collection)

Captain Thomas W. Barnett. (Courtesy of Capt. and Mrs Thomas Barnett)

Captain James de Coverly. (Courtesy of Capt. and Mrs James de Coverly)

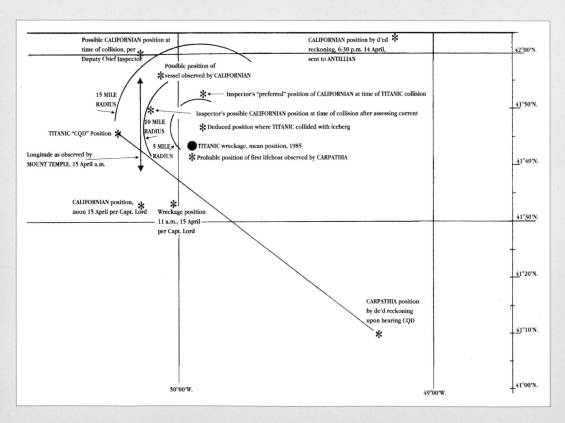

Lawrence Beesley, from a photograph taken aboard the rescue vessel *Carpathia*. (Mr and Mrs George A. Fenwick)

Joseph Groves Boxhall dies in 1967, aged 83. (Authors' collection)

Demolition of Harland & Wolff's Arrol gantry in 1971. (Harland & Wolff collection, Ulster Folk and Transport Museum)

Saturday, 18 February 1967

THE DEATH OCCURS in Lincoln, England, at the age of 89 of Mr Lawrence Beesley, whose book *The Loss of the SS Titanic* is considered by many to be the most authoritative account of the disaster by a survivor.

Mr Beesley, a former science master at Dulwich College, used his skills as a trained observer to record not only the details of the dreadful night, but also his own feelings during and following the sinking.

The success of his book, still a best-seller among those newly interested in *Titanic*, made him an accepted expert on every aspect of the disaster.

Tuesday, 25 April 1967

JOSEPH GROVES BOXHALL, late fourth officer of *Titanic*, dies at the age of 83 in Christchurch, Hampshire, England. Commander Boxhall's remains are cremated at Mortlake Crematorium and on 12 June his ashes are scattered

on the sea from the deck of the Cunard motor vessel *Scotia*, stopped at position 41°46'N, 50°14'W.

With former fifth officer Harold Godfrey Lowe having died at the age of 61 in 1944, all four of *Titanic*'s surviving officers – Lowe, Lightoller, Pitman and Boxhall – had now passed away.

After serving aboard *Titanic*, each had continued in the employment of White Star (or its successor Cunard-White Star) until their respective retirements. Although each gave many years of efficient and exemplary service, not one was ever appointed to command one of the company's vessels.

Spring 1971

IN BELFAST, NORTHERN IRELAND, demolition begins of the great Arrol gantry at Harland & Wolff's Queen's Island yard. Begun in 1906 and

completed in 1908, the combined dimensions of the gantry's two slips – 840ft long, 270ft wide and 230ft high – extended across the width of three former slips. It was beneath this gantry, on slip number 3, that *Titanic*'s keel was laid, her hull completed, and from which she was launched with such high hopes and aspirations on 31 May 1911.

Thursday, 19 March 1981

IN AN ARTICLE appearing in the *Southern Evening Echo*, Mr James Beasley, an American insurance company executive, announces his intention to invest upwards of a billion pounds in a scheme to build three luxury ships, replicas of the *Titanic*. Mr Beasley's company, Transit Risk Corporation, is apparently in the final stages of putting together the financial package.

Having studied plans and photographs of the lost liner, Mr Beasley says that he wants the new vessels to resemble *Titanic* as closely as possible, but that inside the emphasis will be on luxury. A Harland & Wolff spokesman says that Mr Beasley has been in contact with the company twice, and the shipyard are now awaiting firm proposals before deciding whether the plan is feasible.

Monday, 30 May 1983

THE DEATH OCCURS in Portsmouth, England, of *Titanic*'s last surviving crewman, Mr Sydney E. Daniels, who, at the age of 18, was a lift operator aboard the liner.

In this 1970s photograph, Sidney Daniels points to the position of the lifeboat in which he left *Titanic*. (Courtesy *The News*, Portsmouth, UK)

Wednesday, 30 May 1984

HAROLD THOMAS COTTAM, *Carpathia*'s telegraphist, whose interception of *Titanic*'s wireless distress signals enabled the rescue vessel to set a course to the drifting survivors, dies at the age of 93 in Nottingham, England.

Sunday, 1 September 1985

IN THE NORTH ATLANTIC, in the vicinity of 41°43'N, 49°56'W, *Titanic*'s wreck is found lying in two sections at a depth of 12,460ft.

Monday, 23 September 1991

IN A CEREMONY AT Halifax, Nova Scotia, attended by civic leaders and the public, the names of six *Titanic* victims, for nearly 80 years unknown, are unveiled on their grave markers in Fairview Lawn Cemetery. Identifications were researched and confirmed by members of Titanic International, an organisation based in New Jersey.

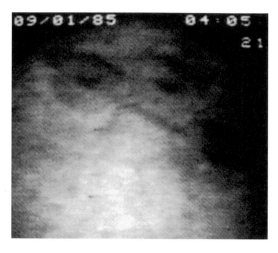

The ghostly, low-resolution televised image of a *Titanic* boiler is the first identifiable sight of the liner's wreckage. (© 1985 Woods Hole Oceanographic Institution)

Officials from *Titanic* International and the city of Halifax dedicate six *Titanic* gravestones at the city's Fairview Cemetery. Among those shown is Russ Lownds (second from right), whose father, an employee of White Star's Halifax agency, assisted in the 1912 identification of the victims. (Edith Gamba collection)

TEN

THE SEARCH FOR *TITANIC*

'WELL, MY LORD, we are not quite satisfied about the exact place of the collision; we think there may be a substantial difference.'

Mr Frederick Laing (Counsel to the White Star Line), Board of Trade *Titanic* Inquiry, page 12

For more than 60 years the allure of finding and exploring *Titanic*'s wreck attracted theorists and dreamers. Some plans were ludicrous, others selfish. All were highly speculative. Almost all ignored science and historic fact. But *Titanic*'s mystique beckoned, and the dreamers responded ...

Saturday, 20 April 1912

THE NEW YORK JOURNAL reports: 'A plan to blow up the wreckage of *Titanic* with a powerful explosive is being considered today by Vincent Astor, son of the late Colonel.'

J.J. Merritt of the Merritt-Chapman Wreckage Company states that he feels the plan is feasible once the wreck is located. However, the discovery on 21 April of the late Colonel's body by the *Mackay-Bennett* obviates further development of this scheme.

Summer 1953

AS MENTIONED IN the previous chapter, Risdon Beasley Ltd (a Southampton, England, marine salvage firm) attempts to use high explosives to form a sea-bottom profile. Their ship, *The Help*, is on site at 43°65'N, 52°04'W from 30 July to 5 August.

October 1968

DOUGLAS WOOLLEY, A British *Titanic* salvage enthusiast, makes his first public announcement. A frequent subject of human interest stories in the British press, Woolley is noticeably active during the next decade or so.

In 1970 he forms The Titanic Salvage Company, followed in 1972 by the Seawise Salvage Company and Seawise Under Water Video Survey Systems Co. (see 1 September 1974 below). In 1979 he is Seawise & Titanic Salvage Ltd (see 1979 below), and in 1980 Delftpoint.

Vincent Astor at Halifax after claiming his father's body. (*Harper's*)

1974

MARK BAMFORD, SON of Joe Bamford (founder of JCB, the well-known British manufacturer of earth-moving equipment), as Titanic Salvage, expresses an interest in the vessel's salvage, perhaps to augment his own theatrical and cinema interests. Beyond commissioning an 18ft model of *Titanic* from the professional model-makers Bassett-Lowke, he does not seem to have pursued his interest in salvage.

1 September 1974

DOUGLAS WOOLLEY'S Titanic & Seawise Salvage Company scheme is announced, using the ship *Cynthia-Yvonne* (formerly *Rosebud*).

Purchased for £500, *Cynthia-Yvonne*, a 55-year-old, 38-ton fishing vessel, is to be used to survey the *Titanic* wreck site in preparation for raising the sunken vessel. Before attempting the *Titanic* survey, Mr Woolley plans to rehearse his crew in Hong Kong Harbour to survey the *Queen Elizabeth*, sunk and wrecked by fire on 9 January 1972.

The scheme is dropped on 7 September 1974.

March 1977

THREE WEST BERLIN businessmen, as Titanic-Tresor, apparently wish to back Douglas Woolley. They withdraw their support in September 1977.

1978

ARTHUR HICKEY, A haulage contractor from Walsall, Staffordshire, England, advocates freezing the interior of the sunken liner's hull and floating it to the surface.

In the same year 'Big Events', Joe King and Spencer Sokale of Sausolito, California, offer to fund and promote several scientific groups that are attempting to organise searches for the *Titanic*.

During the 1970s many plans are proposed to locate *Titanic*'s wreck. Some are only bizarre schemes; others are mainly announcements made to raise capital for the pursuit of nebulous dreams.

However, the wreck begins to attract credible members of the scientific

Alcoa Seaprobe. (© Woods Hole Oceanographic Institution)

community, and some proposals are serious plans employing scientific skill and state-of-the-art equipment. Developments in undersea equipment and search techniques now make such a project feasible. The time for exploitation of mere theory is past and the stage is set for serious exploration.

August 1977

SEAONICS INTERNATIONAL LTD (Robert Ballard, Emery Kristof, Alan Ravenscroft and William Tantum) proposes 'To raise money to build deep-towed visual-imaging vehicles to find the *Titanic*'.

October 1977

THE WOODS HOLE Oceanographic Institution, under expedition leader Dr Robert Ballard, sends the *Alcoa Seaprobe* to 41°40'N, 50°01'W. The vessel, owned by the Aluminum Company of America and developed by Scripps's ocean engineer William Bascom, does not reach the search area due to equipment failure.

May 1978

WALT DISNEY PRODUCTIONS, in collaboration with National Geographic, spends approximately $70,000 on feasibility studies conducted by Alcoa. The plan is rejected in June 1978.

1979

SEAWISE & TITANIC SALVAGE (Philip Slade and Clive Ramsey, former associates of Douglas Woolley;

underwater photo expert Derik Berwin;
Commander Gratton, Fathom Line,
diving consultant; and Dr Nick Fleming,
Marine Advisory Information Service at
Wormley) are on site at 41°40'N,
50°03'W ('subsequently revised').

Spring 1979

NAMED AFTER THE temptress in
Greek mythology, the 'Project Circe'
expedition (Robert H. Gibbons and
Charles Ira Sachs with the ship RV
Valdavia) plans to use an underwater
camera system leased from Hydro
Products, which includes still and
television capability. The system is to
be lowered by armoured cable and will
transmit images up the cable to the
surface ship. A magnetic device will
leave a memorial plaque on *Titanic*'s
hull and pluck up a small metallic
object to be brought to the surface.
The target date is 15 April 1979, when
live transmissions of television images
to the networks of the world will take
place on the disaster's anniversary.

The research vessel is available; the
satellite TV transmitter is available;
but the $600,000 needed to pay for
the ship, equipment and crew
is not.

July–August 1980

TITANIC '80, INC. (Jack Grimm, Mike
Harris and the Lamont-Doherty/Scripps
Institute ship *H.J.W. Fay*) are on site at
41°40'–41°50'N, 50°–50°10'W from
29 July to 17 August. The expedition
searches unsuccessfully for *Titanic*,
thwarted almost continuously by
bad weather.

Top *H..IW. Fay*. (Tracor Inc.)

Above *Gyre*. (Department of Oceanography,
Texas A&M University)

Right The Grimm/Harris expedition uses Deep
Tow, a sidescan sonar package, to search the
ocean floor. (Authors' collection)

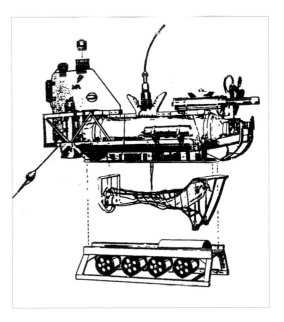

April 1981

FRED KOEHLER, DESCRIBED as 'an
electronic tycoon' from Coral Gables,
Florida, plans to use a 14ft submersible,
Seacopter, for direct salvage of cargo,
especially 'the diamonds in the
purser's safe'.

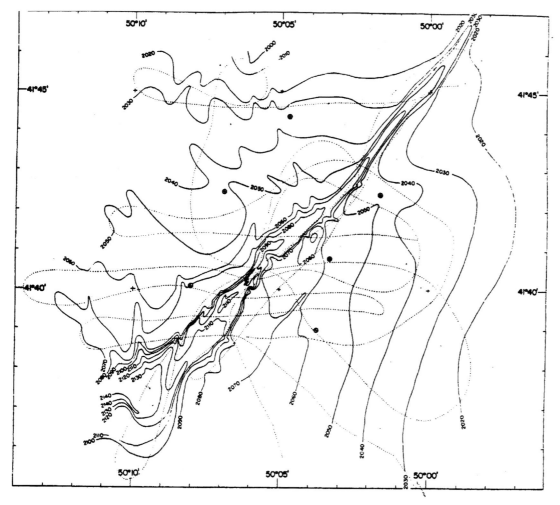

Koehler had been unable to reach agreement with Grimm and Harris in 1980, but in 1981 is unable to secure funds for his own exploration.

July 1981

THE SECOND expedition led by Jack Grimm and Mike Harris, aboard the Lamont-Doherty/Scripps Institute ship *Gyre* is on site in the vicinity of 41°39'–41°44'N, 50°02'–50°08'W from 9 to 18 July, but yet again the expedition is buffeted by storms and fails to locate *Titanic*.

July 1983

THE THIRD Grimm/Harris expedition and the Lamont-Doherty ship *Robert D. Conrad* are on site '380 nautical miles south-east of Cape Race and about 820 miles east of Cape Cod' (vicinity of 41°08'N, 50°03'W) from 20 to 24 July. High winds and heavy seas again frustrate the Texas oilman's efforts to locate *Titanic*.

Early summer 1985

ACCORDING TO A REPORT in a St John's, Newfoundland, newspaper on 4 September 1985, during a scientific voyage in 1980 the Canadian research vessel *Hudson* detected a 180-metre

Top The depth contour map of the 1981 Grimm/Harris expedition shows the area of the expedition's unsuccessful search for *Titanic*. (Authors' collection)

Left The US Navy oceanographic research vessel *Robert D. Conrad* as seen in 1962. (Naval Historical Society, Washington DC)

object in an underwater canyon off the tail of the Grand Banks, subsequently described as 'in the general area where the *Titanic* is thought to have been found'.

The report continues, 'Several attempts to find the object again and identify it failed, including one a few months ago when geologist George Fader of the Bedford Institute [of Oceanography, Dartmouth, Nova Scotia] and a crew aboard the vessel *Pandora* brought the three-man submarine *Pisces II* to the area in hopes of combing the canyon. Poor weather abbreviated the search.'

However, *Pisces II* would have had a difficult time 'combing the canyon'. Launched in September 1968 by the International Hydrodynamics Co. Ltd of Vancouver, BC, it had a maximum operating depth of 3,500ft, with a collapse depth of 5,000ft.

Tuesday, 9 July 1985

THE INSTITUT FRANÇAIS de Recherches pour l'Exploitation des Mers (IFREMER) research vessel *Le Suroit*, under project leader Jean Jarry and expedition co-leader Captain Jean-Louis Michel, arrives at the vicinity of 41°43'–41°51'N, 49°55'–50°12'W and begins a systematic examination of the area before returning to the French colony of St Pierre, off Newfoundland, for supplies on 19 July.

Top *Le Suroit*. (IFREMER)

Middle Aboard *Le Suroit*, expedition co-leader Jean-Louis Michel (standing, right) consults with navigating officer Bernard Jegot about the towed sonar device's position as the 1985 search for *Titanic* continues. (Jean Jarry Collection, courtesy La Cité de la Mer, Cherbourg)

Right ARGO. (© Woods Hole Oceanographic Institution)

room, the scientific crew, under the command of the watch chief, Captain Jean-Louis Michel, continues its search, reading the endless data and images being transmitted from the scanning equipment more than 12,000ft below.

At 12.48am, unexpectedly there appears on the screens images of man-made objects, then more and more components, until suddenly the image of an immense boiler fills the screen. Excitedly the scientists watch as the fascinating forms flow across their monitors.

Their voices, raised in triumph and astonishment, attract other nearby members of the crew. Captain Michel quickly acts to raise the altitude of the instruments being towed, lest they strike the wreck. Someone suggests that

Dr Robert D. Ballard of the Massachusetts-based Woods Hole Oceanographic Institution (WHOI) now joins the expedition, returning with the French team to mid-Atlantic on 26 July. Again the search is unsuccessful (although a later examination of navigational reports shows that *Le Suroit* had come to within 3,300ft of the wreck).

The French vessel again withdraws on 7 August, this time in favour of WHOI's research vessel *Knorr*, which arrives on site on 24 August from its supply base in the Azores. Its equipment includes Deep Tow packages ANGUS and ARGO. Along with several French colleagues Captain Jean-Louis Michel transfers over as co-leader of the expedition with Dr Ballard, each having joint and equal responsibilities of command.

The exploration resumes its stultifying daily routine, more exhausting to many than hard manual labour. They are on site until 5 September.

Sunday, 1 September 1985

ON THE NIGHT OF 31 August/1 September, his watch over, Dr Ballard leaves the bridge and repairs to his cabin, where he relaxes over a book in preparation for sleep. In the control

Above left RV *Knorr*. (© Woods Hole Oceanographic Institution)

Below *Titanic*'s bow, as viewed during the 1985 IFREMER/Woods Hole Expedition. (© Woods Hole Oceanographic Institution)

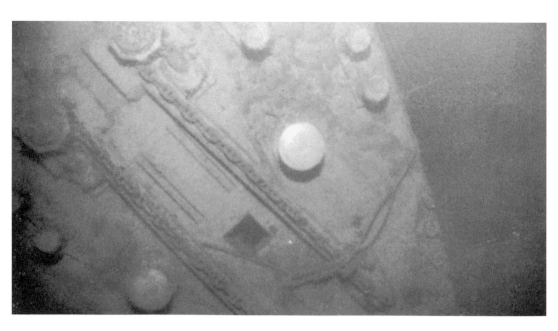

Dr Ballard be summoned; the ship's cook is despatched.

Roused from his near-sleep, Dr Ballard rushes to the control room and takes over command of the watch. Later, in the crowded space, someone remarks that it is now 1.40am, close to the hour that *Titanic* sank.

Dr Ballard leads the way to *Knorr*'s stern, where he leads the entire crew in a brief service of remembrance. Then it is back to stations – there is work to be done, images to be recorded, the world to be told …

The wreck's nautical coordinates (the centre of the bow section is located at 41°43'57"N, 49°56'49"W) are, at the request of Dr Ballard – and with the cooperation of the scientific community – kept secret. They are not revealed until the publication in the autumn of 1987 of Dr Ballard's book, *The Discovery of the Titanic*.

Monday, 2 September 1985

SOME TELEVISION FILMS of the wreck are received at St John's, Newfoundland, aboard a helicopter that had left there and returned the same day.

Tuesday, 3 September 1985

READERS OF THE St John's newspaper *The Evening Telegram* are able to see for themselves a very close approximation of the wreck's coordinates.

During an interview, the helicopter's crew disclose to the *Telegram* that they

'… had been given the location of N41°46', W50°14' [*sic*] but the actual location was N41°43'6", W49°56'7" – a difference of 13 miles.' However, the secret is not disseminated further, and it is remarkable that, during the intervening two years, the site's location appears not to be known or discussed by the general public. (Although not familiar at the time with the *Telegram*'s story, the authors learned of the wreck's location the same week. While assisting a major US news magazine with the *Titanic* story, they were handed a business card by a photographer who had taken a picture from the air of RV *Knorr* at the wreck site. On the back of the card were written the wreck's coordinates. The authors, too, kept the secret.)

Considerable rancour arises between French and American media interests regarding the preemptive showing of the wreck films – those that arrived at St John's on 2 September – by Canadian Television (CTV) and the American television network CBS. CTV says that it arranged exclusive film rights with a French consortium, L'Etoile Blanche (White Star), which, according to reports, 'has been dealing with the expedition'. CBS, it is stated, purchased the rights outside Canada.

During *Knorr*'s return voyage to Woods Hole, the French and Americans reach a mutual agreement to fly the pictures and films by helicopter from on board *Knorr* to Woods Hole. There, copies of the photographs taken by ANGUS and the film footage shot by ARGO would be released simultaneously to French and American media the next day.

On his return from the North Atlantic, Dr Robert Ballard briefs the press at the National Geographic Society's Washington headquarters. (Authors' collection)

Once on shore, however, the American networks urge Woods Hole into releasing the films at once. While the material is still en route to Paris by air, for what had been expected to be a simultaneous morning release, French viewers are already seeing images transmitted from the United States by satellite from the premature American television broadcasts.

This situation, combined with the already sensitive French reaction to the untimely CTV and CBS broadcasts, causes an enmity between IFREMER and Woods Hole that severely weakens the previous spirit of cordial cooperation.

ELEVEN

EXPLORATION AND EXHIBITION

Wednesday, 11 September 1985

A BILL IS INTRODUCED in the United States House of Representatives. Its short title is 'The RMS Titanic Memorial Act of 1985', also known as HR3272 of the 99th Congress.

99TH CONGRESS
1ST SESSION **H. R. 3272**

IN THE SENATE OF THE UNITED STATES

DECEMBER 3 (legislative day, DECEMBER 2), 1985
Received; read twice and referred to the Committee on Foreign Relations

AN ACT

To encourage international efforts to designate the shipwreck of the R.M.S. Titanic as an international maritime memorial and to provide for reasonable research, exploration and, if appropriate, salvage activities with respect to the shipwreck.

1   Be it enacted by the Senate and House of Representa-
2 tives of the United States of America in Congress assembled,
3 **SECTION 1. SHORT TITLE.**
4   This Act may be cited as the "R.M.S. Titanic Maritime
5 Memorial Act of 1985".

The 'RMS Titanic Memorial Act of 1985' is introduced in the House of Representatives. (Authors' collection)

Public hearings are held at Washington, DC, on 29 October 1985. The amended bill is presented to the full House of Representatives on 21 November and again on 2 December 1985. The bill is passed on 3 December 1985 and introduced in the Senate on 27 January 1986.

99TH CONGRESS
2D SESSION   **S. 2048**

To encourage international efforts to designate the shipwreck of the R.M.S. Titanic as an international maritime memorial and to provide for reasonable research, exploration, and, if appropriate, salvage activities with respect to the shipwreck.

IN THE SENATE OF THE UNITED STATES

FEBRUARY 5 (legislative day, JANUARY 27), 1986
Mr. WEICKER (for himself and Mr. PELL) introduced the following bill; which was read twice and referred to the Committee on Foreign Relations

SEPTEMBER 11 (legislative day, SEPTEMBER 8), 1986
Reported by Mr. LUGAR, without amendment

A BILL

To encourage international efforts to designate the shipwreck of the R.M.S. Titanic as an international maritime memorial and to provide for reasonable research, exploration, and, if appropriate, salvage activities with respect to the shipwreck.

1   Be it enacted by the Senate and House of Representa-
2 tives of the United States of America in Congress assembled,

The bill passes into law. (Authors' collection)

Referred to the Committee on Foreign Relations, it emerges on 9 September 1986. Minor amendments necessitate its return to the House. The amended bill is passed on 6 October 1986 and signed into law by President Ronald Reagan on 21 October 1986.

The legislation calls primarily for an international study of *Titanic*'s situation and has no other specific authority.

July 1986

ALTHOUGH INVITED BY Dr Robert D. Ballard of Woods Hole Oceanographic Institution (WHOI) to join the 1986 expedition to the wreck site, the French organisation IFREMER pleads 'insufficient funding' and does not participate. The expedition, under the leadership of Dr Ballard, comprises the ship *Atlantis II*, the manned submersible *Alvin*, and the remote-operated vehicle (ROV) *Jason Junior* ('*JJ*'), and is on site in the vicinity of 41°43'N, 49°56'W from 12 to 24 July.

The expedition completes extensive still, film and video photography of the wreck, completing 11 out of 12 planned dives.

The submersible *Alvin*, suspended from the A-frame crane at the stern of the research vessel *Atlantis II*, is used to convey the first observers to *Titanic*'s wreck. (© Woods Hole Oceanographic Institution)

The manned submersible *Nautile* is employed to recover the first *Titanic* artefacts. (Authors' photo © 1993 RMS Titanic, Inc.)

IFREMER's research vessel *Nadir*. (IFREMER)

July 1987

THE PARTICIPANTS IN Expedition Titanic 1987 are Oceanic Research and Development Ltd, a general partner in Titanic Ventures Ltd; Westgate Productions; Taurus International; LBS Communications, Inc; and Compagnie Générale Maritime. Technical operations

February 1987

AN EXPEDITION UNDER Steve Bilsby and Jack Grimm announces plans to depart Ocean Village in Southampton, England, aboard the *Waterwitch* around the end of March, to arrive at the wreck site on 15 April and take possession of the wreck on the disaster's 75th anniversary. After a 'six-month blitz on the boat', operations to raise the wreck are to begin.

Participating is Douglas Woolley, Bilsby's foster father, who claims to have salvage rights to the wreck. The expedition does not take place.

Far left A grey floor tile with a red insert offers valuable information about *Titanic*'s interior colour schemes. (© 1987 RMS Titanic, Inc.)

Left The sea floor's corrosive actions over 75 years have etched a noticeable line across the ship's bell recovered from the debris field. (© 1987 RMS Titanic, Inc.)

Middle left The luxury of First Class is recalled by this marble sink. (© 1987 RMS Titanic, Inc.)

Middle right Second Class plates glow following their restoration to their original condition at the laboratories of LP3 Conservation. (© 1987 RMS Titanic, Inc.)

Bottom A pillar supporting the grand staircase's ceiling, flanked by two ghostly chandeliers, is already perforated by corrosion in 1987. (© 1987 RMS Titanic, Inc.)

are undertaken by IFREMER and preservation by Electricité de France. Vessels used are *Nadir*, the manned submersible *Nautile*, and the remote-operated vehicle *Robin*.

The Expedition is at 41°43'N, 49°56'W and vicinity from 22 July to 11 September, and a total of 32 dives to the wreck is completed and approximately 1,800 artefacts recovered.

Monday, 3 August 1987

SENATOR LOWELL WEICKER Jr introduces a Senate bill, S-1581, 'to prohibit the importation of objects from the RMS *Titanic*'. The bill passes the Senate and is then tabled. The House of Representatives takes no further action on the matter.

Monday, 19 October 1987

A SUIT IN THE US District Court at Tampa, Florida, attempting to enjoin the showing of a forthcoming film about *Titanic*'s recovered artifacts, is filed by five promoters and investors. The group is led by Michael Harris, an explorer and adventurer who produced the 1980 film *Search for the Titanic* (qv).

According to an article in the St Petersburg, Florida, *Times*, in his suit Harris contends that early in 1987 he created along with Carlos Piaget, a financier and investor, the corporation Oceanic Research & Exploration Ltd, with each partner receiving stock and a share of future profits. Piaget was named sole director but had no power to transfer shares other than his own. Both Piaget and Harris distributed some of their own shares to other partners.

However, on 28 July, Harris contends, Piaget broke the deal and represented himself as the sole owner of Oceanic's stock to a group of Connecticut businessmen and John Joslyn, president of a film production company based in California, who together created Titanic Ventures, a Connecticut-based limited partnership that now claims all rights to *Titanic*'s artefacts. The television show, according to the suit, will cause irreparable harm because the novelty of the artefacts will wear off.

On 21 October US District Court Judge William Terrell Hodges, in a three-page ruling, declares that 'any financial loss sustained by Harris and his partners from the telecast can be recovered later if their suit against Piaget and his associates is successful.' Piaget and his associates stand to lose hundreds of thousands of dollars if the show is cancelled. Hodges rules 'that their interests outweigh those of Harris and his group because Harris can still go to court to recover his losses.'

An agreement is subsequently reached.

Wednesday, 28 October 1987

RETURN TO THE TITANIC ... LIVE, a television broadcast from the Paris Museum of Science and Industry in Paris, France, purports to show articles being removed from a safe that had been taken from the ocean floor near the *Titanic*'s wreck. The programme opens with the host, actor Telly Savalas,

Recovered from the debris field, a safe's door is featured in the 28 October 1987 TV programme. (© 1987 RMS Titanic, Inc.)

on a mock shipboard set. 'Welcome to Paris,' he says, 'and the adventure of a lifetime.'

In a review of the programme that appears in the *New York Times*, critic John Corry states, 'What followed was a combination of the sacred and profane and sometimes the downright silly.'

Articles removed from the safe, being displayed publicly for the first time, include a small leather bag found inside the safe at the time of recovery by the conservation team. Another bag, removed with great solemnity from a modern vault (into which it had apparently been placed for safekeeping), contains a leather satchel that holds banknotes and pieces of jewellery. The latter are examined on the air by professional experts, who proclaim one of the pieces to be a diamond bracelet. 'Diamonds are a girl's best friend,' confides Mr Savalas. Moments later the programme fades to a close.

Wednesday, 18 April 1990

AN EXHIBITION ORGANISED by the Ulster Folk & Transport Museum, Holywood, Northern Ireland (just outside Belfast) opens at the South Street Seaport Museum in downtown New York. On display is original *Titanic* material from the Museum's archives, including Thomas Andrews's own draughtsman's instruments, construction working plans, and a diorama of the sinking vessel.

This first major exhibition of *Titanic*-related material in the United States runs through 21 January 1991.

Summer 1990

Following conservation and preservation of *Titanic* artefacts recovered during the 1987 expedition, a representative group of the objects is placed on display at the French Government's Musée de la Marine in Paris as a 'farewell and thank you to the people of France'.

Spring 1991–May 1992

FOR A LITTLE more than a year objects from *Titanic*'s wreck, carefully preserved by Electricité de France, are exhibited at several maritime museums in Sweden and Norway. Thousands of enthusiastic visitors flock to the exhibitions:

Early Spring 1991: Sea Historical Museum, Stockholm, Sweden; 69,000 visitors

4 May–4 August 1991: Sea Museum, Malmö, Sweden; 79,100 visitors

19 November 1991–2 February 1992: Sea Museum, Göteborg, Sweden; 61,000 visitors

3 March–10 May 1992: Norsk Seamuseum, Oslo, Norway; 84,350 visitors

Top The South Street Seaport Museum building housing the *Titanic* exhibition had blazing white stars in the windows, beckoning to visitors. (Catherine Minot, *Seaport Magazine*, South Street Seaport Museum)

Middle Artefacts recovered in 1987 are displayed in the Musée de la Marine (shown on the left in the Palais de Chaillot). (Authors' collection)

Left The Sea Historical Museum, Stockholm, is the first of four Scandinavian venues for the *Titanic* artefact exhibition.(© Gunnel Ilonen, Stockholm Maritime Museum)

June–July 1991

THE PARTICIPANTS IN the IMAX *Titanic* expedition are the P.P. Shirshov Institute of Oceanography of Moscow, Underseas Research Ltd, and Titanic Films, who in turn have engaged White-Pix Productions. The vessels used are the Russian RV *Akademik Mstislav Keldysh* (commonly known as 'the *Keldysh*'), and the manned submersibles *Mir 1* and *Mir 2*. They are on site at 41°43'N, 49°56'W and vicinity from 28 June to 16 July.

In an agreement between Imax Systems Corporation and the P.P. Shirshov Institute, signed 26 April 1991, an understanding is reached that 'during the Expedition to the *Titanic*, no treasures, artifacts or items other than approved scientific samples will be removed from the wreck.'

Seventeen dives to the wreck are completed, and more than 40,000ft of film is shot in the IMAX® format. The footage is incorporated in the production of a wide-screen motion picture by Stephen Low Productions, Inc., called *Titanica*. Since its 1995 release the film has continued to play to international acclaim.

During the dive sequence, five pieces of metal and several 'rusticles' are recovered from the wreck by *Mir 2*. This authorised removal allows analysis of the specimens by Canadian laboratories in Dartmouth, Nova Scotia.

Top and middle The dramatic setting for one of the earliest artefact exhibitions at Malmö, Sweden, displays *Titanic*'s beautiful objects to great advantage. (Courtesy of Sea Museum, Malmö, Sweden)

Right *Akademik Mstislav Keldysh*. (By Wusel007 via Wikimedia Commons)

Summer 1992

MAREX-TITANIC, INC., a corporation based in Memphis, Tennessee, among whose leaders is explorer and Texas oilman Jack Grimm, lay claim to the *Titanic*'s wreck site, stating that Titanic Ventures (which had established their claim to the wreck during their own 1987 expedition) have not revisited the wreck since 1987, and have thereby, in effect, abandoned the wreck and their salvage efforts on it. Marex now lay claim to the wreck and engage a US salvage service (Eastport International) to conduct the salvage operation.

Marex bases another part of their claim on the fact that Ralph B. White, an underwater camera operator who identifies himself as a 2.5% owner of Marex and also an employee of that corporation, had, in 1991, while 'conducting' the IMAX-Russian venture, 'brought up' from the wreck site a piece of metal and a glass medicine bottle. Marex contend that these items represent salvage by a principal and therefore establish their ownership of the wreck that Titanic Ventures had (they claimed) abandoned in 1987.

Below The US District Court, Eastern District of Virginia, Norfolk. (Courtesy of Bonnie N. Pryor)

Bottom *Sea Mussel* seen here as *Putford Sea Mussel* after a subsequent change of ownership. (Courtesy Putford Enterprises Ltd, Simon Hasher, Director)

Friday, 7 August 1992

IN THE US DISTRICT COURT, Eastern District of Virginia, Norfolk, Marex-Titanic, Inc. files a claim to ownership and salvage rights to 'The Wrecked and Abandoned Vessel ... believed to be the RMS *Titanic*' as well as the entire wreck site and previously recovered artefacts.

Wednesday, 12 August 1992

DEPUTY MARSHAL Frederick J. Cox 'arrested and took into his custody the alleged artifacts of The Wrecked and Abandoned Vessel', as well as the vessel itself. The court states that anyone who wishes to contest the claim must file its answer within 30 days.

Titanic Ventures are not long in filing an intervening complaint, asking for exclusive salvage rights. Their answer expresses continued interest in the wreck; describes professional aspects of their salvage and preservation of the artefacts; speaks of their public exhibitions of the artefacts in the recent past and in the future; and declares the corporation's intent, then in an advanced planning stage, to explore the wreck further in 1993.

In an effort to further assert their claim on the wreck, Marex-Titanic despatch a salvage ship, *Sea Mussel*, to the wreck site prior to the hearing set for 29 September 1992 in the court of Judge J. Calvitt Clarke Jr, US District Court at Norfolk, Virginia.

Tuesday, 29 September 1992

IN JUDGE CLARKE'S court, attorneys for Titanic Ventures argue that Marex-Titanic have no legitimate claim to *Titanic*'s wreck, as Marex have never been to the vessel. Titanic Ventures base their claim on the artefacts recovered from the wreck during the 1987 expedition.

Marex-Titanic base their claim on the fact that Titanic Ventures have not been to the wreck in five years. Further, they say that they are in possession of a small glass bottle and a fragment of the hull that were salvaged from the wreck in 1991 and turned over to the District Court in August 1992.

Titanic Ventures, in turn, argue that the objects were either illegally retrieved by an undersea photographer who participated in the joint IMAX-Russian 1991 expedition, during which there was a solemn agreement not to remove any unauthorised items from the wreck or wreck site, or they are not genuine artefacts.

Judge Clarke tells Marex-Titanic that their group can do no *Titanic* salvage work before final judgment of the court.

Wednesday, 30 September 1992

WITH MAREX-TITANIC'S salvage ship, *Sea Mussel*, actually on site, 2½ miles above *Titanic*'s wreck, Judge Clarke reaffirms his previous day's injunction; he wishes to consider the facts presented to him and determine which group has the right to salvage the wreck. The date for his ruling is not set.

The Marex group state that they will keep their vessel on site for the entire two weeks planned for their expedition at a rumoured cost of more that $1,000 (£606) an hour. Later that day they ask Judge Clarke for the right to do limited preparatory work until a decision is rendered in the case.

'My injunction is still in place,' Judge Clarke says. 'And if I find that someone has dropped so much as an anchor overboard, someone's going to jail.'

US District Court Judge J. Calvitt Clarke Jr. (Courtesy of Judge Clarke)

Friday, 2 October 1992

JUDGE J. CALVITT CLARKE renders his decision. He upholds the five-year-old claim of Titanic Ventures, rendering permanent the injunction he had earlier granted against Marex-Titanic, Inc.

Judge Clarke approves the form of judgement on 13 October 1992.

During the hearings, Marex-Titanic, Inc. file a motion for voluntary dismissal of the case, which Judge Clarke denies.

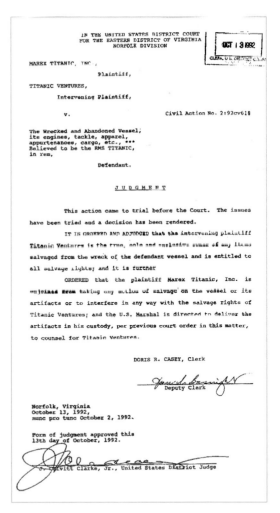

Judge Clarke's decision. (US District Court, Eastern District of Virginia)

Titanic Ventures, their claim to the wreck's salvage assured by Judge Clarke's ruling, proceed with plans to mount a second exploratory expedition for the spring or summer of 1993.

Wednesday, 16 December 1992

FRENCH LAW REQUIRES that ownership claims be invited before the objects are returned to Titanic Ventures. The law is invoked because of Titanic Ventures' involvement with the French Government-supported IFREMER, and because the objects were taken to France for restoration by Electricité de France, a state-owned utility.

NOTICE

In 1987, items taken on the wreck of the TITANIC were landed on French territory in Lorient.

Pursuant to its laws, the French State is applying the procedure which allows assigns of the shipwrecked to secure the restitution of these items.

Interested persons may immediately contact:

— either   the French Embassy In the USA
4101 Reservoir road
NW WASHINGTON DC 20007

— or   the Secretariat d'Etat a la Mer In Paris
Direction de la Flotte de Commerce
3, Place de Fontenoy
75007 PARIS

They will find all the necessary information, at the above-mentioned locations, regarding the procedure and the evidence required for proving the claims, as well as a list of the items and a form for the request for restitution.

A set of photographs may be inspected on location.

Potential requesting parties are reminded of the fact that they must:

— send in their request within a period of 3 months from the date of publication of this notice

— establish proof of ownership,
— participate in the costs of finding the items.

The advertisement inviting ownership claims in *Titanic* artefacts. (© 1987 RMS Titanic, Inc.)

A notice inviting claims is published in the *New York Times*, the London *Times* and three French newspapers. Potential claimants are invited to view photographs of the objects at the French embassies in London and Washington and at the Merchant Marine Secretariat in Paris.

March 1993

A BRIEF BY Marex-Titanic, Inc. asking the US Appeals Court to overturn the District Court's earlier decision in favour of Titanic Ventures by Judge J. Calvitt Clarke is filed at Richmond, Virginia.

The brief by Marex's attorneys claims that Judge Clarke had granted Titanic Venture's salvage rights even after Marex's request for voluntary dismissal and their full compliance with court rules allowing such voluntary dismissal.

Titanic Ventures' attorney files a brief asking the appeals court to reject Marex's argument.

Tuesday, 6 April 1993

AT THE VANCOUVER Maritime Museum, British Columbia, Canada, the exhibition '*Titanic*: Then and Now' opens. It includes a full-scale recreation of the wireless room with original period equipment and a full-scale section of the boat deck near Captain Smith's cabin as it looked in 1985 when the wreck was discovered.

Other features of the exhibition include film clips from *A Night to Remember*, and from *Titanica* showing dives on the wreck; also featured are several objects recovered as surface debris from the wreck site in 1912 by Canadian ships retrieving bodies.

Wednesday, 5 May 1993

IN THE FOURTH US Circuit Court of Appeals in Richmond, Virginia, Marex-Titanic, Inc. and Titanic Ventures continue to argue over rights to *Titanic*'s wreck. A three-judge panel hears arguments for about 15 minutes before telling lawyers that they already have enough information from the written briefs.

Lawyers for Marex-Titanic persist in their claim that Titanic Ventures had abandoned the wreck and their rights to it.

Titanic Ventures' attorney states that their client had maintained reasonable presence.

The Court adjourns to consider its judgement.

May 1993

TITANIC VENTURES IS reorganised as a public company, RMS Titanic, Inc.

June 1993

THE RESEARCH AND Recovery Expedition 1993 is on site at 41°43'N, 49°56'W and vicinity from 8 to 23 June. The participants are RMS Titanic, Inc. and IFREMER. Technical operations are undertaken by IFREMER, and artefact preservation by LP3 Conservation, Semur-en-Auxois, France. The vessels are RV *Nadir*, the manned submersible *Nautile* and ROV *Robin*.

Fifteen dives are made to the wreck, several of which are devoted solely to orientation, observation and research, including one each by the authors of the present work. Approximately 800 objects are recovered during the remaining dives.

Tuesday, 22 June 1993

F. BRADFORD STILLMAN, attorney for RMS Titanic, Inc., presents a lead crystal decanter to the keeping of Judge J. Calvitt Clarke Jr of the US District Court, Norfolk, Virginia. The decanter serves as evidence of salvage. Mr Stillman then files for the arrest of *Titanic* and the artefacts.

Tuesday, 29 June 1993

RETURNING FROM HER voyage to the *Titanic*'s site, the IFREMER research vessel *Nadir* visits the city of Norfolk, Virginia. There, for the first time in the United States, artefacts recovered from the wreck's debris field are put on public exhibition, including the ship's whistles and their manifold; a crystal vase, probably from the ship's First Class dining room; a soup bowl from the ship's Third Class service; a cut glass decanter from First Class; and a metal bathroom towel rack.

Among the distinguished guests welcoming *Nadir*, her crew and the artefacts are Jean Jarry, IFREMER's operations leader on the French search expedition of August 1985; Jean-Louis Michel, IFREMER oceanographer, who was in command of the watch aboard *Knorr* when *Titanic* was found at 12.48am, 1 September 1985; the Mayor of Norfolk, Mason C. Andrews; together with Arnie Geller, President and CEO, and George Tulloch, Chairman, of RMS Titanic, Inc.

Wednesday, 25 August 1993

IN RICHMOND, VIRGINIA, a three-judge panel of the Fourth US Circuit Court of Appeals says that US District Court Judge J. Calvitt Clarke Jr erred when, despite Marex-Titanic having filed at the last minute for a voluntary departure from the trial, he granted exclusive *Titanic* salvage rights to Titanic Ventures.

However, the Appeals Court does say that Marex-Titanic introduced misleading evidence at hearings on the rights, perhaps influencing Judge Clarke's decision.

Below F. Bradford Stillman, attorney for RMS *Titanic*, Inc., aboard RV *Nadir* during the summer 1993 expedition. (Courtesy of Bonnie N. Pryor/RMS Titanic, Inc., collection)

Bottom Participating in the Fourth US Circuit Court of Appeals hearings on behalf of Titanic Ventures/RMS Titanic, Inc. is attorney Mark Davis. (Courtesy of Bonnie N. Pryor)

'As the facts unfolded, the district court made no secret of its feelings that Marex had misled the court in the initial hearings held August 12, 1992,' Judge Kenneth K. Hall writes in the panel's decision. 'Marex realised "the way the wind was blowing" and filed a motion for voluntary dismissal,' Hall continues.

Titanic Ventures filed an intervening complaint and asked for exclusive salvage rights. Judge Clarke granted the request, even though Marex complied with court rules allowing voluntary dismissal.

Since Marex did comply with court procedures for dismissal, 'The district court had no discretion to allow Titanic Ventures to intervene in the [therefore] defunct action filed by Marex,' Hall writes.

The appeals judge adds, however, that Marex had misled the court, and footnotes that finding by indicating what the District Court might do: 'The plaintiffs' [Marex's] behavior has been dissembling if not downright fraudulent. [The] District Court may still impose sanctions.'

Thursday, 26 August 1993

RMS TITANIC, INC. again files its claim in Judge Clarke's US District Court; within the statutory time of ten days the claim is advertised. Anyone who wants to challenge the claim has ten days after that date to do so. Marex-Titanic do not respond to RMS Titanic's claim, nor do they renew their own claim.

However, one of the original British underwriters of the ship's insurance, The Liverpool & London Steamship Protection & Indemnity Association, does intervene, much as RMS Titanic,

Inc. (then Titanic Ventures) had intervened against Marex in August 1992 to file a claim against *Titanic* and her artefacts.

Wednesday, 20 October 1993

AN ADMINISTRATOR IN the French Office of Maritime Affairs (Ministry of Equipment, Transportation and Tourism) in Lorient, France awards Titanic Ventures, Ltd title to 1,892 artefacts from the *Titanic* wreck site. These artefacts were recovered during the course of 32 dives to the wreck in 1987, conducted by Titanic Ventures with the assistance of the Institut Français de Recherche Pour l'Exploitation de la Mer (IFREMER); they were taken by IFREMER to France for conservation and restoration, and become known as the 'French Artefacts' or the 'French Collection'.

Thursday, 23 December 1993

IN NORFOLK, VIRGINIA, in keeping with the Circuit Court's suggestion that 'District Court may still impose sanctions', Judge J. Calvitt Clarke assesses court costs and attorneys' fees in the amount of $60,000 (£36,300) against Marex-Titanic, Inc. of Memphis, Tennessee. Judge Clarke says

that Marex-Titanic misrepresented facts to the Court when it sought sole ownership of the wreck in 1992.

Tuesday, 7 June 1994

US DISTRICT COURT Judge J. Calvitt Clarke Jr dismisses the claim on *Titanic*'s wreck and artefacts by the Liverpool & London Steamship Protection & Indemnity Association.

RMS Titanic, the only group that has recovered artefacts from the shipwreck, is granted the right to 'salvor in possession' by the Court.

July 1994

RMS TITANIC, INC. and IFREMER take part in the *Titanic* 1994 Expedition. Again, technical operations are by IFREMER and preservation by LP3 Conservation, Semur-en-Auxois, France, and the craft involved are *Nadir*, *Nautile* and *Robin*. The Expedition is on site at 41°43'N, 49°56'W and vicinity from 11 to 31 July.

A total of 18 dives is made and approximately 1,000 objects are recovered; in addition, 2.385 metric tons of coal are salvaged.

Tuesday, 4 October 1994

'THE WRECK OF THE Titanic Exhibition' opens at the National Maritime Museum, Greenwich, England; more than 150 artefacts from *Titanic*'s wreck are displayed. The exhibition features objects from the ship itself as well as items directly associated with the ship's passengers and crew. Generally favourable press reviews as well as high praise from all who attended are received.

Originally scheduled to run only until 2 April 1995, the exhibition is twice extended by popular demand to 1 October 1995. By the time it closes more than 750,000 visitors have seen the historic display.

Right 'Wreck of the *Titanic*' exhibition brochure cover. (© 1994 RMS Titanic, Inc.)

Below The National Maritime Museum, Greenwich, England. (© National Maritime Museum, Greenwich)

Top A poignant reminder of a passenger's personal effects is this small ceramic Dutch boy and shoe. (RMS Titanic, Inc.)

Above The authorised sale of pieces of coal from *Titanic*'s debris field provides funds for the restoration of artefacts. The coal was declared a non-artefact by government institutions in Britain and France. (The largest piece shown measures approximately 18 inches (46cm) in length.) (RMS Titanic, Inc.)

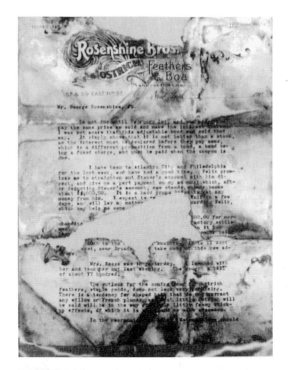

Saturday, 15 April 1995

A MEMORIAL GARDEN is dedicated in the grounds of the National Maritime Museum, Greenwich, England, recalling those who were lost on the *Titanic*. Attending the simple but emotional ceremony are *Titanic* survivors Edith Brown Haisman and Eva Hart.

A monument carved from Cornish granite and bearing a bronze plaque commemorates the loss of the liner and

Left The remarkable preservation work of LP3 laboratories is demonstrated by this typewritten letter retrieved from *Titanic* passenger George Rosenshine's luggage. (© RMS Titanic, Inc.)

Below left Among the many beautiful items on display is this delicate glass carafe. (© RMS Titanic, Inc.)

Above left *Titanic* survivors Edith Brown Haisman and Millvina Dean are present at the opening of the NMM exhibition. Also present is the producer of the film *A Night to Remember*, William MacQuitty (right), who, as a boy, witnessed *Titanic*'s Belfast departure. (© 1994 Robert M. DiSogra collection)

Below Survivors Edith Haisman and Eva Hart. (Private collection)

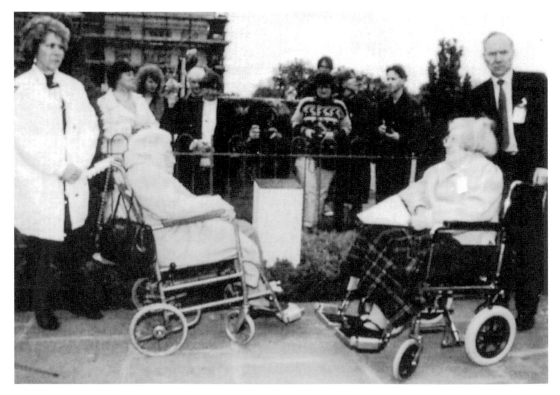

her victims and is the heart of the simple garden of Peace roses, rosemary, purple sage and Irish golden yew.

Tuesday, 25 April 1995

IN ANTRIM, NORTHERN IRELAND, Mivan Marine announce in the pages of the *Business Telegraph* that they have completed a computerised design of the 'Mark Two *Titanic*' for a Japanese client who wishes to replicate the ship for use as a floating convention centre in Hakodate, the northernmost island of Japan. An exhibition venue is planned, as are four different styles of chapel, making it an attractive setting for weddings, a big business in Japan. Presently in the hands of the client, the plan awaits completion of financial arrangements.

Summer 1995

BUDGETED AT MORE than $4 million (£2.425 million), American businessman and financier John Joslyn's proposed 40-day summer expedition to *Titanic*, 'Titanic Eagle – '95', plans to search for artefacts in the debris field as well as inside the wreck and to probe the wreck's interior.

The exhibition organiser is Phoenix Oceanographic Services Ltd, with technical operations by Oceaneering Technologies. The vessels to be used are RV *Rockwater I* and ROVs incorporating the Gemini and Magellan robotic systems. The location is to be 'North Atlantic Ocean 375 miles South of Newfoundland'.

Sales of television rights as well as photographic, literary and other rights will finance the expedition through Phoenix Oceanographic Services Ltd, an offshore company. Exhibitions of recovered artefacts are planned, and a major American television network appears eager to participate.

The expedition is subsequently postponed until 1996, but does not take place.

Late summer 1995

CANADIAN FILM-MAKER James Cameron charters the Russian research vessel *Akademik Mstislav Keldysh* and her two submersibles *Mir 1* and *Mir 2* to dive to *Titanic* in order to film the wreck for his motion picture about the disaster.

During dives involving the filming, *Titanic*'s superstructure is apparently breached in order to provide footage of the ship's interior. In addition, apparently the crew of one of the Russian submersibles displaces and damages the Marconi room's skylight frame. More damage is inflicted in the opening where the dome over *Titanic*'s forward grand staircase once stood: pieces of the submersible's Kevlar propeller shroud are actually broken off; they fly in several directions, lodging themselves in *Titanic*'s superstructure.

However, the worst damage is the destruction of the external bulkhead of Captain Smith's quarters, his 'suite' of cabins on the boat deck's forward starboard side. The bulkhead is flattened, and the cabins' interiors exposed.

Only those fortunate enough to have visited the wreck before September 1995 have seen significant and historically important parts that no longer exist; history and future generations have been denied a sight of the wreck as it was. Nothing remains of

RMS Titanic, Inc.'s Matthew Tulloch displays grim evidence of the Russian assault on *Titanic*'s superstructure – a piece of *Mir*'s propeller cowling, recovered from *Titanic*'s deck in 1996. (Authors' photo © 1996 RMS Titanic, Inc.)

these areas save a trail of destruction. Those who view *Titanic*'s wreck as a tomb now have a truly damaged tomb over which to shed their tears. Those from RMS Titanic, Inc. and IFREMER, who have come in gentle exploration, touching only pieces separated from the wreck, have tears to shed as well – tears of anger and frustration and pity, for those others whose action has left an irreparable gap in the heritage they wished to leave.

February 1996

IN NORFOLK, VIRGINIA, John Joslyn, whose Westgate Productions had been an element of Titanic Expedition 1987, begins proceedings in the US District Court to set aside RMS Titanic, Inc.'s rights as sole salvor in possession. Joslyn wishes to conduct a photographic expedition at the wreck site without including RMS Titanic, Inc. in his plans. His premises are that RMS Titanic, Inc. had not mounted an expedition in 1995, and that they had no apparent ability or intention to conduct a 1996 expedition.

Friday, 19 April 1996

CHERBOURG, FRANCE: Dedication of a memorial monument to *Titanic* and her passengers.

Titanic stopped briefly at Cherbourg during the late afternoon and early evening of 10 April 1912, debarked 24 cross-Channel passengers and took aboard a total of 274 passengers of all classes.

Located on the quay of the Old Arsenal, the former spot where train passengers transferred to tenders, the monument is dedicated in the presence of Mle. Louise Laroche, one of two living French *Titanic* survivors. (Mle. Laroche died 25 January 1998.)

Friday, 10 May 1996

SENIOR FEDERAL COURT Judge Clarke, in whose Norfolk, Virginia, court Joslyn's claim was filed, grants a preliminary injunction and reaffirms the status of RMS Titanic, Inc. as sole salvor in possession of *Titanic*. He promises a short written opinion in August.

Tuesday, 13 August 1996

IN HIS WRITTEN opinion granting the injunction in favour of RMS Titanic, Inc., Judge Clarke declares that the court is ruling in consistency with its two previous orders regarding *Titanic*, on 7 June 1994 and May 1996, in which RMS Titanic, Inc. was granted and should remain the sole salvor in possession.

In his opinion, Judge Clarke writes, 'RMS Titanic has expended time, efforts, money, and ingenuity over a period of approximately nine years in locating the wreck, starting salvage operations, and continuing salvage operations. The Court granted RMS Titanic possession of the wreck site for monetary gain to compensate it for these efforts and to encourage their continuation.

'... The activity Joslyn contemplates is exactly the type of activity the Court contemplated in its May 1996 Order giving RMS Titanic exclusive possession. The Court specifically referred to video sales, film documentaries and television

The research vessel *Nadir* and the submersible *Nautile* return to the site in 1996. (Authors' photo © 1996 RMS Titanic, Inc.)

broadcasts as inventive marketing ideas that RMS Titanic must resort to since it is not selling the artefacts. It is clear that the presence of another in the marketplace would diminish the rights the Courts granted RMS Titanic.

'If RMS Titanic is not selling artefacts like traditional salvors, it must be given the rights to other means of obtaining income. The Court finds that in a case such as this, allowing another "salvor" to take photographs of the wreck and wreck site is akin to allowing another salvor to physically invade the wreck and take artefacts themselves.'

August 1996

TITANIC EXPEDITION 1996 is undertaken by RMS Titanic, Inc. and IFREMER, together with Aqua Plus; Stardust Visual; The Discovery Channel; Polaris Imaging, Inc; Bass Ale; SCI; and Ellipse Programme. Technical operations are by IFREMER, with technical support from Aqua Plus (Ellipse). The ships are *Nadir* and *Nautile* (on site at 41°43'N, 49°56'W and vicinity from 3 to 31 August), *Ocean Voyager* (4 to 27 August), *Jim Kilabuk* (26 to 30 August) and *Ballymena* (5 August to 8 August). The cruise ships *Island Breeze* and *Royal Majesty* also attend from 27 to 29 August.

Nautile completes several dives of diverse natures to the wreck in the first full-scale scientific inquiry into its condition.

Dr David Livingstone, Senior Projects Engineer, Harland & Wolff, Belfast, becomes the first marine architect ever to view the wreck and make professional observations; Paul Matthias, President of Polaris Imaging, Inc., completes a sonar profile of

Titanic's bow in the vicinity of the iceberg's impact; and microbiologist Dr Roy Cullimore collects examples of the 'rusticles', enabling him to analyse the organisms in the cascades of rust that flow down areas of *Titanic*'s hull. Co-author of the present work, Charles Haas, conducts a 'guided tour' of *Titanic* for the Discovery Channel cameras during his dive.

However, the majority of the dives are devoted to examining a large, freestanding portion of *Titanic*'s hull. This section weighs an estimated 19.5 metric tonnes (22 tons) and measures 4 x 7 metres (13 x 23ft). The 'Big Piece' is to be fastened to an intricate web of cables and buoyancy bags in the hope of lifting it to the surface. Unfortunately, when the lift bags bring the piece to within 80 metres of the surface, full retrieval is thwarted by an unfortunate combination of bad weather, equipment failure and lift bag loss.

The piece now lies in a known location marked by an underwater beacon. With appropriate equipment, perseverance and a modicum of luck, its retrieval and preservation at some future date appear assured.

Top *Ocean Voyager* serves as an accommodation ship and floating television studio for the expedition. (Authors' photo © 1996 RMS Titanic, Inc.)

Middle left *Nautile* is launched from *Nadir*'s fantail. (Authors' photo © 1996 RMS Titanic, Inc.)

Middle right Dr David Livingstone, senior naval architect from Harland & Wolff, *Titanic*'s builders, boards *Nautile*. (Authors' photo © 1996 RMS Titanic, Inc.)

Right Dr Roy Cullimore from the University of Regina prepares to study the ship's 'rusticles'. (Authors' photo © 1996 RMS Titanic, Inc.)

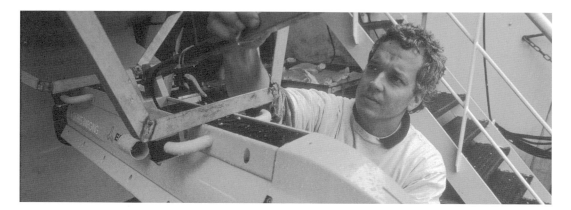

Paul Matthias, president of Polaris Imaging, Inc., checks the underwater sonar imaging device newly installed on *Nautile*. (© 1996 RMS Titanic, Inc.)

An artist's rendering shows 1912's popular misconception of the iceberg's damage. (*The Sphere*)

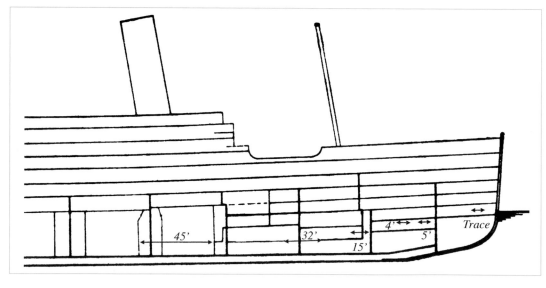

As represented on this diagram, the 1996 sonar scans conducted by Paul Matthias show the location and size of the damage actually inflicted by the iceberg. (Authors' collection)

Right Cruise ships *Island Breeze* (right) and *Royal Majesty* (far right) join the expedition on 27 August 1996. The 1,700 on board witness the expedition's scientific activities at the site. (Authors' photo © 1996 RMS Titanic, Inc/Michael V. Ralph collection)

Middle right Edith Brown Haisman and Michel Navratil, *Titanic* survivors, return aboard *Island Breeze* to the place where their fathers were lost in 1912. (Michael A. Findlay collection)

Far right Survivor Eleanor Shuman graces the passenger complement aboard *Royal Majesty*. (Authors' photo © 1996 RMS Titanic, Inc.)

Below right The submersible *Nautile*'s crew rigs the 'Big Piece' for its 1996 journey to the surface. (© 1996 RMS Titanic, Inc.)

Below Not the cavern of a lurking sea monster, but a far more destructive force is represented by this electron microscope photograph of micro-organisms that have so far devoured approximately 20 per cent of the iron in *Titanic*'s hull. The photograph depicts a width of approximately 75 micrometres. (Courtesy Dr Henrietta Mann, Dalhousie University, Halifax, NS)

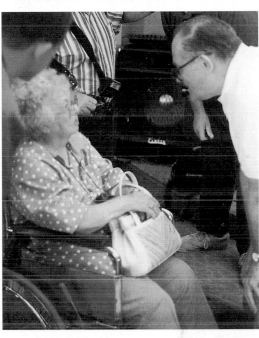

Far left Brochure for the Norfolk, Virginia, exhibition. (© 1996 RMS Titanic, Inc.)

Left Brochure for the Memphis exhibition. (Courtesy Wonders, Memphis, TN)

Below The Memphis exhibition displays china, ceramics and fine porcelain. (© 1997 RMS Titanic, Inc.)

Bottom Displayed with a thrust bearing journal from one of the ship's reciprocating engines are objects from the ship's engine and boiler rooms: a Kilroy's stoking indicator (left wall), pieces of coal (centre floor), and a hook from the engine room's hoist (right). (Authors' photo © 1997 RMS Titanic, Inc.)

Wednesday, 27 November 1996

'TITANIC: THE EXPEDITION' opens at Nauticus, The National Maritime Center at Norfolk, Virginia in association with RMS Titanic, Inc. The exhibition includes artefacts from all four expeditions conducted by Titanic Ventures/RMS Titanic, Inc. It also includes a light tower (used during 1996 to illuminate the wreck's exterior); a large lift bag of the sort used to recover heavy objects from the wreck; and portions of the propeller shroud from the Russian submersible that caused damage to *Titanic* during the commercial filming of the wreck in 1995 which had been recovered during RMS Titanic, Inc.'s 1996 expedition.

The exhibition is well-mounted, and contains several 'wet cases' displaying artefacts that have not yet undergone conservation. The retrieved portions of the Russian submersible are documented in photographs and detailed captions, as is the damage they inflicted. Among the exhibition's other features is a series of lectures during February featuring attorneys, authors and expedition leaders.

The exhibition is enthusiastically received by the public. It closes on 31 March 1997.

Thursday, 3 April 1997

'TITANIC', PRESENTED BY RMS Titanic, Inc. in association with Wonders, The Memphis International Cultural Series, opens at the Pyramid convention and exhibition centre on the banks of the Mississippi at Memphis, Tennessee. By its closing on 30 September, more than 837,000 people have attended the exhibition.

Monday, 14 April 1997

SPONSORED BY THE Ulster Titanic Society (UTS), an international convention and symposium, 'Titanic at Home', is held in Belfast, Northern Ireland, under the gracious and efficient leadership of John Parkinson, UTS President, and Una Reilly, UTS Chairman.

A series of lectures by prominent *Titanic* experts – literary, administrative, technical and historical – each followed by a question-and-answer session, are among the convention's highlights.

A rare public tour of the Harland & Wolff shipyard precedes the convention's opening. The tour provides a last opportunity to visit many of the old, familiar red-brick buildings that characterised the shipyard during its many years of prominence and productivity, and which were demolished soon thereafter.

Left Authors Eaton and Haas were privileged to participate in 'Titanic at Home'. During the shipyard tour they pause at the sloping ramp that once supported *Titanic*'s launching ways. (Photo by Philip Armstrong, Authors' collection)

Above The engine works, one of 'the old, familiar red-brick buildings' at Harland & Wolff's Queen's Island yard, was where *Titanic*'s engines were built and tested. (Authors' collection)

Below Poster for the Broadway musical *Titanic*. (© Doug Johnson/Dodger Endemol Productions. Published by permission)

Wednesday, 23 April 1997

ITS PREVIEWS AND opening postponed because of technical problems with its spectacular scenery, the long-awaited Broadway musical *Titanic* opens at New York's Lunt-Fontanne Theatre.

Even the first two scheduled previews were cancelled for technical reasons: the elaborate scenery would not function properly, and the ship simply *would not sink*.

Originally scheduled for a 10 April opening, the production, with book by Peter Stone and music and lyrics by Maury Yeston, is budgeted at $10 million (more than £6 million). It receives decidedly mixed reviews, but goes on to become one of the most financially successful musical productions in Broadway history.

Two months later it wins five Tony Awards, presented by the American Theatre Wing, including that for Best Musical.

Thursday, 8 May 1997

THE EXHIBITION 'Expedition Titanic' opens in the Kehrwieder of the historic free port district of Hamburg, Germany. Housed in a picturesque warehouse well over 100 years old, the display, in association with RMS Titanic, Inc., includes some 600 artefacts from *Titanic*'s debris field. A specially designed sound system and an outstanding musical score composed especially for the show bring an air of presence to the exhibition that would be lacking in a more formalised setting.

Lighting variations among galleries and diverse display techniques present the objects congruent to their roles in the wreck's story, and culminate in an

During Act I of the hit Broadway musical *Titanic*, passengers sing 'I Must Get on That Ship' as they board the liner. (© Joan Marcus. Printed by permission)

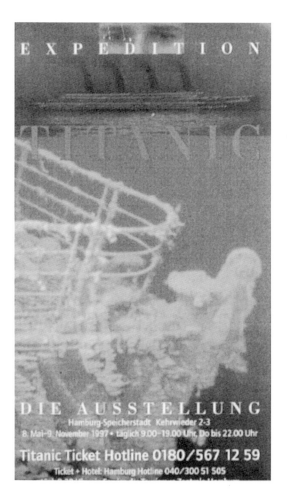

Brochure for Hamburg's 'Expedition Titanic' exhibition. (© 1997 RMS Titanic, Inc.)

emotional, almost cloister-like display of the ship's bell, alone, surrounded only by reflective music.

Well represented in the final gallery are depictions of the science of deep-sea diving and object retrieval, and the science and art of artefact restoration and conservation.

Scheduled to close on 9 November, 'Expedition Titanic' is twice extended. By November 1998, a year past its original planned closing date, the exhibition has been seen by more than one million people.

Sunday, 1 June 1997

AN EXHIBITION OF *Titanic* artefacts opens in the exhibition hall aboard RMS *Queen Mary* in Long Beach, California in association with RMS Titanic, Inc. Somewhat similar in concept and content to the Nauticus exhibit of November 1996, the display meets with great public approval and is so well attended that its projected closing date of January 1998 is twice extended, until September 1998.

Saturday, 15 November 1997

'TITANIC: THE EXHIBITION' opens at the Florida International Museum in

Top right An immense photomural of *Titanic*'s bow adorns the exterior of Hamburg's artefact exhibition. (Authors' collection)

Middle right Portions of the Hamburg exhibition cause visitors to feel a presence aboard *Titanic*. (© 1997 RMS Titanic, Inc.)

Right RMS *Queen Mary* at Long Beach, California, becomes the site of the 1997–98 RMS Titanic, Inc. artefact exhibition. (Authors' collection)

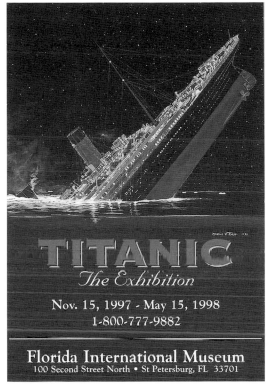

Postcard for the St Petersburg, Florida, exhibition. (Courtesy Michael V. Ralph and Florida International Museum)

This bronze cherub, from *Titanic*'s after grand staircase, was featured at the St Petersburg, Florida exhibition. Following conservation, its grace and beauty are preserved for eternity (Michael V. Ralph © 1997 RMS Titanic, Inc.)

St Petersburg, Florida, for a six-month run, subsequently extended. It is a modification of the Memphis exhibition, and by the time of its closing on 31 May 1998 has attracted 750,000 visitors, the highest attendance at any event in the Museum's history.

Tuesday, 6 January 1998

THE DEATH OCCURS in Abilene, Texas, at the age of 72 of Jack Grimm, Texas oilman, who once described his life as 'a continuous search for the unknown'.

As already described in Chapter 10, in 1980, 1981 and again in 1983 Grimm and his partner Michael Harris mounted unsuccessful expeditions in search of

Titanic, their efforts being hampered by extremely bad weather and inadequate historical preparation. To the end of his life, Grimm contended that a photograph of a sea-bottom rock was indeed one of *Titanic*'s propellers.

Nonetheless Mr Grimm did provide the scientific members of his expeditions with the opportunity to procure invaluable data about the configuration of the ocean's floor.

Saturday, 24 January 1998

'TITANIC: FORTUNE & FATE' opens at the Mariners Museum in Newport News, Virginia. The exhibition permits visitors to participate in such activities as entering a lifeboat and sending a wireless message on equipment similar to *Titanic*'s. The exhibition also includes letters written from the liner, period costumes, a recreation of part of the ship's First Class dining room and one of three existing *Titanic* life jackets.

In keeping with the immense popularity of *Titanic*-related activities, the exhibition's closing date is extended from 7 September to 1 November 1998.

Wednesday, 28 January 1998

TITANIC SURVIVOR LOUISE Laroche dies at age 87 in Paris. Just one year and nine months old when she and her

Eleanor Ilene Shuman on board MV *Royal Majesty* during the 1996 Titanic Research and Recovery Expedition Cruise. (Steven B. Anderson Collection)

family set out for Cap Haitien, Haiti, in *Titanic*'s Second Class, she, her mother Juliette (22) and her sister Simonne (3) were saved, but her father, 25-year-old Haitian engineer Joseph Laroche, was lost.

Monday, 9 March 1998

ELEANOR ILEEN SHUMAN (née Johnson) dies, aged 87, in Elgin, Illinois. Eighteen months old, she, her mother Alice (26) and her brother Harold (4) travelled in *Titanic*'s Third Class and were returning home after visiting family in Finland. All were saved.

Monday, 6 April 1998

THE FIRST GENERAL public announcement is made in New York regarding the proposed building of a full-size replica of *Titanic*. A spokesman for the Swiss-based company White Star Line Ltd states that the oil-fuelled replica will 'look the same, but it will be

Jack Grimm. (Photo by Anita Brosius, courtesy Lamont-Doherty Geological Observatory, Palisades, NY)

The Mariner's Museum exhibition logo. (Courtesy of the Mariners' Museum, Newport News, Va)

adapted to modern regulations'. The project's partners hope to engage the services of Harland & Wolff, builders of the original ship, 'in an attempt to hire them as shipbuilder'.

A spokeswoman for G&E Business Consulting & Trust, the Swiss-based hotel developer that is the project's chief shareholder, states additionally that, 'The replica *Titanic* would cost $400 to $500 million' (£242 to £303 million), that tickets for the maiden voyage will cost from $10,000 to $100,000 (£6,060 to £60,600) and 'will be for people who are rich and crazy about the *Titanic*'.

A spokeswoman for the project's United States partner, Titanic Development Corporation, based in Las Vegas, Nevada, says, 'Some investors are already lined up, but many more will be needed.'

At almost the same time, a South African company, RMS Titanic, announces plans to build its own *Titanic* replica. According to an American magazine, 'They'll reproduce the lavishness – and add air conditioning, new engines and, of course, enough lifeboats.'

A contest between the two companies appears to be developing: 'White Star has set its sail date for April 10, 2002 – exactly 90 years after the first *Titanic* left shore. RMS Titanic vows to beat that by more than two years.'

Monday, 13 April 1998

A SYMPOSIUM SERIES begins at the United States National Archives in Washington, DC, in observance of the 86th anniversary of the *Titanic* disaster. Recognised experts in their respective fields discuss such subjects as official documents and transcripts of the 1912

US Senate investigation; an examination of photographs taken aboard *Titanic*; and the creation and application of digital visual effects used in the James Cameron film *Titanic*.

An evening with Walter Lord (16 August 1998) and a report by authors and historians Charles A. Haas and John P. Eaton on the 1998 expedition and wreck dives (14 September 1998) complete this interesting series.

Wednesday, 15 April 1998

IN CONJUNCTION WITH the full membership meeting of the British Titanic Society held at Southampton, England, Onslow's, the London auction house, conducts one of its world-famous sales of *Titanic* memorabilia. Containing 137 lots, the auction realises

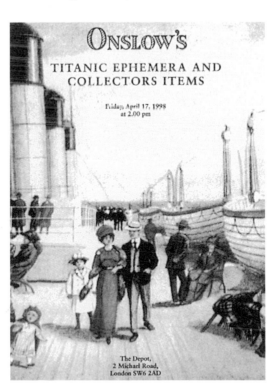

The catalogue for the Onslow's *Titanic* auction. (Courtesy Onslow's Auctions Ltd)

a total value in the vicinity of £111,000 ($185,000). Added to the auction at the last minute, a letter posted at Queenstown by one of *Titanic*'s stewards fetches the highest price ever paid for a *Titanic*-related letter, £4,400 ($7,260).

In keeping with the ever-increasing worldwide interest in the subject, the highest price ever paid for a *Titanic* item is realised with the sale of the former property of Edmond Stone, a *Titanic* steward, lost in the disaster – his watch, its hands stopped forever at 2.16, is sold for £15,000 ($24,750) to an American collector.

Saturday, 13 June 1998

RMS TITANIC, INC. (RMST) was the corporate entity created in 1993 to sell to the public OTC (over-the-counter) shares in *Titanic*-related activities, namely to explore, retrieve, conserve and exhibit items removed from and around *Titanic*'s wreck. Several other individuals and corporations also desired to dive and recover artefacts from the wreck site.

A decision in the United States District Court for the Eastern District of Virginia, in Norfolk, Virginia, by District Court Judge J. Calvitt Clarke, Jr on this date grants exclusive rights to RMST to pursue their goals, and barred all other claimants.

Tuesday, 23 June 1998

DURING THE SPRING of 1998 a commercial venture, Deep Ocean Expeditions, is formed in Norfolk, Virginia, to provide members of the public with transportation to *Titanic*'s wreck site and the opportunity to dive and photograph the wreck.

Mike McDowell, the trip's organiser, plans to lead a group of 60 tourists, who will pay $32,500 (£19,700) per person for the trip and the dive. For their daily dives to the wreck the organisers intend to use Finnish-built *Mir* submersibles – supplied, together with support technicians and scientists, by the P.P. Shirshov Institute of Oceanology at Moscow – each submersible holding a technical crewman and two observers. The observers' own photographic efforts are to be augmented by 'separate dives for scientists and professional photographers, who will be recording the wreck'.

At least two travel firms, the Connecticut-based Quark Expeditions and the UK-based WildWings Worldwide Travel, issue promotional material for the expeditions, and a number of paying participants sign on for the voyage.

On 4 May RMS Titanic, Inc., who in 1994 had been granted rights to the wreck as 'salvors in possession', file a motion in the United States District Court for the Eastern District of Virginia, Norfolk Division, for a preliminary injunction to prevent Deep Ocean Expeditions from visiting the site and photographing the wreck. The hearings are held on 27 May. Senior District Court Judge J. Calvitt Clarke Jr, in whose court the procedure is conducted, reserves his opinion until he can study and consider the facts.

On 23 June, in a brilliantly written 47-page Opinion and Order, Judge Clarke rules that the Deep Ocean Expeditions venture would devalue RMS Titanic, Inc.'s photographic rights, and would threaten that company's ability to control and preserve the wreck. The Judge orders Deep Ocean Expeditions and others to stay away from the *Titanic* site for purposes of photographing,

videotaping, searching, surveying or salvaging the wreck. He defines the wreck zone as a rectangular box about 14 miles by 21 miles around *Titanic*.

Clarke concludes that RMS Titanic, Inc. is salvaging artefacts from the wreck 'for the benefit of all mankind ... RMST is not exploiting the wreck for profit. It does not sell artefacts.'

In his ruling, Judge Clarke commends RMS Titanic, Inc. for 'maximizing the wreck's historical value and returning the wreck's artefacts to society for the general use and education of all mankind.'

An attorney for Deep Ocean Expeditions says that Norfolk's federal court has no jurisdiction over the wreck, which lies in international waters, and cannot control public picture-taking at the historic site.

'The law of the sea requires freedom of navigation,' the attorney says. 'If we want to go down and visit the ship, that is part of freedom of navigation.' Deep Ocean Expeditions says that the company will appeal against Judge Clarke's ruling.

Wednesday, 24 June 1998

A NEW AND EXPANDED permanent *Titanic* exhibition opens at the Maritime Museum of the Atlantic in Halifax, Nova Scotia. Photographs and text emphasise the Halifax connections with the *Titanic* disaster, as well as its place in shipwrecks and maritime safety.

Augmenting the museum's own impressive collection of documents and wood from *Titanic*'s public rooms, the new exhibition includes the following 'new' items, among others: an original wireless log from Cape Race recording the ship's first CQD and subsequent calls to *Carpathia*; a piece of wood from

the liner's Second Class smoking room; two new models of the ship, including an illuminated diorama of the sinking; and *Titanic*'s bow as seen through a submersible's window.

Increased public interest in *Titanic*, as well as the prominent rôle played by Halifax in the disaster, assure the success of this significant exhibition.

Elsewhere in Halifax, municipal authorities authorise an extensive programme, funded by federal, provincial and local grants, to repair and restore the 150 *Titanic* graves in Fairview, Baron de Hirsch and Mount Olivet cemeteries, and to improve facilities to deal with a large increase in the number of visitors to the cemeteries, attributed to the success of the Cameron movie *Titanic*.

Wednesday, 1 July 1998

IN CONJUNCTION WITH the World Trade Center, Boston, Massachusetts and RMS Titanic, Inc., 'Titanic: The Exhibition' makes its Northeastern US debut. Spectacularly displayed and tastefully exhibited, more than 250 *Titanic* artefacts are presented inside a substantial, specially constructed enclosed marquee with an evocative atmosphere enhanced by superb lighting.

Brochure for the Halifax exhibition. (Maritime Museum of the Atlantic, Halifax)

Right A 17ft model of the ill-fated liner greets visitors to RMS Titanic, Inc.'s Boston artefact exhibition. (Authors' photo © 1998 RMS Titanic, Inc.)

Middle Among the largest objects yet recovered from the debris field is this mooring bitt. It is exhibited in a special nitrogen-filled case to prevent metallic deterioration. (Authors' photo © 1998 RMS Titanic, Inc.)

Bottom In the 'Titanic's Voices' hall, a central pylon bears photographs and quotations of some of *Titanic*'s passengers and crew. A man's suit (left), recovered from a debris field suitcase, provides the opportunity for contemplation and conjecture; its conservation took more than two years, assuring its place in history. (Authors' photo © 1998 RMS Titanic, Inc.)

Below Prior to the Boston exhibition's opening, skilled workers install one of eight etched glass panels in the 'Hall of Reflections'. The panels contain the 2,231 names of *Titanic*'s passengers, crew members, and three shipyard workers killed during the liner's construction (Authors' photo © 1998 RMS Titanic, Inc.)

"It's the first time that we have had to deal with artifacts that have been in water so deep and so long. It is not easy to practice precision while you learn."

Chief of Titanic Conservation, Dr. Stéphane Pennec
LP3 Conservation Laboratory

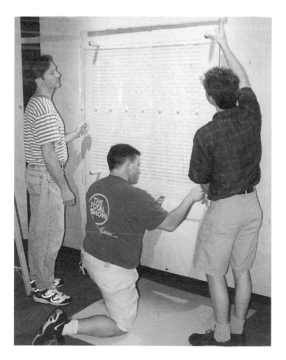

"I've seen it all, but those memories of that night in the North Atlantic will never go away."

Edith Brown Haisman
2nd Class Passenger, Survivor

As in earlier American exhibitions of similar context (Memphis, Tennessee, and St Petersburg, Florida), fine china and crystal, delicate jewellery and paper objects, and massive parts of the ship itself are on display. An outstanding item in the show is a 30ft-long cross-section drawing of *Titanic*, used as an exhibit during the British Board of Trade Inquiry headed by Lord Mersey (see page 154). The fragile drawing is generously loaned by a private collector.

A large section of *Titanic*'s hull plating (recovered from a depth of more than 11,000ft) arrives at Boston aboard the *Abeille Supporter* on 20 August. After careful examination by LP3's conservators, the piece is stabilised and exhibited beneath a specially designed water irrigation system. Displayed in an annex to the main exhibition, the piece becomes an instant hit with the public.

Scheduled to close on 1 November, 'Titanic: The Exhibition' is extended to 15 November. When it finally closes, it has been seen by hundreds of thousands of visitors.

Plans are made to take the exhibition to St Paul, Minnesota, with Atlantic City, New Jersey, and additional cities under consideration.

Tuesday, 7 July 1998

COBH, IRELAND: Unveiling of a *Titanic* memorial monument dedicated to the Irish passengers lost in the great liner's sinking.

Titanic visited Cobh (then Queenstown) 11 April 1912, where she debarked seven 'local' passengers and took aboard 120 passengers, including 113 First Class, of whom 73 were lost.

The memorial, located at Cobh's Pearse Square, bears two bronze plaques mounted on a plinth of Kilkenny limestone.

Friday, 24 July 1998

A TRAVELLING EXHIBITION of *Titanic* artefacts in association with RMS Titanic, Inc., 'Titanic Exhibition: Japan' opens in Tokyo, Japan. The ship's history and her fateful voyage, together with wreck exploration and the recovery and conservation of artefacts, are told through approximately 200 objects on display. The exhibition travels through Japan's largest cities, making stops of several weeks at each: Tokyo (32 days); Yokohama (48 days); Kyoto (60 days); Kobe (30 days); Hiroshima (30 days); and Sapporo (30 days).

The exhibition concludes its Japanese cycle in July 1999.

August 1998

THE 1998 RESEARCH and Recovery Expedition of RMS Titanic, Inc. takes place. The participants are IFREMER; Discovery Communications; Stardust Visual; the National Broadcasting Company/*Dateline;* Aquaplus; Polaris Imaging; Oceaneering Technologies; Woods Hole Oceanographic Institution; Les Abeilles International; and LP3 Conservation Laboratories. Technical operations are the responsibility of IFREMER. The principal ships involved are *Nadir*, *Ocean Voyager*, *Abeille Supporter* and *Petrel V*, together with *Cape Branden* and *Verna and Gean*; the manned submersible *Nautile* is also employed. Underwater vehicles (Remote Operated Vehicles – ROVs) involved are *Robin*, *Magellan*, *T-Rex*, *Abyssub* and *Remora*. The location is 41°43'N, 49°56'W and vicinity.

The logistics required to assemble personnel, supplies, equipment, electronic gear and ships for the 1998 expedition are indeed formidable. To the body of researchers and scientists

The French recovery vessel MV *Abeille Supporter* recovers a 22-ton section of *Titanic*'s hull during the 1998 Research and Recovery Expedition. (Jamie Roberts © 1998 RMS Titanic, Inc.)

routinely present on previous expeditions are added the staff members and complex apparatus to support two separate television broadcasts, one of which includes live segments from the wreck site itself, and another the taping of the expedition's activities for broadcast at a later date.

Departing from such diverse ports as Ponta Delgada in the Azores, Boston, Massachusetts, St John's, Newfoundland, and Bayonne, France, the vessels rendezvous at the wreck site. *Nadir* is first on the scene, arriving on Monday 3 August. Dives using the submersible *Nautile* commence at once. *Nadir* is joined the following day by *Ocean Voyager*, and four days later, on 8 August, by both *Petrel V* and *Abeille Supporter*.

One of *Nautile*'s primary functions during this 1998 expedition is to prepare a scientifically detailed mosaic of the entire wreck – bow section, debris field and stern section – to augment the grid of the area delineated during previous expeditions.

Ocean Voyager, carrying broadcast personnel and equipment, is next on the scene. *OV* also has on board the ROVs *Magellan* and *T-Rex* ('Titanic Remote Explorer'), which will be used to photograph the wreck in detail. It is hoped that the minuscule *T-Rex* (designed by high school teacher Bill Willard and his engineer wife Susan Willard) can enter previously unseen areas of *Titanic*'s interior and transmit colour images of the scenes.

Manoeuvred from its own control centre, the 4,500lb *Magellan 725* Remote Operated Vehicle, from Oceaneering Technologies Inc., is a deep-ocean advanced ROV system (7,000-metre rated) designed for high-quality work, inspection and recovery operations. It is to be used during this expedition to

transmit from the debris field and the wreck's bow and stern sections extremely high-quality video images through its fibre-optic link to the surface.

For almost two weeks the energies of the expedition's participants are devoted to the recovery of a large piece of *Titanic*'s hull and to preparations for a

television programme to be broadcast live from the wreck and from the decks of the surface vessels.

The 'Big Piece', a separate 25ft by 13ft, 22-ton section of *Titanic*'s hull, was measured and rigged for recovery during the 1996 expedition (qv), but its retrieval was thwarted by stormy

DEPLOYMENT OF VESSELS USED DURING THE 1998 RESEARCH AND RECOVERY *TITANIC* EXPEDITION

Nadir
Departs Ponta Delgada, San Miguel, the Azores, Wednesday 29 July

On site Monday 3 to Sunday 16*, and Saturday 22 to Monday 31 August

Arrives St John's, Newfoundland, Thursday 3 September

Ocean Voyager
Departs Boston, Massachusetts, Thursday 30 July

On site Tuesday 4 to Sunday 16*, and Saturday 22 to Monday 31 August

Arrives Boston Saturday 5 September

Abeille Supporter
Departs Bayonne, France, Friday 31 July; at Ponta Delgada, San Miguel, the Azores, Tuesday 4 August

On site Saturday 8 August to Sunday 16 August

Arrives Boston Thursday 20 August

Petrel V
Departs St John's Thursday 6 August
On site Saturday 8 August to Sunday 16 August

Arrives St John's Tuesday 18 August

Verna and Gean
Out of St John's

On site Tuesday 4 August, 2.13am to 2.35am**

Cape Branden
Out of St John's

On site Monday 31 August, 9.20pm to 9.35pm***

* *Nadir* and *Ocean Voyager* temporarily departed the site on Sunday 16 August for a four-day round-trip voyage to St John's, Newfoundland, with a one-day lay-over to refuel and pick up supplies. Each departed finally from the site on Monday 31 August.

** The 100ft *Verna* and *Gean* sailed out of St John's with replacement parts for *Ocean Voyager*'s differential global positioning system, navigation gear that enabled *Voyager* to maintain a fixed position over *Titanic*.

*** *Cape Branden* delivered an engine part to *Ocean Voyager*. Because of deteriorating weather, it departed very quickly.

weather. It was towed to an area approximately 10 miles from *Titanic* when the lift cable broke, sending the piece gently back to the ocean floor at or about position 41°36.2'N, 49°45.5'W. The 1996 expedition's final dive by *Nautile* marked the piece with a transponder (electronic buoy) and determined that it was undamaged in its decent to the bottom.

The recovery of the 'Big Piece' offers a dramatic example of the cutting edge of late-20th-century deep-sea salvage.

Monday 3 August: *Nautile* begins to attach petrol-filled lift bags to the rigging of the 'Big Piece'; altogether six are installed. The work is completed by 8 August.

Sunday 9 August: The lift bags are triggered acoustically to begin their ascent. After several frustrating hours it is apparent that the 'Big Piece' is not rising. Dispatched to discover the problem, *Nautile* finds the piece upright and moving, but not lifting. That evening another lift bag is sent to the bottom to provide additional buoyancy.

Top MV *Ocean Voyager* serves as a floating laboratory and television studio, transmitting the first live television pictures from *Titanic*'s wreck more than 12,500ft below the Atlantic to millions of viewers in 100 countries. (Authors' photo © 1998 RMS Titanic, Inc.)

Middle The French oceanographic research vessel MV *Nadir*, a veteran of the 1993, 1994 and 1996 expeditions, is the command ship during RMS Titanic, Inc.'s 1998 expedition, and provides support for the submersible *Nautile*. (Authors' photo © 1998 RMS Titanic, Inc.)

Left MV *Petrel V*, built in 1947, provides spartan dormitory accommodation for some expedition personnel during the 1998 expedition. (Authors' photo © 1998 RMS Titanic, Inc.)

Above Giant lift bags bob gently in the North Atlantic beneath *Abeille Supporter*'s stern frame crane, and the lift rope stretches taut as recovery of the 'Big Piece' begins. (Authors' photo © 1998 RMS Titanic, Inc.)

Above right As *Abeille Supporter*'s crew watch intently, chains at the end of the hoisting cable appear, indicating that the 'Big Piece' is just below the surface. (Authors' photo © 1998 RMS Titanic, Inc.)

Middle For the first time in 86 years, daylight touches *Titanic*'s hull. In the background, crew begin to collect the detached lift bags that have brought the piece to the surface. (Authors' photo © 1998 RMS Titanic, Inc.)

Right As lifting continues, portholes come into view off *Abeille Supporter*'s stern. (Authors' photo © 1998 RMS Titanic, Inc.)

Monday 10 August: The sixth lift bag is attached and triggered at about 2.30pm, and word is received that the piece is ascending. At 3.15pm three orange lift bags break the ocean's surface, and *Abeille Supporter* manoeuvres into position to recover the 'Big Piece'. With *Abeille Supporter*'s crane hook attached, the three uppermost lift bags in the array are cut away from the lifting cables and float away, to be recovered later.

At 5.40pm *Abeille*'s winch starts to reel in the main cable to which the lift bags have been attached. One after another the three remaining bags are detached (a dangerous task that involves separating the heavy bags from the lifting cable with only the sea's swells to create the necessary slack).

At 6.18pm the rusted piece of *Titanic*'s steel hull plating emerges into the air for the first time in over 86 years. Waves wash gently across the scarred, pitted and rust-encrusted surface, and the glass of the portholes reflects the late afternoon sun.

Fully lifted from the water, the dripping piece swings high over *Abeille*'s fantail, but before it can be

Top Gradually, the piece's full width is revealed. In the foreground a bed of manila hawsers waits to cushion the 'Big Piece' when it is lowered to *Abeille Supporter*'s deck. (Authors' photo © 1998 RMS Titanic, Inc.)

Middle Hoisting continues as *Abeille Supporter*'s crew move closer, providing an idea of the size of the piece. (Authors' photo © 1998 RMS Titanic, Inc.)

Left As *Abeille Supporter*'s A-frame crane pivots inward, guidelines are tightened to bring the piece on board. (Authors' photo © 1998 RMS Titanic, Inc.)

lowered to the spot prepared for it on the vessel's deck, a stray breeze catches the piece, despite the crew's best efforts at stabilising it, and bumps it into the leg of *Abeille*'s A-frame crane. For a breathless moment time seems frozen, and there is a chill fear that the 'Big Piece' might break loose and return to the ocean's depths. However, the crane operator's skilled and gentle touch and a co-ordinated pull on the control lines by the deck crew quickly control the piece, and it is gently lowered to its padded cradle on

Top The upper part of the giant hull piece is now completely above water. The arrangement of the portholes and subsequent examination of attachments on the piece's reverse side confirm authors Haas and Eaton's 1996 assessment that the piece was once the outer wall of cabins C-79 and C-81 on *Titanic*'s starboard side. (Authors' photo © 1998 RMS Titanic, Inc.)

Middle left As lifting continues, the segment of plating that once extended down to *Titanic*'s First Class dining room is revealed. The 22-ton piece is now supported entirely by *Abeille Supporter*'s lifting system and twists slightly in the wind. (Authors' photo © 1998 RMS Titanic, Inc.)

Middle right After gently bumping *Abeille*'s stern during lowering, the 'Big Piece' rests on deck as crew move to detach the lifting chains. Later, ashore, the piece's lower section will be successfully straightened. (Authors' photo © 1998 RMS Titanic, Inc.)

Right A proud moment is shared as expedition co-leaders George Tulloch and Paul-Henri Nargeolet congratulate Pierre Valdy, IFREMER's *Titanic* Project Head and designer of the lift bag system. In the right background is *Abeille Supporter*'s Captain Louis Deshommes. (Authors' photo © 1998 RMS Titanic, Inc.)

Left While the brass forming the portholes of the 'Big Piece' looks almost new, extensive corrosion is evident on most steel surfaces. This photograph was taken through a water 'shower' arranged by the onboard conservator to begin stabilising the piece and to protect it from exposure to the air. (Authors' photo © 1998 RMS Titanic, Inc.)

Below left In just two years, segments of chain attached to the 'Big Piece' during the 1996 recovery effort have been heavily corroded by the same underwater bacteria that have caused *Titanic*'s disintegration. 'Rusticle' activity appears heaviest at the thin plates joining *Titanic*'s ribs and beams to the main plates (left). *Titanic* is literally and rapidly disassembling herself. (Authors' photo © 1998 RMS Titanic, Inc.)

Below Harland & Wolff senior naval architect Dr David Livingstone examines the 'Big Piece' on *Abeille*'s deck. The webframe plate on the right was among the features confirming that the piece came from *Titanic*'s starboard C deck. (Authors' photo © 1998 RMS Titanic, Inc.)

Abeille's after deck. A conservator from LP3 quickly takes charge, and the 'Big Piece' is soon entirely bathed in a sea-water spray, the first of many steps in the conservation process.

In 1996 the 'Big Piece' was identified by naval architects and historians as being from *Titanic*'s starboard side in the vicinity of cabins C-79 and C-81. However, in 1998, after some further analysis, one naval architect postulated that it may have come from the port side, and this information is reported to the public during the live television broadcast. But once the naval architects have a chance to examine the previously hidden back side of the piece on the surface, they are able to demonstrate conclusively that the piece is indeed from the starboard side, as originally believed.

The 'Big Piece' retrieval having been successfully completed, the expedition's several groups of workers return to more routine matters.

Tuesday 11 August: *Nautile* descends to the wreck to explore the stern. Aboard is microbiologist Dr Roy Cullimore, who is engaged in an on-going study of how several types of bacteria are at work literally devouring *Titanic*'s hull at the rate of 200lb a day.

Wednesday 12 August: On yet another dive to the wreck, *Nautile*'s own ROV, *Robin*, is sent inside *Titanic*'s bow through existing openings to explore previously unexamined interior portions of the wreck. Large areas of B deck are examined and *Robin* is sent further down the area of the forward grand staircase than it had previously gone. Remarkable video footage is obtained.

On this day preparations are also begun for the complex task of broadcasting a live television image from *Titanic*'s wreck, 2½ miles deep. Technicians aboard *Abeille Supporter*

lower a special basket containing 6,500ft of fibre-optic cable to the ocean floor, in a location about 5,000ft from the wreck, to avoid any possibility of snagging *Nautile* and her crew.

Friday/Saturday, 14/15 August: During the night, *Abeille* drops a metal cage connected to a live fibre-optic up-link to the ship. At 5.45am on the 15th, the cage is positioned 2,600ft equidistant from *Titanic*'s bow and stern.

Saturday 15 August: At 1.45pm *Nautile* retrieves the fibre-optic basket and carries it in its robotic arms about half a mile to connect it with the up-link in the cage. Shortly after 5.30pm the connection is made and for the first time live colour images from *Titanic*'s wreck are viewed and incorporated into a live television network programme, seen in more than 100 countries worldwide.

On Sunday 16 August the 1998 expedition's first phase ends with the departure from the site of *Abeille Supporter* for Boston, carrying the 'Big Piece'. Broadcast engineers and technicians who have successfully completed the live programme are transferred to *Petrel V* for the return to St John's, Newfoundland. *Nadir* and *Ocean Voyager* also set out for St John's, but at a somewhat slower speed.

After a day at St John's to take on fuel, water and supplies, *Nadir* and *Ocean Voyager* return to the wreck site. Upon their arrival on Saturday 22 August, the expedition's second phase begins, and proves to be equally productive, but more in keeping with practices and procedures established during earlier expeditions. In one way, however, it is far more dramatic.

The days are occupied with a number of tasks. Artefacts are retrieved, documented and prepared for shipment to the conservation laboratory. The mosaic of the wreck and its debris field is carefully undertaken. *Magellan*'s amazing colour images from the wreck are received, recorded and interpreted. Segments of a film depicting the expedition's projects and achievements are shot on a daily basis: interviews, individual and group; analyses of wreck images; commentary on historical and present-day occurrences – all to be edited for a future television programme and a tape of the expedition's accomplishments in the historic context of *Titanic*'s never-ending story.

All activities are curtailed by two days with the approach from the west-south-west of Hurricane Bonnie. Underwater vehicles are retrieved and secured; staff members and crew prepare for the converging storm; delicate electronic equipment is carefully stowed; and moveable objects (medium and large) are tied down. The preparations are not in vain. Even as *Nautile* departs from the site for St John's and *Ocean Voyager* for Boston, the storm strikes with ferocious fury. For more than 24 hours, winds of up to 65 knots (76mph) and waves of 40 to 50ft buffet the vessels. Even after the storm passes, its wake is marked by high seas and higher than normal winds.

Nadir reaches St John's on Thursday 3 September, and *Ocean Voyager* enters Boston Harbor on the morning of Saturday 5 September.

In coming years there is yet more to be done with and for *Titanic*'s wreck. Data from earlier expeditions, combined with research conducted during the 1998 expedition, clearly indicates that *Titanic* is deteriorating far more rapidly than previously estimated. If the wreck's interior is to be additionally examined, if the causes of the disaster are to be further evaluated, if *Titanic*'s future can be safeguarded by a closer over-all scrutiny, if the scientific methods so well accomplished during previous expeditions are to be extended to their most beneficial realisation – if these ends are to be met, future exploration, goals and techniques will have to be re-examined.

Titanic was once the culmination of man's scientific and industrial achievement. Its documentation, and its rescue from deterioration and destruction, can be part of a similar fulfilment.

Let this be the challenge.

Thursday 10 September 1998

THE RESEARCH VESSEL *Akademik Mstislav Keldysh* departs from St John's, Newfoundland, for the *Titanic* wreck site. The ship carries 12 tourists – five German, five American, one Australian and one Briton – who have paid up to $32,500 (£19,700) for the opportunity to dive to the wreck.

Before his appeal is decided, and in defiance of the court order by United States District Court Judge J. Calvitt Clarke Jr (see 23 June 1998), expedition organiser Mike McDowell hopes to lead his group of inquisitive tourists to the wreck with the use of the Russian submersibles *Mir 1* and *Mir 2*. On their way to and at the wreck site, participants are treated to lectures on oceanography and *Titanic*'s history.

They arrive at the site on Saturday 12 September, and the dives commence. Instead of the customary two pilots and single observer (for safety purposes), each submersible now carries two observers and a single pilot. One observer during the second dive is a German television camera operator.

After eight dives, during which 16 observers are carried to the wreck, the expedition departs the location on 15 September.

TWELVE

PAST, PRESENT, FUTURE . . .

SINCE THIS BOOK'S original publication in 1999, *Titanic*'s present has become her past.

The past – the first generation: people who saw or sailed on her – have all passed on. Many important members of the second generation – people who recorded her actual history, people who *discovered* her, those who first explored the wreck, recovered and exhibited her material objects – have departed.

The present – the third generation, preservationists, historians, genealogists – all work to discover (or rediscover) details heretofore missing, adding a piece to the puzzle, a tile to the mosaic, until a fully authentic representation can take its appropriate place in history.

The future? As this book is being prepared, the legal owners of *Titanic*'s salvaged artefacts are petitioning a US court for the right to disperse some of the recovered artefacts through individual sale. Also, a promised replica of *Titanic*, planned for construction at a Chinese shipyard and due for a maiden voyage within two years, appears in doubt, perhaps due to its sponsor's reported financial difficulties.

All is not well for *Titanic*'s immediate future. But the present, and the recent past – the month-by-month and even the day-by-day events – are sufficient to keep the subject recognisable to the public.

There are always '15 April' observances and the well-known 'rearrangement of the deck chairs' ...

There is perhaps no more joyous way to pick up the thread, as it were, of *Titanic*'s recent sequence of significant events than that which took place 20 February 1999 at St Paul, Minnesota:

Sunday, 20 February 1999

TITANIC'S WHISTLES WERE recovered during the 1993 expedition, and were carefully restored by the Braun Intertee Corporation in Eden Prairie, Minnesota. Over a three-day period they are mounted and displayed in the plaza outside St Paul, Minnesota's Union Depot, where an exhibition of *Titanic* artefacts is in progress.

A few moments after 4.05pm, after a ceremony of dedication, the whistles are sounded before a crowd local police estimate as between 80,000 and 100,000 spectators. The proceedings are broadcast by radio and television to a worldwide audience.

(In 2015, to mark the 30th anniversary of the discovery of *Titanic*'s wreck, a recording of the whistles' sound is reintroduced at the non-travelling artefact exhibitions in Buena Park, California; Las Vegas, Nevada; and Orlando, Florida.)

Wednesday, 24 March 1999

THE UNITED STATES Court of Appeals for the Fourth Circuit, Richmond, Virginia, reverses the June 1998 ruling of the US District Court judge in Norfolk, Virginia, granting RMS Titanic, Inc. exclusive rights to the wreck. The three-judge panel rules the District Court's decision does not apply to visitors.

The appellant in the case, Deep Ocean Expeditions, begins plans for tourist dives to the wreck, charging $35,000 per visitor.

RMS Titanic, Inc. appeals the decision to the United States Supreme Court.

Friday, 3 September 1999

ARGOSY INTERNATIONAL LTD, headed by Graham Jessop, announces

Titanic's rescue ship *Carpathia* sinks approximately 120 miles (190km) south of Fastnet on the morning of 17 July 1918. (Wikimedia Commons)

it has located the rescue ship *Carpathia*'s wreck, 185 miles south-west of Cornwall, England, having been sunk on 17 July 1918 by two torpedoes from German submarine *U-55*. Bad weather forces the expedition to abandon the site before its discovery can be verified using underwater cameras.

(When Jessop later returns to the wreck site, it is found that the remains are not those of *Carpathia*, but rather those of the Hamburg-America Line vessel *Isis*, sunk 8 November 1936 after being flooded by a broken hatch.)

May 2000
American author and diver Clive Cussler and his organisation, the National Underwater and Marine Agency (NUMA), discover *Carpathia*'s actual wreck, standing upright at a depth of 500ft (150m). The approximate location is given as 120 miles (190km) south of Fastnet, Ireland.

Tuesday, 5 October 1999

THE UNITED STATES Supreme Court rejects RMS Titanic, Inc.'s appeal to prohibit others' visits to the wreck site. The ruling allows Deep Ocean Expeditions to offer tourist dives to the wreck. By 2012, the company is charging $60,000 per person per dive.

Sunday, 28 November 1999

CLAIMING THAT RMS Titanic, Inc.'s stock is worth more than its $51 million (£30 million) current value, a group of dissident stockholders accumulates 51 per cent of the company's shares by proxy or ownership. The company's president and its general counsel are removed and new management installed.

January 2000

CANADA, THE UNITED STATES, the United Kingdom and France prepare a draft agreement establishing rules regarding the preservation of *Titanic*'s wreck site.

Thursday, 6 November 2003
The United Kingdom signs the pact to preserve *Titanic*, the first nation to do so.

Sunday, 17 June 2004
In London, the United States signs the treaty to preserve *Titanic*. Between 2007 and 2011, the treaty is submitted to three sessions of Congress, but remains to be ratified by the United States Senate.

Tuesday, 10 June 2008
The Canadian Government says it will join the effort to protect *Titanic*'s site.

Friday, 21 July 2000– Monday, 21 August 2000

ABOARD THE CHARTERED Russian research vessel *Akademik Mstislav Keldysh* (commonly referred to as 'the *Keldysh*'), RMS Titanic, Inc. conducts an expedition to perform mapping surveys and retrieve artefacts from *Titanic*'s wreck site.

The entire expedition is plagued by bad weather, and is cut short by two weeks.

More than 800 artefacts are recovered during 28 dives, and are referred to in the future as 'the American artefacts'.

Wednesday, 2 August 2000

A LEATHER-BOUND NOTEBOOK is stolen from the *Titanic* artefact exhibition at Chicago, Illinois' Field Museum of Science.

A guard is apprehended, arrested, and the notebook is returned unharmed to the exhibit.

Sunday, 28 January 2001

TEN GOLD COINS and nine banknotes are stolen from a *Titanic* artefact exhibition at the Opryland Hotel, Nashville, Tennessee.

The crime is never solved.

Tuesday, 30 January 2001

MICHEL NAVRATIL, AGE 92, *Titanic*'s last male survivor, dies at his home in Montpellier, France.

Michel Navratil, one of the '*Titanic* orphans', in 1997. (Courtesy of Michele M. Marsh)

Titanic's picture darkens and becomes less distinct with the deaths of significant members of its 'family'.

Joseph Groves Boxhall	25 Apr 1967	67	Last surviving *Titanic* officer
Sidney Daniels	30 May 1982	89	Last *Titanic* crewman
Edith Eileen Haisman (née Brown)	20 Jan 1997	100	Second-longest lived survivor
Walter Lord	19 May 2002	85	Author of *A Night to Remember*
George Tulloch	31 Jan 2004	59	Former president of RMS Titanic, Inc.
William MacQuitty	4 Feb 2004	99	Producer of film *A Night to Remember*. In 1912, saw *Titanic* being towed to her trials.
J. Calvitt Clarke, Jr	6 May 2004	83	US District Court judge, made decisions re: RMS Titanic, Inc.'s status as salvor-in-possession of *Titanic*'s wreck
Lillian Gertrud Asplund	6 May 2006	99	Last American survivor
Barbara Dainton (née West)	16 Oct 2007	95	Last Cross-Channel *Titanic* passenger
Elizabeth Gladys 'Millvina' Dean	21 May 2009	97	In 1912, age 11 months, youngest survivor; in 2009, final *Titanic* survivor
Roy Ward Baker	5 Oct 2010	93	Director of film *A Night to Remember*

1 Edith Haisman (née Brown) was 15 when she and her parents Thomas (age 60) and Elizabeth (40) sailed from Southampton aboard *Titanic* in Second Class. She returned to *Titanic*'s sinking site on 1 September 1996 during the 'Titanic Research and Recovery Expedition Cruise', dropping a wreath on the ocean's surface in her father's memory. Edith was *Titanic*'s oldest living survivor at the time of her passing in January 1997. (David F. Hutchings)

2 Author of 11 books, Walter Lord is best known for *A Night to Remember* (1955) and *The Night Lives On* (1986). (Michael A. Findlay)

3 George Harmon Tulloch, co-leader of five *Titanic* expeditions. (Charles A. Haas)

4 Lillian Gertrud Asplund, the final American *Titanic* survivor. (Asplund family photo via Henry Aldridge & Son, Auctioneers)

5 Gladys Elizabeth 'Millvina' Dean, the youngest and final living *Titanic* survivor, in March 2009. (Charles A. Haas)

Thursday, 17 May 2001–June 2011

Body No. 4, 'The Unknown Child'
Wednesday, 17 May 2001

The remains of the 'Unknown Child' in Halifax's Fairview Lawn Cemetery are exhumed for DNA analysis and positive identification.

The examination takes more than a year.

Friday, 3 May 2002

News is released that 'Unknown Child' is not Gösta Leonard Pålsson, a Third-Class passenger from Sweden, as many had believed, but no further identification is offered.

Wednesday, 20 November 2002

An American television programme identifies the remains as Third Class passenger Eino Viljami Panula from Finland.

(A final, official report cites urgency of the programme's imminent broadcast as a factor in its conclusion.)

Monday, 30 June 2003

Shoes removed from Body No. 4 before the original 1912 interment and subsequently donated to Halifax's Maritime Museum of the Atlantic become a clue in the DNA identification.

Sunday, 15 April 2007

A leading investigator into Body No. 4's identification reveals the child's name to be Sidney Leslie Goodwin, from Wiltshire, England; his parents and five siblings also died in the disaster.

Wednesday, 1 August 2007

Evidence and explanation regarding the Unknown Child's identification are made by key scientists involved in the DNA inquiry.

Misgivings about the Panula determination had arisen based on the size and development of a tooth recovered during the exhumation at Body No. 4's gravesite. Also, the size of the shoes donated in 2003 and evaluated by the analysts were more likely the correct size for an older child (Goodwin's 19-month age) rather than for the Panula child's 13 months.

June 2011

Having been previously published online on 10 April 2010, the final formal report, along with scientific and genetic records, is published in the peer-reviewed journal *Forensic Science International: Genetics*.

Tuesday, 14 August 2001–Saturday, 29 September 2001

ABOARD THE RESEARCH vessel *Keldysh*, James Cameron – producer, writer and director of the 1997 film *Titanic* – leads a group of more than 50 technicians and researchers in dives to examine and photograph *Titanic*'s wreck.

The 2003 film *Ghosts of the Abyss* depicts their work.

Friday, 7 December 2001–11 October 2002

Salvage rights

Friday, 7 December 2001

RMS Titanic, Inc. announces it wishes to sell the entire *Titanic* artefact collection.

Tuesday, 26 February 2002

RMS Titanic, Inc. appeals against the US District Court's ruling barring it from selling artefacts.

Friday, 12 April 2002

The United States Court of Appeals for the Fourth Circuit in Richmond, Virginia rules RMS Titanic, Inc. is only a temporary caretaker, does not own the artefacts, and may not sell them.

Monday, 15 April 2002

A group of dissident shareholders sues RMS Titanic, Inc. for mismanagement.

Tuesday, 30 April 2002

US District Court Judge Rebecca Beach Smith dismisses the dissident shareholders' suit, ruling there is insufficient evidence.

Tuesday, 24 September 2002

RMS Titanic, Inc., of which Arnie Geller is now president, notifies the district court and the Securities and Exchange Commission that it will surrender salvage rights and conduct no further expeditions to the wreck.

Friday, 11 October 2002

Judge Smith orders RMS Titanic, Inc. to explain why it wishes to give up its salvage rights.

November 2002 – October 2006

Illicit Salvage

Friday, 22 November 2002

Arnie Geller, president of RMST, Inc., states in Judge Smith's court that he is unaware of any unauthorised activities or dives to *Titanic*.

Tuesday, 11 March 2003

The possibility is suggested that the wreck may have been plundered by Ocean Resources, Inc., headed by Graham Jessop, formerly of RMST.

Saturday, 1 May 2004

The Times of London reports that during March 2003 ('18 months earlier') a ship, the *Northern Horizon*, equipped with the remote-operated vehicle *Abyssub*, visited the wreck site and removed distinctive artefacts.

Monday, 30 October 2006

A sidelight from *Titanic* is put on the market by a German antiques dealer, as reported by the BBC. The item appears genuine, although its source is not substantiated.

Thursday, 22 November 2002

RMS TITANIC, INC. announces that a shareholders' meeting is called for 5 February 2003 to decide whether to give up the company's salvage rights.

Monday, 26 November 2002

JUDGES CLARKE AND SMITH remind and caution RMS Titanic, Inc.'s president, Arnie Geller, that the company must protect the wreck.

Tuesday, 1 April 2003

A PROPOSED PROJECT, the 'Titanic Quarter', to redevelop land on and adjacent to the former site of the Harland & Wolff shipyard, Belfast, Northern Ireland, is first announced.

November 1995

American President Bill Clinton officially opens 'Titanic Park' during a peace mission to Northern Ireland.

September 2002

Developer Mike Smith is appointed chief executive of the Titanic Quarter.

2005

The site becomes the home for Northern Ireland Service Park, affiliated with Queen's University. It is also the site for Titanic Studio, a film studio centre.

July 2006

Work begins on Phase One of the development. Belfast Metropolitan College plans to build a £44 million campus in the Titanic Quarter.

October 2007

Planning permission is given for Titanic Quarter's second phase, which includes the Odyssey Complex, a sports and entertainment venue, and 2,000 homes adjacent to the Titanic Quarter.

The Belfast Harbour Marina is completed in Harland & Wolff's Abercorn Basin.

The Premier Inn, Titanic Quarter's first hotel, opens and begins operations.

April 2011

The Public Record Office of Northern Ireland (PRONI) opens its new £30 million facility at 2 Titanic Boulevard.

Saturday, 31 March 2012

'Titanic Belfast' is a visitor attraction whose contents were created by the *Titanic* Foundation and designed by London-based Events Communications to educate people on Belfast's heritage through *Titanic*'s story.

To the 'Titanic Quarter' (begun in 2001), plans were added in 2005 for a museum to depict the history of not only Belfast city, but also the company that built the world-famous ship and her illustrious sisters; construction begins in May 2009 and the exhibit opens to the public 31 March 2012.

Designed by Eric Kuhne and Associates, the eight storey, 38.5m-high (126ft) building contains 11,000 sq. metres (118,000sq. feet) of exhibition space and costs in excess of £100 million ($140 million), including £77 million ($108 million) for the building and the balance for upgrading the public land, which was supported by £60 million in public funds.

The building's exterior is clad in 3,000 silver anodised sheets folded into complicated shapes and sizes, 2,000 panels being completely unique. The building's design reflects Belfast's history of shipbuilding and Harland & Wolff's industrial legacy; its angular form suggests the shape of ships' prows, with the main 'prow' pointing towards the middle of the *Titanic* and *Olympic* slipways, some 100m (330ft) away.

Inside, exhibition space is devoted to interactive galleries: Belfast, the city; the shipyard; *Titanic*'s launch; the fitting out (which includes a computer-generated tour through all of the vessel's decks from engine room to bridge); the maiden voyage; the sinking; the aftermath (which enables a searcher to investigate passengers, crew and company backgrounds); myths, legends and popular culture aspects of the disaster; and the final gallery, '*Titanic* Beneath' (which shows views of the wreck as it exists today, and the logistics and mechanics of dives to the site).

Ocean Exploration of the US government's National Oceanic and Atmospheric Administration (NOAA) sponsors an 11-day research cruise to *Titanic*'s wreck site.

The mission's primary objective is to provide a photo-mosaic of the structure, especially of the stern, a site not previously examined in detail. More than 24 running hours of video footage is obtained.

A second project involves a thorough study of the microbial communities called 'rusticles' that permeate the wreck.

Titanic Belfast is the story of *Titanic* and her people, past and present:

- The ship – from lines on a preliminary sketch to an alive and active wreck.
- The people – who built the ship and sailed aboard her.
- Today's visitors – who simultaneously learn and enjoy.

Crowds gather as 'Titanic Belfast' opens on 31 March 2012. The building's remarkable design suggests the bows of ships. (Ardfern via Wikimedia Commons)

Aboard the research vessel *Ronald H. Brown*, scientists mapped *Titanic*'s wreck site during a 2004 expedition sponsored by the National Oceanic and Atmospheric Administration. (NOAA via Wikipedia.com)

Thursday, 27 May 2004– Saturday, 12 June 2004

AT THE WRECK SITE again between 30 May and 9 June, aboard the NOAA research vessel *Ronald H. Brown*, members of NOAA's staff continue to map *Titanic*'s wreck site and observe the extent of the wreck's deterioration.

Monday, 21 April 2003

RMS TITANIC, INC. proposes donating its artefact collection to the Mariners Museum, Newport News, Virginia.

Due to many legal and moral obligations, negotiations with the museum end without result.

Sunday, 22 June 2003– Wednesday, 2 July 2003

ABOARD THE CHARTERED Russian research vessel *Keldysh*, the Office of

Friday, 18 June 2004

IN WASHINGTON, DC, John F. Turner, Assistant Secretary of State for Oceans and International Environmental and Scientific Affairs, signs an international agreement to protect the *Titanic* wreck site from unregulated salvage operations.

The agreement was first called for in the Titanic Maritime Memorial Act, signed into law by President Ronald Reagan in 1986. The United States began negotiating this agreement in 1997 with the United Kingdom, Canada and France.

Tuesday, 24 July 2007

THE US STATE DEPARTMENT sends proposed legislation to the United States Senate for consideration and ratification ...

Wednesday, 25 August 2004–Wednesday, 8 September 2004

ABOARD THE RESEARCH VESSEL *Mariner Sea*, RMS Titanic, Inc. conducts its seventh research-and-recovery expedition. For the first time, a deep-sea remote-operated vehicle is used instead of a manned submersible. Seventy-five artefacts are recovered and the site is mapped for future retrievals.

Thursday, 14 October 2004

PREMIER EXHIBITIONS, INC. becomes the holding company for RMS Titanic, Inc. Premier will plan, develop and operate exhibitions on a variety of subjects, including those featuring *Titanic* artefacts, while RMS Titanic, Inc. will continue its 'salvor-in-possession' rights granted to it in 1994 by a federal court.

Wednesday, 20 October 2004

THE UNITED STATES Securities and Exchange Commission fines six RMS Titanic, Inc. shareholders.

Two RMST officers are named in a civil injunctive action, and in a related case, four shareholders are named in a civil penalty action.

The SEC complaint alleges that in obtaining proxy votes to effect the 1999 management change, the defendants acted without the required disclosure to the Commission and to RMST shareholders; that RMST shareholders did not learn of the defendants' plan to acquire control of the company until such control changed; and that shareholders were then powerless to prevent the change.

Without admitting or denying the Commission's findings, the defendants consent to the entry of final judgements.

Wednesday, 22 June 2005–Thursday, 18 August 2005

DURING THIS PERIOD'S 56 days, five expeditions visit the *Titanic* wreck site. All expeditions use the Russian research vessel *Keldysh*. Each departs from, and returns to St John's, Newfoundland.

24 June–7 July 2005
Discovery Channel Television / Earthship Production – Phase One
Led by James Cameron, the expedition's object is to photograph the wreck's exterior and interior using the best possible equipment. The resulting footage is incorporated in a television programme about the wreck, *The Last Secrets of the Titanic*.

7–17 July 2005
Deep Ocean Expeditions
Twenty tourists pay $35,650 (£20,000) apiece to dive to the wreck. On each of five dive days, each of the two *Mir* submersibles carry two guests and the submersibles' pilots to the wreck.

The Russian research vessel *Akademik Mstislav Keldysh* is the primary surface support ship for five different *Titanic* expeditions in 2005. (Wikimedia Commons)

18–27 July 2005
Discovery Channel Television /
Earthship Production – Phase Two
James Cameron completes his plan to film exterior and interior views of *Titanic*. Using the two *Mir* submersibles and two remote-operated wireless 'camera bots', Cameron obtains superb footage for inclusion in the television programme *The Last Secrets of the Titanic*.

31 July–8 August 2005
G. Michael Harris Expedition
Florida-based entrepreneur Harris dives to the wreck site to photograph *Titanic* for his Orlando exhibition venue, *Titanic: The Experience*.

10–18 August 2005
History Channel Television /
Chatterton-Kohler / Lone Wolf
Productions
A group of three dives to the wreck and wreck site documents the purported discovery of two 'missing' pieces from the wreck. The story of the dives is broadcast as the History Channel's *Titanic's Final Moments: Missing Pieces* on 28 February 2008.

Sunday, 4 December 2005

IN AN ARTICLE printed in *The [London] Sunday Times*, Dr Robert D. Ballard writes that he intends to cleanse *Titanic*'s crumbling and 'rusticle'-covered hull and spray it with a special anti-fouling, anti-bacterial paint. He

The last surviving vessel of the White Star Line, *Nomadic* undergoes restoration in Belfast's Hamilton Graving Dock in 2012, before her masts are installed and upper works completed. (Charles A. Haas)

repeats his proposal in his 2008 book, *Archaeological Oceanography*.

Thursday, 26 January 2006

BUILT IN 1911 at Belfast's Harland & Wolff, the tender *Nomadic* (later renamed *Ingenieur Minard*) served as a passenger tender at Cherbourg. She saw honourable service in both world wars, and in 1968 this last vessel of the great White Star Line was retired.

Saved from breakers, she was privately converted to a floating restaurant and moored at Paris on the River Seine near the Eiffel Tower, for many years.

Sadly, over the years, the owner allowed the vessel to deteriorate. In 1974 her superstructure was rebuilt, but in 1999, Paris harbour inspectors demanded a hull inspection. When the owner refused, the harbour authorities seized the vessel, removed her upper decks so the hull could pass beneath the Seine's low bridges and, in April 2003, towed her out of Paris to Le Havre for demolition.

International pressures demanded an auction: In November 2005 the first auction occurs, but no bids are received meeting the reserve price of £500,000 ($880,000).

Thursday, 26 January 2006
At a second auction, an offer of £100,000 made by the Belfast City Council does not meet the reduced reserve of £171,320 ($301,573).

The Northern Ireland Department for Social Development, however, does make an offer of £263,000 ($462,880), which is accepted.

Wednesday, 12 July 2006
At Le Havre, after inspection and preparation, *Nomadic* is loaded aboard the 300ft (91m) submersible barge AMT *Mariner* for transport to Belfast.

Friday, 21 July 2006
Nomadic's hull returns to the water at Belfast's Harland & Wolff shipyard, her 1911 place of birth. Repairs and restoration are begun, and are ongoing.

Sunday, 2 June 2013
After a £7 million ($12.3 million) restoration, *Nomadic* is officially opened to the public at Belfast.

Tuesday, 31 January 2006

IN RICHMOND, VIRGINIA, the United States Court of Appeals for the Fourth Circuit affirms the 2004 ruling by the US District Court for the Eastern District of Virginia, in Norfolk, that the 'law of salvage', not the 'law of finds', applies to the *Titanic* case and rules that the District Court must provide RMS Titanic, Inc. with an appropriate award, full ownership of the artefacts, and future rights to salvage.

Saturday, 15 April 2006

HOUSED IN A nearly full-size reproduction of the ill-fated ship's forward half, and entered through a replica of a huge iceberg, a *Titanic* 'museum attraction' opens in Branson, Missouri. It contains a comprehensive exhibit of the ship's history and the disaster that befell it, but no recovered artefacts. The museum is favourably received and becomes a popular tourist site.

Wednesday, 28 February 2007

PREMIER EXHIBITIONS AGREES to sell its ownership interests in RMS *Carpathia*. Its subsidiary, RMS Titanic, Inc., receives $500,000 (£303,000) from Seaventures for the sale, which includes the right to display objects recovered from *Carpathia*'s wreck and certain *Titanic* artefacts.

Seaventures is owned by Joseph Marsh, who owns more than 5 per cent of the company's common stock.

On 15 April 2008, a second payment of $2,500,000 (£1,515,000) is received from Seaventures.

Friday, 13 April 2007– Sunday, 15 April 2007

MORE THAN 100 MEMBERS of *Titanic* organisations from seven countries – the UK, the US, Switzerland, Ireland, Sweden and the host country, Canada – meet in Halifax, Nova Scotia, to mark the liner's 95th anniversary.

The convention's most significant presentation is made by *Titanic* historian Alan Ruffman, who reveals publicly for the first time the correct identity of the 'Unknown Child' as Sidney Leslie Goodwin. (See 17 May 2001.)

Saturday, 19 May 2007

HAROLD FROELICH dies at age 85, in Minneapolis, Minnesota. Froelich headed the design team that produced the submersible vehicle *Alvin*, the miniature submarine used by Robert Ballard in his dives to *Titanic*.

Named after Allyn Vine of the Woods Hole Oceanographic Institution, *Alvin* made more than 4,000 dives to *Titanic* and other locations.

Saturday, 25 August 2008
Being developed at Woods Hole, a replacement for *Alvin* designed by the US Navy is expected to transport a pilot and two observers 4 miles (6.4km) deep, providing access to 99 per cent of the oceans' depths.

Tuesday, 24 July 2007

THE US STATE Department again sends to the US Senate a treaty to implement *Titanic*'s protection. The legislation will control access to and salvage of the wreck and will be implemented by the National Oceanic and Atmospheric Administration (NOAA). (See 18 June 2004).

November 2007

OPERATED BY WORLD Tourist Attractions, the so-called Wheel of Belfast, a 200ft (60m) version of the famous London Eye Ferris wheel, is placed by the Northern Ireland Planning

The Titanic Memorial at Belfast's City Hall is completely engulfed by the Belfast Wheel for more than two years until efforts to remove it succeed. (Una Reilly)

Office directly above and surrounding the city's main *Titanic* memorial at the east side of Belfast's Victorian-era City Hall.

Sunday, 11 April 2010
Strenuous objections led by Una Reilly, co-founder of the Belfast Titanic Society, and by the UK's Environmental Agency lead to the wheel's shutdown on this date, and its subsequent removal.

Tuesday, 19 February 2008

LESTER F. WEBER, a former archivist at the Mariners Museum, Newport News, Virginia, pleads guilty to theft and sale of museum property between 2000 and 2006. He stole more than 1,500 museum items and sold them on eBay for $162,959 to buyers across the country.

Among the material stolen and sold are several of the 115 items acquired in 1986 from Frank Philip Aks, a *Titanic* survivor, including original letters and lawsuit papers.

Wednesday, 17 December 2008
In the US District Court for the Eastern District of Virginia, Judge Rebecca Beach Smith sentences Weber to four years in a federal prison.

Saturday, 2 June 2008

IN HIS SEARCH for *Titanic*'s wreck in 1985, Robert Ballard used US Navy equipment that had been secretly used earlier during the same mission to check the status of two nuclear submarines – USS *Thresher* and USS *Scorpion* – that had sunk in the Atlantic in the 1960s.

Although the US Navy knew of this mission, it is not well known by the general public until the National Geographic Channel on this date nationally televises the programme *Undercover Titanic with Bob Ballard*.

November 2008–January 2009

MARK SELLERS, a venture capitalist and a member of the board of Premier Exhibitions (see 14 October 2004) seeks to oust Arnie Geller, RMST's president, because of sagging profits.

January 2009
In a quick series of financial moves, and with stockholders' approval, Sellers Capital takes over RMST and Premier Exhibitions, and removes Arnie Geller as president. Sellers is assisted by

Christopher J. Davino, who becomes the company's new CEO.

Friday, 26 October 2009

BEFORE JUDGE REBECCA Beach Smith of the United States District Court for the Eastern District of Virginia, in Norfolk, Premier Exhibitions, parent company of RMS Titanic, Inc., asks the court to award it sole possession of the artefacts recovered from the ship's wreck site and thus end the decade-long controversy surrounding ownership.

Friday, 23 November 2009
Judge Smith agrees to make a decision 'sometime after January 4th' regarding disposition of the wreck's artefacts.

(The court gained jurisdiction over the case in 1992 [q.v.] when, under Judge J. Calvitt Clarke Jr, it granted sole 'salvor-in-possession' rights to the original RMS Titanic company, which had applied for this protection. Judge Smith worked with Judge Clarke for seven years, and on the latter's retirement, assumed jurisdiction in the case herself.)

She gives attorneys until 4 January 2010 to file any follow-up briefs, and says she will then come to a decision.

Monday, 13 July 2009

INTENDING TO DEPICT the story of Southampton's maritime heritage and, in particular, the connection between the city and *Titanic*, the Southampton City Council announces plans for a new city museum, and appoints the design team, naming Wilkinson Eyre as lead.

Wednesday, 2 September 2009
Assisted by a grant of £499,000 from the Heritage Lottery Fund, the City Council unveils the project's details, for a museum, gallery and exhibition space, to cost £28 million.

Friday, 18 December 2009
To be located in the civic centre's west wing, site of the former magistrates' courts, the new SeaCity Museum's entrance hall will include shops and a café. Another area, 'Gateway to the World', will depict the city's past 600 years; and in the exhibit hall, 'Southampton's *Titanic* Story', the tale of the ship and the disaster will be told through the eyes of the city, where 609 of the 908 *Titanic* crew members lived or lodged.

Monday, 29 March 2010
A National Heritage Lottery Fund grant of £4,600,000 to the City of Southampton enables the city to proceed with construction of the SeaCity Museum.

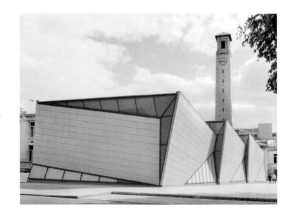

The SeaCity Museum, including this new pavilion for temporary exhibitions, opens in April 2012 as an addition to Southampton's Civic Centre. (Hahnchen via Wikimedia Commons)

Tuesday, 10 April 2012

Southampton's SeaCity Museum opens for its first visitors.

Tuesday, 6 October 2009

THE 'TITANIC MEMORIAL CRUISE' is announced on the internet. Without mentioning the operator's name, a description of the cruise notes that the ship, Fred Olsen Cruise Line's MV *Balmoral*, is to depart Southampton, England, 'in April' 2012 and retrace *Titanic*'s original 1912 voyage. A memorial service is planned for the sinking site on the disaster's anniversary. Prices for the trip start at $3,900 (£2,785) per person.

Monday, 15 March 2010

DESIGNED BY HUGH TURNER and dedicated on 15 April 1914, the cloister and fountain to *Titanic* telegraphist Jack Phillips in his hometown of Godalming, Surrey, England, is found to have been vandalised.

Local efforts to refurbish the memorial (said to be the largest monument to an individual victim of the disaster) prove inadequate.

July 2010
A gift of £280,000 ($462,000) from England's Heritage Lottery Fund enables the council to restore the memorial in time for the observance of the disaster's centennial in 2012.

Thursday, 8 April 2010

SIMILAR TO AN EXHIBIT in Branson, Missouri, a *Titanic* museum, built to

The forward half of *Titanic* has 'docked' as a museum attraction in Pigeon Forge, Tennessee. (Billy Hathorn via Wikimedia Commons)

duplicate the dimensions of the forward half of the original ship, opens on this date in Pigeon Forge, Tennessee, just north of the Great Smoky Mountains National Park. The exhibition holds 400 pre-discovery artefacts in twenty galleries. The structure cost $25 million (£14.2 million) to build.

Thursday, 15 April 2010

MILES MORGAN TRAVEL announces details of the 2012 'Titanic Memorial Cruise'. The ship MV *Balmoral* will depart Southampton 8 April, sail to Cherbourg and then on to Queenstown (now Cobh); it will arrive at the sinking site on the night of 14–15 April, where a memorial observance will be conducted. Passengers will then travel to Halifax, Nova Scotia, for a day-long visit to the cemeteries where some 150 of *Titanic*'s victims are buried. The trip will end at New York.

With a minimum fare of $3,900 per person, the cruise quickly sells out. (See also 8 April 2012.)

22–31 August and 6–17 September 2010

SPONSORED BY RMS TITANIC, INC. and the Woods Hole Oceanographic Institution, and using the latest technology and equipment, an expedition is to generate a three-dimensional map of the wreck and surrounding debris field, creating an archaeological plan for the site.

The expedition's departure is delayed briefly when, on 18 August, a fire is discovered aboard the 250ft research vessel *Jean Charcot* at its St John's, Newfoundland, mooring. There is no damage. The fire – likely caused by welding sparks – is quickly extinguished by the city's firefighters, and the mission departs on schedule.

The mapping is completed during the first five days at the site, when the group must leave the area in advance of Hurricane Earl and returns to St John's.

The group returns on 6 September and for nine days conducts a detailed examination of the wreck itself. More than 130,000 digital photographs are taken of the entire vessel; these will be used to identify the precise locations from which each artefact was originally removed.

Since the wreck's September 1985 discovery 25 years earlier, this 23rd expedition to the site is perhaps the most successful, and its results will be studied for many years.

Tuesday, 7 December 2010

THE STEEL ON *Titanic*'s wreck is covered with streamers of ferric oxide, named 'rusticles', that are teeming with life. Using material recovered during a 1991 dive to the wreck, researchers at Dalhousie University, Halifax, Nova Scotia, the Ontario Science Centre, Canada, and the University of Seville, Spain, isolate an iron-oxide-eating organism – a species of bacteria never before seen. The newly discovered life form is given the name *Halomonas titanicae*.

Tuesday, 31 May 2011

BELFAST HARBOUR IS central to the city's observance of the 100th anniversary of *Titanic*'s launch. Hundreds of people gather at 12.13pm along the banks of the River Lagan to mark the moment with cheers and song as many ships in the harbour sound their whistles, just as others had as the great liner glided into the water a century earlier.

Monday, 15 August 2011

IN A RULING issued by Judge Rebecca Beach Smith of the United States District Court, Eastern District of Virginia, RMS Titanic, Inc., a wholly owned subsidiary of Premier Exhibitions, Inc., is granted title to *Titanic*'s artefacts.

After many years of contentious legal procedures, the company now has uncontested ownership of the more than 5,000 artefacts recovered on expeditions during 1993, 1994, 1996, 1998, 2000 and 2004. (The collection also includes artefacts recovered jointly with the French in 1987 and awarded to the company in 1993 by a French maritime tribunal.)

In her decision, Judge Smith also rules that RMS Titanic, Inc. must continue to maintain the artefacts in perpetuity, and may sell them only as an intact collection under restricted terms and with the court's approval.

September 2011

PREMIER EXHIBITIONS, PARENT company of RMS Titanic, Inc., establishes a separate subsidiary, Premier Exhibition Management, and a content division, the existing RMS Titanic, Inc.

October 2011

PREMIER EXHIBITION MANAGEMENT announces it will buy the assets of '*Titanic*: The Experience', a 20,000sq. ft space in Orlando near Walt Disney World, Sea World and Universal Studios.

Sunday, 19 September 2011

POLICE WORK TO recover a gold-plated necklace stolen from the exhibition of *Titanic* artefacts at Copenhagen's Tivoli Gardens. The showcase was unbroken and the alarm did not sound.

Thursday, 29 December 2011

CHRISTOPHER DAVINO, current president of RMS Titanic, Inc., announces the forthcoming sale of *Titanic*'s entire artefact collection. Appraised in 2007 at $189 million, it will be auctioned on 15 April 2012 by Guernsey's Auctioneers in New York. Potential buyers (who must bid for the entire collection; no individual pieces are listed) will be selected through an application process open until 1 April. Final sale must be approved by the US District Court for Eastern Virginia's judge, who has ultimate control of the artefacts.

Sunday, 29 January 2012

IN RESPONSE TO earlier inquiries, about 120 interviews are conducted at the BBC South studios in Southampton of descendants of *Titanic*'s former crew. Additional interviews are planned for 10 April at the SeaCity Museum's opening.

Excerpts from the interviews will be broadcast during BBC's centennial observance of *Titanic*'s loss.

Tuesday, 10 April 2012

PREMIER EXHIBITIONS AND its subsidiary RMS Titanic, Inc. announce in Atlanta that they are in discussions with multiple parties for the sale of its collection of more than 5,000 *Titanic* artefacts recovered from the wreck site. The company refuses further discussion, stating it is conducting negotiations in confidence and will release updated information as soon as practical.

It had intended to sell the collection through Guernsey's Auction House in early April.

Friday, 20 April 2012

AUSTRALIAN MINING BILLIONAIRE Clive Palmer signs an agreement with the state-owned CSC Jinling shipyard in Nanjing, Jiangsu, China, to construct a replica of the 1912 White Star liner *Titanic*.

Monday, 30 April 2012

Palmer formally announces in a Canberra, Australia press conference that he has commissioned a Chinese shipyard to build a replica of the 1912 White Star liner *Titanic* for his company, named Blue Star Line Pty, Ltd.

The plan is to build a vessel as similar as possible to the original, but using modern technology and meeting all current safety regulations.
The new vessel will have a gross tonnage of 56,000 compared with 46,000 of the 1912 original.

It will be 4.2m (13ft 9in) wider than the original, but the same length.

Titanic II will cost £300 million ($528 million) (compared with the £1.5 million original 1912 cost).

The new vessel is scheduled to sail to New York in 2016, if all goes as planned.

Who is Clive Frederick Palmer?

- Born 26 March 1954, Melbourne, Australia
- Residence: Sovereign Islands, Gold Coast, Queensland, Australia

Australian billionaire Clive Palmer proposes building *Titanic II*, replicating the lost liner to the extent that modern safety standards permit. (Jwmcdonald81 via Wikimedia Commons)

- Married: 1983–2005. First wife died; 2007, remarried. Four children
- Member of the Australian Parliament for Fairfax, 7 September 2013–9 May 2016
- Owner of Mineralogy, a company with large iron ore reserves; 2008, Waratah Coal; 2009, Queensland Nickel (which, in January 2016, enters voluntary administration)
- 2012, *Titanic II*
- 2013, *Palmersaurus*, a park that features animatronic dinosaurs

Tuesday, 19 June 2012

Finnish naval architecture firm Deltamarin Ltd is commissioned to design the new ship.

Tuesday, 17 July 2012

The ship's preliminary general arrangement is published. Lower deck cabins are to be 'typical for a modern

cruise vessel', while cabins and public rooms from D deck upwards will be 'as in the original ship'.

October 2012

A design consultant and historian are appointed by Clive Palmer. Also appointed are members of an advisory board who will provide suggestions and recommendations to ensure that *Titanic II* would appropriately and respectfully pay homage to *Titanic*, her crew and passengers.

Tuesday, 28 May 2013

Clive Palmer announces that Tillberg Design, a Swedish company, will design the ship's interior.

Wednesday, 17 July 2013

Palmer appoints Lloyd's Register to review key *Titanic II* drawings.

Monday, 9 September–Thursday, 12 September 2013

At the Hamburgerische Schiffbau Versuchsanstalt (HSVA) (Hamburg Ship Model Basin), a 9.3m (31ft) long wood model of *Titanic II* is subjected to propulsion and power tests at speeds up to 23 knots. The results 'will be ready in a few months'.

February 2014

In an interview, Palmer claims keel laying will occur in September 2014. He cautions that the original *Titanic* had taken seven years to build, while his project's team has been working for only two and a half years, and they would have liked to start sooner, but 'wanted to make sure we didn't make any mistakes'. He claims that a selection of cabins is being constructed on land for approval and that this would be completed by July 2014.

As part of its 2013 press kit, Clive Palmer's Blue Star Line Pty Ltd issues this artist's rendering of *Titanic II*, eastbound from New York City, passing the Statue of Liberty. The dark rectangles on the two forward funnels, both dummies, are observation rooms' windows. Below the 'historic' but non-functional lifeboats, a flotilla of modern rescue craft helps assure compliance with the latest safety regulations. (Blue Star Line Pty Ltd)

At 2.20am, 15 April 2012, 100 years to the minute after *Titanic* sank, passengers and crew gather in silence on the after decks of MV *Balmoral* for a memorial service directly above *Titanic*'s wreck during the 'Titanic Memorial Cruise'. (Charles A. Haas)

March 2015

Deltamarin tells an Australian broadcast journalist that work on *Titanic II* has been halted. It is reported that no work has begun at the Chinese shipyard identified as the likely site of construction, and that shipyard officials doubt the project would advance beyond the proposal stage.

Thursday, 26 March 2015

The Blue Star Line trademark is listed as 'abandoned'.

September 2015

A spokesman for Palmer says the project has merely been delayed, and that the ship will be launched in 2018. The vessel's maiden voyage now will be from Jiangsu, China, to Dubai, United Arab Emirates, where Blue Star was 'developing licensing partnerships for its *Titanic II* trademark'.

Saturday, 7 May 2016

Administrators for Queensland Nickel, purportedly in bankruptcy, reveal that Mr Palmer's former company poured almost AUD$5.9 million (£3.34 million, US$4.44 million) into the project from

2012 until April 2014, when cash slowed to a trickle. Project management fees accounted for AUD$1.9 million (£1.07 million, US$1.43 million) while AUD $3.3 million (£1.87 million, US$2.49 million) was spent on lavish marketing of the venture in the US and Britain.

Monday, 23 May 2016

Mr Palmer rules out a bid for re-election to the Australian Senate, a position he has held since 2013.

As of August 2016 there is no signed construction contract with any shipyard, and Deltamarin refers all questions regarding the project to the Blue Star Line.

2012

DURING THE PERIOD leading to and including the 100th anniversary of *Titanic*'s loss, several countries commission postage stamps to mark the vessel's construction, voyage and loss. Among these countries are Canada, Eire, Batum, Bahamas, Gambia, Micronesia, Nevis, Turkmenistan, Somaliland and St Vincent.

Photographs and original artwork depict the ship and her people on the stamps. Scenes from James Cameron's film *Titanic* are employed; countless cachets and special cancellations are also utilised, to say nothing of labels that imitate pre-existing photographs and drawings.

It is a field day for collectors of minutiae.

April 2012

CENTENARY OBSERVANCES IN memory of *Titanic* and the people she carried are conducted worldwide throughout the month, by many groups from South Africa to Southampton, from Belfast to New York, to Halifax, to 41°43'N, 49°56'W.

Cobh (Queenstown), 11–15 April: A centennial observance of *Titanic*'s only visit to Queenstown, including a special service at St Colman's Cathedral.

Southampton, 12–15 April: Wreath laying at significant locations and memorial sites throughout Southampton; a special convention of members of the British Titanic Society.

New York (Secaucus, NJ), 27–29 April: The annual convention of Titanic International Society, including a special New York Harbor tour, a visit to Ellis Island, and a gala banquet.

Two special memorial cruises, managed by Miles Morgan Travel:

Aboard MV *Balmoral*, built 1988, refitted 2008; 715ft, 45,537grt

8 April	Departs Southampton, 1,309 aboard. During the days the ship is at sea, eleven guest speakers present sixteen lectures on *Titanic* and her people
9 April	Cobh (Queenstown), Ireland
10–13 April	At sea
14 April	Arrives at 41°43'N, 49°56'W, the spot beneath which *Titanic* lies. Rendezvous with *Azamara Journey*, which had left New York 10 April
15 April	2.20am, *Titanic* memorial service in conjunction with *Azamara Journey*
16–17 April	At Halifax

The Phillips Memorial Cloister in Godalming, Surrey, has been repaired after being damaged by vandals (Ian Taylor via Wikimedia Commons)

18 April	At sea
19 April	Arrival and docking at New York

Aboard M/S *Azamara Journey*, built 2000, refurbished 2007; 592ft, 30,277grt

10 April	Departs New York, 680 aboard
11 April	At sea, for Halifax, Nova Scotia. While at sea, nine guest speakers present talks on *Titanic*, her people and artefacts
12 April	At Halifax, Nova Scotia
13 April	At sea
14 April	Arrives at 41°43'N, 49°56'W, the spot where *Titanic* lies. Rendezvous with *Balmoral*
15 April	2.20am, *Titanic* memorial service in conjunction with *Balmoral*
16–17 April	At sea, for New York
18 April	Arrival and docking at New York

Sunday, 15 April 2012

THE MEMORIAL CLOISTER erected in 1913–14 in Godalming, Surrey, to the memory of Jack Phillips, *Titanic* wireless operator, was badly damaged in 2010 by vandals. Thanks to fundraising efforts led by *Titanic* researcher Mandy LeBoutillier and local volunteers, the memorial (largest of all *Titanic*-related memorials) is repaired and refurbished to nearly its original state. It is rededicated, with affection, on this day – the centennial date of *Titanic*'s loss.

Wednesday, 18 April 2012

MADELYN WILS, PRESIDENT and CEO of the Hudson River Park Trust, announces that New York City's historic Pier 54, where survivors from *Titanic* had been landed by *Carpathia*, has been closed almost completely, with only the landward 300ft of the 800ft-long pier remaining open, for fears the remainder could collapse into the river.

Thursday, 31 May 2012

SOMETIME BEFORE THE death of Elizabeth Gladys Dean (known the world over as Millvina Dean) – *Titanic*'s youngest and final survivor – her countless friends and admirers around the world raised funds through contributions to assist with her nursing home costs.

After her 2009 death, the remaining proceeds in the Millvina Fund are sufficient to provide a garden in her memory, adjacent to the newly opened Southampton museum, SeaCity.

The garden consists of a grass-covered elliptical open space bisected by a pathway, with an engraved plinth alongside. At each end of the ellipse, curved benches offer places of respite. Surrounding the open space are a green-and-gold privet hedge and flowerbeds featuring plants of many colours, aromas and textures.
The garden is situated north-west of Southampton's SeaCity Museum, where Havelock and Commercial roads intersect.

A century after *Titanic*'s survivors disembarked from *Carpathia* at New York City's Pier 54, in this July 2012 view, all that remains of the historic structure was its platform, supporting pilings and a steel arch where once the words 'Cunard Line' had appeared. Since then, amid fears of imminent collapse, much of the platform has been demolished, leaving only the arch. (Mike Peel via Wikimedia Commons)

Thursday, 5 July 2012

OUTSIDE THE CLUBROOMS of Harland & Wolff's Welders' Club in Belfast, Northern Ireland, a plaque is unveiled in memory of the eight men who had died in and around *Titanic* during the vessel's construction (six in the yard, two in the works.)

The names of the five known dead are inscribed on the plaque. Research is continuing on the three remaining men's names.

Tuesday, 16 October 2012

PREMIER EXHIBITIONS ANNOUNCES it has found a group of buyers for the more than 5,000 artefacts it owns that were recovered from *Titanic*'s wreck. It has signed a non-binding letter of intent to sell the collection for $189 million and, while it did not name the buyers, says it believes it will satisfy all of the federal court's conditions.

headquarters on West 48th Street in New York City for display.

Friday, 25 January 2013

ON 3 NOVEMBER 1912, at their New York union headquarters on East 86th Street in Manhattan, the Musical Mutual Protective Union dedicated a graceful 2ft by 3ft, 70lb bronze plaque honouring *Titanic*'s lost musicians. In 1921, the union became Local 802, American Federation of Musicians (AFM), and some time later moved their headquarters to 229 West 52nd Street, taking the plaque with them. In 1982, Local 802 left West 52nd Street for new quarters, leaving the plaque behind. The building at West 52nd Street was torn down.

In 1989, Douglas Turner moved to Naples, Florida, where he joined the Collier County Sheriff's Department as a criminal investigator. To relieve the pressures imposed by his job, he enjoyed visiting regional antique dealers and scrap yards with his wife, looking for unusual items.

The Millvina Dean Memorial Garden in Southampton, England. (David F. Hutchings)

One Friday in January 2013, Turner finds a plaque – covered with grease and dust, corroded and flecked with verdigris – leaning against a basket of scrap metal awaiting disposal. Leaving the object behind, he returns and purchases it for about $1.60 (£1.10) per pound, being told by the scrap dealer that someone had brought it in together with another 'Local 802 war memorial plaque', and that 'within days I would have thrown it in the scrap basket to be melted down'.

June 2016
Having retrieved and rescued both plaques from destruction, Turner arranges with Local 802 AFM's lawyer for the latter to purchase them and return them to the union's

Tuesday, 26 February– Sunday, 3 March 2013

IN SEVERAL ELABORATE presentations, Clive Palmer reveals to travel agents, media persons, and interested parties the exterior and interior plans for the projected *Titanic II*.

Among those attending, *Titanic* historical groups are well represented.

New York – Tuesday, 26 February, an 11-course dinner aboard the museum ship USS *Intrepid*

Halifax – Friday, 1 March, breakfast at the Lord Nelson Hotel

London – Saturday, 2 March, dinner at the Natural History Museum

Macau, China – Sunday, 3 March, dinner at The Venetian Macau

Southampton – Sunday, 3 March, breakfast at the South Western Hotel.

Monday, 9 September 2013

IT IS OFFICIALLY announced that Albion House, the 116-year-old former Liverpool home of *Titanic*'s owner, the White Star Line, is being converted to a 64-room, 11-floor luxury apartment hotel. To be called '30 James Street', the facility contains an indoor pool and a restaurant. The upper ground floor and basement are *Titanic*-themed, as are many of the rooms.

The development and conversion are done by Signature Living Hotels, owned by Lawrence and Katie Enright. It opens in February 2014.

The Musicians Mutual Protective Union's plaque after its rescue and cleaning by then-owner Douglas Turner. (Charles A. Haas)

The violin is sold to an anonymous British buyer for £900,000 (about $1.78 million) far beyond the original estimate of between £200,000 and £300,000 ($320,000 and $480,000).

Sunday, 27 October 2013

SEVEN STAR ENERGY investment announces construction by Wuchang Shipbuilding of a *Titanic* replica intended as the main attraction at the Romandisea Theme Park at Suing City, Sichuan, China. The replica will contain rooms similar in size to the original *Titanic*'s; it will be anchored on the River Daying Qi. It is expected to cost around 1 billion juan ($165 million), and should open in October 2017.

Wednesday, 9 October 2013

PREMIER EXHIBITIONS ANNOUNCES its failure to sell *Titanic*'s artefacts: the purchase agreement was ended because the buyers' consortium could not secure financing. The principals in the consortium are not revealed, but some of the involved parties continue to express an interest.

The sales price in the now-ended letter of intent was not expressed, although in the past the collection has been valued at between $100 million and $200 million.

Saturday, 19 October 2013

... The music ceased, then began again, thinly, as Hartley, perhaps in reverie, pulled his bow across the strings for a final time. He was joined as, one by one, the other players picked up the familiar tune – the hymn played at graveside for brother musicians departed, and Hartley's own favourite, *Nearer, My God, To Thee ...*

(From *Falling Star*, by John P. Eaton and Charles A. Haas)

AFTER AN EXHAUSTIVE seven-year historical and forensic scrutiny that included, among other probes, an examination for the salinity of moisture in the instrument, the authenticity and ownership of the violin are satisfactorily determined, as well as the true tale of its journey from *Titanic*'s decks to storage rooms throughout northern England.

Andrew Aldrich, of Henry Aldrich and Son, conducts the violin's authentication, perhaps the most personal and intimate of all associated *Titanic* memorabilia, as well as the auction.

Thursday, 2 January 2014

IN 1912, TWO-YEAR-OLD Helen Loraine Allison was the only child from First or Second Class lost in *Titanic*'s sinking, which also claimed the lives of her wealthy parents, Hudson and Bessie Allison.

In 1940, a woman named Helen Loraine Kramer appeared on the radio programme *We the People*, claiming to be the lost child, saved when put in a lifeboat by her father. When challenged by family members, Kramer refused to identify herself further, but continued to pursue her claim. Eventually she moved to the 'western United States' and was not heard from again.

In 2012, a woman, Debrina Woods, who claimed to be Kramer's granddaughter, purportedly was in possession of 'a suitcase full of letters' between her grandmother, a lawyer and the Allison family, proving she was related to them; she also asserted she had DNA evidence and 'proof from a museum' that the documents were legitimate – although she never provided the name of the museum or the laboratory where the DNA was examined.

It is only after the 'Loraine Allison Identification Project' carries out its own DNA tests (through a forensic scientist at Laurentian University in Canada, and a *Titanic* researcher) that Debrina Wood's claim is proven false.

Adjacent to the 'Titanic Belfast' exhibition, left, the former Harland & Wolff drawing offices (right) will become a boutique hotel set for opening in 2017. (Una Reilly)

Wednesday, 16 April 2014

A MEMORIAL GARDEN to commemorate passengers who boarded *Titanic* by way of the tenders *America* and *Ireland* is opened at Cobh (formerly Queenstown), Ireland. The garden contains a glass wall that overlooks a view across the harbour to the distant Roches Point, where *Titanic* had anchored from 11.30am to 1.30pm on 11 April 1912 to take aboard mail and passengers.

Saturday, 26 April 2014

AT AN AUCTION of *Titanic*, White Star Line and ocean liner memorabilia conducted by auctioneers Henry Aldridge and Son, a letter by Esther Hart with a postscript by her daughter Eva sells for $200,000 (£119,000). The letter is handwritten on RMS *Titanic* stationery and dated 'Sunday afternoon' [14 April]. In her postscript, Eva wishes, 'Heaps of love and kisses to all.'

At the same auction, a Second Class breakfast menu for 11 April 1912, mailed from Queenstown by Second Class saloon steward Jacob Gibbons, is sold for $147,000 (£87,000).

Friday, 29 August 2014

PREMIER EXHIBITIONS, the parent company of RMS Titanic, Inc., announces the resignations on Monday, 25 August of three of its six-member board of directors; on Friday, 28 August a new executive chairman, Samuel S. Weiser, is named.

Monday, 13 October 2014

DR ROBERT BALLARD, co-leader (with IFREMER's Jean-Louis Michel) of the French–American expedition that discovered *Titanic*, announces the end of his fifteen-year relationship with the Mystic Aquarium in Connecticut. The aquarium enabled Ballard to show exhibits relating to *Titanic*, as well as items from his other subsequent expeditions.

Ballard will soon open the east coast headquarters of the Ocean Exploration Trust – founded in 2008 – and will continue working closely with the United States Coast Guard and with the University of Rhode Island; he will also continue his magazine and television work with *NOVA* and *National Geographic*.

Tuesday, 14 October 2014

SAMUEL WEISER, present executive chairman of Premier Exhibitions, Inc., parent company of RMS Titanic, Inc., states the present value of *Titanic*'s artefacts is $218 million. (The collection had been appraised in 2007 at $189 million.) The current appraisal was performed by The Alesko Company on 17 September 2014, and does not include the value of intellectual property and archaeological assets compiled during the company's 2010 dives.

Wednesday, 15 October 2014

MARK SELLERS, president of Northbrook, the investment management firm for Sellers Capital LLC, reaches an agreement to sell his approximately 14.4 million shares (31 per cent) of Premier Exhibitions to Armada Group – a Palm Bay, Florida-based investment firm led by George Wight Jr – for about $16.2 million. The agreement is publicly announced on 22 October.

But on 25 November, in a Form 13D filing with the United States Securities and Exchange Commission, Sellers states that, as of 20 November, the buyer had not met all the closing conditions and by his 25 November filing, Sellers concludes that Armada did not plan to fulfil its obligations.

Right The silver loving cup presented to *Carpathia*'s Captain Arthur Rostron by Margaret 'Maggie' Brown on 29 May 1912 is sold at auction in October 2015. (Henry Aldridge and Son, Auctioneers)

Far right The loving cup presented *to Carpathia*'s Captain Arthur Rostron by a passengers' committee headed by Margaret Tobin Brown is sold for £129,000 ($198,000) in October 2015. (Henry Aldridge and Son, Auctioneers)

Sellers, age 46, had served on Premier's board of directors since July 2008 and was chairman of the board from January 2009 to August 2014.

Tuesday, 17 February 2015

Using a £4.9 million grant from the Heritage Lottery Fund's Heritage Enterprise programme, the former Harland & Wolff headquarters and drawing offices will be turned into a *Titanic*-themed hotel with 84 rooms and related public heritage space.

Located on Belfast's Queens Road and adjacent not only to the 'Titanic Belfast' exhibition but also the slipways where *Titanic* was built and launched, the headquarters building was constructed in three stages between 1889 and 1922; it was partially restored in 2008 by Titanic Quarter Ltd for use as its own headquarters and office space.

The hotel is expected to open in 2017.

Wednesday, 2 April 2015

PREMIER EXHIBITIONS ANNOUNCES it will merge with the Canadian company Dinoking Tech (DK) of Richmond, British Columbia. Under the agreement's terms, Premier will acquire outstanding shares of DK, of which Daoping Bao is the principal shareholder.

Upon the closing of the transaction (expected in August 2015), Dinoking will hold 47 per cent of Premier's outstanding voting shares and the right to nominate four of seven board members. Bao will become executive chairman, president and chief executive officer of Premier, while Dinoking will become an indirect, wholly owned subsidiary.

Saturday, 18 April 2015

AN AUTHENTIC *Titanic* deck chair is sold by Henry Aldridge and Son to a private British collector for $158,000 (just over £100,000).

The chair, one of six salvaged by the recovery ship *Mackay-Bennett*, was given to a French captain, Julien Lemarteleur, who kept it until his death in 1973, when it was given to a colleague, Robin Lee; the present owner acquired it in 2001.

Saturday, 30 May 2015

PREMIER EXHIBITIONS, the parent company of RMS Titanic, Inc., opens an exhibition at 475 Fifth Avenue, New York City, celebrating 40 years of the television variety program *Saturday Night Live*.

The exhibition displays various well-known programmes in the show's 40-year history as well as a 'behind the scenes' view of the six-day process of putting together an individual show, including writing, cast selection, costumes design, make-up, rehearsals and the televising of the programme. The exhibition closes 6 June 2016.

Wednesday, 9 September 2015

(See also 16 October 2014)

MARK SELLERS, a Chicago-based investor, files a lawsuit in Chicago's Northern District Federal Court for $12.4 million against George Wight Jr and his Armada Group for breach of contract of his letter of agreement signed 15 October 2014 to buy 15,409,179 shares of Premier Exhibitions at $1.05 a share.

Per the filing, Sellers claims Wight used his Armada corporate entities as a sham to mislead the Premier board and shareholders into believing he had the money to complete the deal. Sellers

Photographed on the morning of 15 April 1912 by chief steward M. Linoenewald aboard the German liner *Prinz Adalbert*, this berg – with a scar of red paint at its base – has long been called 'the iceberg that sank the *Titanic*'. (Henry Aldridge and Son, Auctioneers)

alleges Wight 'never had sufficient cash on hand' to complete the deal.

Saturday, 24 October 2015

SOLD TO A PRIVATE collector by Henry Aldrich and Son is the silver loving cup presented by *Titanic* survivor Molly Brown to *Carpathia*'s Captain Sir Arthur Henry Rostron on 29 May 1912.

The cup – 12in tall and weighing 39½oz – has been exhibited at the National Museums Liverpool, the Ulster Folk and Transport Museum and at the *Titanic* exhibits at Branson,

Missouri and Pigeon Forge, Tennessee. The cup sells for £129,000 ($197,980).

Sold at the same auction for £21,000 ($32,000) is the photograph identified by experts as the iceberg that sank *Titanic*. Taken 16 April 1912 by the chief steward of *Prinz Adalbert*, the photograph shows at its base a streak of red paint made by the vessel striking the berg. The picture hung at Burlingham, Montgomery and Beecher, the law offices of the firm that defended *Titanic*'s owner, until its closing in 2002.

Saturday, 14 May 2016

AT THE HOLY Name Cemetery, Jersey City, New Jersey's largest cemetery, a headstone is unveiled for the heroic seaman in *Titanic* lifeboat No. 13: Robert John Hopkins, who died in 1943 and was buried in an unmarked grave, is honoured with a polished black granite marker placed in his memory by the Titanic International Society and the Archdiocese of Newark. Seaman Hopkins and Fireman Fred Barrett had to cut lifeboat 13 free from its falls as it drifted directly under lifeboat 15, which was being lowered.

Also remembered are four other *Titanic* survivors buried at this cemetery: Margaret Devaney, Elizabeth Dowdell, Thomas McCormack and Bridget McDermott. (After his death in 1975, McCormack's name and dates were not engraved on his family's stone until Titanic International Society and the Archdiocese of Newark corrected the omission in May 2016.)

Tuesday, 14 June 2016

PREMIER EXHIBITIONS, the Atlanta-based company that owns salvage rights and more that 5,500 *Titanic* artefacts, files for voluntary Chapter 11 bankruptcy protection in the United States Bankruptcy Court, Middle District of Florida, at Jacksonville, Florida. The case is assigned to the Honourable Paul M. Glenn, bankruptcy judge.

As enumerated in the bankruptcy filing, Premier Exhibitions is configured

Judge Paul M. Glenn of the US Bankruptcy Court for the Middle District of Florida is hearing Premier Exhibition's Chapter 11 Bankruptcy filing. (United States Trustee's Office, US Department of Justice)

to present five different types of exhibitions, as reflected in the following table:

According to the filing, the 'Saturday Night Live: The Experience' exhibition, opened in May 2015, was incredibly unprofitable and the debtors closed all exhibitions operating in the space at 417 Fifth Avenue, Manhattan, 'on 6 June 2016, and plan to vacate the premises as soon as practicable'.

The filing includes an exhibit of an appraisal of *Titanic*'s artefacts performed 17 September 2014 by The Alasko Company, Chicago, Illinois (*q.v.* 14 October 2014).

Among the almost countless considerations listed by the debtors in the filing, the following is of interest: 'As of 14 June 2016, the Debtors owe their creditors approximately $12,000,000 in unsecured debts. A sale of just a small subset of artefacts from the French collection would permit the Debtors to pay every creditor in full, and allow every Common shareholder to retain their equity position as the Company emerges from bankruptcy.'

The preliminary hearing for the petition, Number 3:16-bk-02230-PMG, is scheduled for Judge Glenn's court on 20 June 2016, with 163 claims in the initial docket. The deadline date for filing additional claims is 24 October 2016.

Monday, 20 June 2016

The debtors petition the Bankruptcy Court to facilitate such a sales motion, despite the fact that on 12 July 2011 the US District Court's Judge Rebecca Smith – in granting title to the artefacts to RMS Titanic, Inc. – stated that RMST must continue to maintain and conserve the artefacts forever and must sell them *only as a collection*.

Friday, 1 July 2016

The United States government confers with counsel from RMST in an attempt

EXHIBITIONS OWNED OR LEASED – as of 13 June 2016	Stationary	Touring	Total
'Bodies... The Exhibition' and 'Bodies Revealed'	2	2	4
'Titanic: The Artefact Exhibition' and 'Titanic: The Experience'	2[1]	6	8
'Real Pirates'	–	1	1
'The Discovery of King Tut'	–	1	1
'Saturday Night Live: The Exhibition'	1[2]		1

1   Las Vegas, Nevada and Orlando, Florida.
2   Closed 6 June 2016.

to resolve the United States' objection to the sales motion. The parties are unable to resolve the matter.

As part of their objection, the government presents documentation of the original 1987 agreement from IFREMER (*Institut Français de Recherché pour l'Exploitation de la Mer* / French Research Institute for Exploration of the Sea) for the charter of *Nadir*, *Nautile* and *Robin*, the equipment used during the dives to *Titanic* in 1987 by Titanic Ventures Ltd; In the same presentation is a copy of the 1994 revised covenants and conditions set by the US District Court for disposition of objects recovered from the wreck, defining and ensuring the unity and integrity of the *Titanic* collections (i.e. the 1987 French and the 1993, 1994, 1996, 1998, 2000 and 2004) artefacts.

Tuesday, 5 July 2016

In the US Bankruptcy Court, Guy G. Gebhardt, acting United States Trustee for the court's Region 21, files a complaint against RMS Titanic, Inc., calling the court's attention to omissions and non-compliances in RMST's filing, including the following: Does RMST ('the Debtor') have full title to the artefacts (the 'French artefacts') it wishes to sell? There is no inventory of the French artefacts. There is an unspecified 'narrow subset' of artefacts the Debtor wishes to sell; what is it? There is no statement of whether the sale is to be public or private. The French government has not been provided with a notice of the sale motion.

Gebhardt's objections to the sale motion include (among others) all of the foregoing.

He suggests that the sale motion be denied because all proper parties have not been notified and it does not contain the required information.

Thursday, 21 July 2016

Premier Exhibitions, Inc., the parent company of RMS Titanic, Inc., meet at their home office in Atlanta, Georgia, and announces the following:

Michael Little is terminated as chief financial officer and replaced by the chairman of the audit committee, Jerome Hernshall; Mingchen Yao resigns from the board of directors.

Two new directors are appointed: Mark Bains (who takes Henshall's place as audit committee chair), and Gao Ding, who has experience in political and culture affairs, who replaces Yao.

The company also reiterates its bankruptcy motions of 14 and 20 June 2016.

Wednesday, 17 August 2016

Filed through the Florida Bankruptcy Court, RMS Titanic, Inc., sues the French government seeking a declaration that France and all French government agencies have no interest in the French artefacts that would prevent their sale.

(Through an agreement with the Premier Exhibitions subsidiary RMS Titanic, Inc. and France at the time of the first salvage in 1987, the recovered objects were to be called the 'French Artefacts', and were to be kept together as a collection. But Premier/RMS Titanic Inc. argues in the suit that in 1993 France awarded it unconditional ownership of the artefacts and thus the right to sell some.)

The suit will require France to make clear whether it does or does not claim some control over them.

* * *

Wednesday, 15 March 2017

OCEANGATE ANNOUNCES A 2018 EXPEDITION

THE CEO AND CO-FOUNDER of OceanGate®, a privately owned, Everett, Washington-based firm, Stockton Rush, reports that he and his company's research team will use a new, state-of-the-art manned submersible in a seven-week series of trips to *Titanic*'s wreck, the first such manned exploration since 2005.

The expedition will employ *Cyclops 2*®, constructed of carbon fibre and titanium, and designed in collaboration with the University of Washington's Applied Physics Lab. Some 22ft (6.7m) long and weighing 19,000lb (8,600kg), *Cyclops 2* will be capable of diving 13,000ft (4,000m), and will boast the largest viewport of any deep-diving submersible. Using equipment and personnel from the Woods Hole Oceanographic Institution's Advanced Imaging and Visualization Laboratory, the expedition plans to take 3D pictures of the wreck and its debris field, and measure the amount and degree of deterioration that has occurred since the wreck's 1985 discovery.

Cyclops 2 can carry five people – a pilot, a navigator and three 'mission specialists', to include marine biologists and maritime engineers, as well as members of the public who will pay a fee of $105,129 (£82,262) to make a dive to *Titanic*'s wreck.

Experts plan to use laser scanning and photogrammetry techniques to create images of the wreck in multiple formats. Live 'visits' inside the ship's hull using remote-operated vehicles (ROVs) are projected. In accordance with provisions of the April 2012

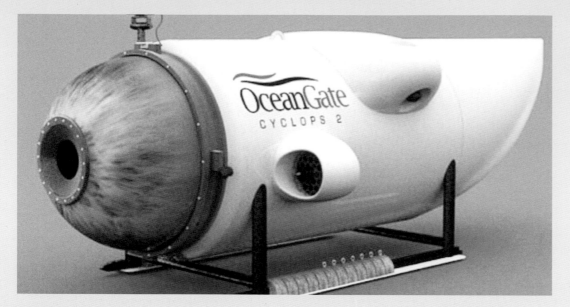

An artist's rendering of the new deep-sea submersible *Cyclops 2*®, which will be deployed during a proposed 2018 expedition to *Titanic*. (OceanGate® Inc.)

designation of *Titanic* as a United Nations Educational, Scientific and Cultural Organization (UNESCO) World Heritage Site, the expedition will not recover any artefacts.

OceanGate plans to complete and test dive the submersible by November 2017, and conduct the expedition in May–June 2018.

* * *

Attempts to recover *Titanic*'s artefacts extend from 20 April 1912 (when Vincent Astor wanted to blow up the wreck where she lay), through Risdon Beasley Ltd's 1953 attempt to investigate the wreck; it travels through Seaonics, of 1977; Woods Hole of October 1977; 'Project Circe' of spring

1979; and Jack Grimm's ill-fated expeditions of 1980, 1981 and 1983. It culminates on 2 September 1985 in the wreck's discovery, and in Titanic Ventures' and IFREMER's 1987 first dives.

James Cameron's film (1997) *Titanic* and his 2003 documentary film of the wreck's interior (*Ghosts of the Abyss*) have brought the ship and its contents to the world's public.

Now, more than thirty years after the wreck's discovery, the 15sq.-mile (38.4sq.-km) wreck site is protected by the United States' National Oceanographic and Atmospheric Administration and by international treaty, while Paul-Henri Nargeolet, co-leader of the 1987, 1993, 1994, 1996, 1998 and 2010 expeditions, continues

to work daily to plot and reconstruct an artefact-by-artefact map of the entire wreck site.

Geologically and historically speaking, *Titanic* soon will die. In 50, 100 or 500 years, the wreck and its debris field will disintegrate, or be absorbed by the ocean's saline atoms.

With the June 2016 proposed sale of some of *Titanic*'s artefacts to protect and to continue public display of objects from the world's most famous shipwreck, there appears to be a means to preserve the wreck. However, such sale will destroy the legal and cultural integrity of the artefact collection. What position the courts will take – can take – remains to be seen …

TITANIC'S AMERICAN FLAG

IN APRIL 1912, the American flag, last modified in 1908, contained 46 stars to indicate the total number of states following Oklahoma's admission to the Union in 1907. (In 1912 the flag was modified to contain 48 stars, six rows of eight stars each, to reflect the admissions of New Mexico [6 January 1912] and Arizona [14 February 1912], but it was not flown officially until 4 July 1912.)

In the American flag of 1908, the 46 stars were arranged as follows:

Aboard British merchant vessels prior to 1914, the national flag hoisted at the foremast of any vessel when the voyage began denoted the country to which she was ultimately bound. The colours were maintained, according to regulations, throughout the voyage, irrespective of how many other countries were visited.

When the voyage neared its end, the masthead ensign was replaced by that of the country from which the vessel had initially departed.

(Renderings of *Titanic*'s various flags may be found amongst the colour illustrations.)

TITANIC STATISTICS

Tonnage:		Height:		Cruising speed	21 knots
Gross	46,329	Waterline to boat deck	60ft 6in	Top speed (estimated)	23–24 knots
Net	21,831	Keel to top of funnel	175ft	Planned capacity:	
Displacement	66,000 tons	Horsepower	46,000	First Class	735
Length overall	882ft 9in	Two reciprocating engines,		Second Class	674
Beam	92ft 6in	indicated hp	30,000	Third Class	1,026
Moulded depth	59ft 6in	Turbine engine, shaft hp	16,000	Crew	885

The starboard profile of *Titanic*, seen at Belfast. (Harland & Wolff Ltd)

CAPSULE CHRONOLOGY

1909 **Friday, 22 March**
Keel laid

1911 **Wednesday, 31 May**
Launched

1912 **Tuesday, 2 April**
Departs Belfast for
Southampton

Wednesday, 10 April
12 noon: Departs Southampton
on maiden voyage

6.35pm: Arrives at Cherbourg,
France
8.10pm: Departs Cherbourg for
Queenstown (Cobh), Ireland

Thursday, 11 April
11.30am: Arrives at Queenstown
1.30pm: Departs Queenstown for
New York; total aboard, 1,317
passengers, 908 crew

Sunday, 14 April
11.40pm: Strikes iceberg

Monday, 15 April
2.20 am: Sinks; 1,513 lost, 712
saved

Thursday, 18 April
Survivors, rescued by Cunard
liner *Carpathia*, are landed at
Pier 54, New York

1985 **Sunday, 1 September**
Wreck discovered, vicinity of
41°43'N, 49°56'W

(New York Tribune)

TIME AND DISTANCE ESTIMATES

Titanic
launched 12.15pm, 31 May 1911
sank 2.20am, 15 April 1912

This time period equals
319.5 days (+2h 05m)
7,760 hours (+05m)
460,205 minutes
27,612,300± seconds

During her life afloat, *Titanic* sailed the following approximate distances (expressed in statute miles):

2 April
Sea trials out of Belfast 120

2–3 April
Belfast to Southampton 570

10 April
Southampton–Cherbourg via Spithead 89

10–11 April
Cherbourg to Queenstown 315

11–12 April
At sea (12 noon to 12 noon) 386

12–13 April
At sea (12 noon to 12 noon) 519

13–14 April
At sea (12 noon to 12 noon) 546

14 April
At sea (12 noon to 11.40pm) 260
Estimated distance following collision 5±

Total 2,810± miles

THE SEARCH FOR *TITANIC*

Boxhall's calculated position
41°46'N, 50°14'W
Incorrect 12.15am transmission
41°44'N, 50°24'W
Californian's position by dead
reckoning, 14 April 1912, 10.21pm
42°05'N, 50°0/'W
Carpathia's position when picking up
survivors, estimated by:
  Californian   41°36'N, 50°0'W
  Birma   41°36'N, 49°45'W

Grimm/Harris, 1980
41°40'–41°50'N, 50°0'–50°10'W
Grimm/Harris, 1981
41°39'–41°44'N, 50°02'–50°08'W
Grimm/Harris, 1983
vicinity of 41°08'N, 50°03'W
IFREMER, 1985
41°43'–41°51'N, 49°55'–50°12'W
Woods Hole, 1985
41°35'–41°46'N, 49°52'–50°10'W

The wreck's position, per Dr Robert
Ballard's book, *The Discovery of the
Titanic*:

Centre of bow section
41°43'57"N, 49°56'49"W
Centre of boiler field
41°43'32"N, 49°56'49"W

Stern section
41°43'35"N, 49°56'54"W

At latitude 41°46'N	1° equals	1' equals
Nautical miles	59.97	0.99
Statute miles	69.01	1.15

Prior to discovery, many people believed *Titanic* to be preserved at the sea's bottom in pristine condition. The wreck proved to be in multiple pieces, their contents emptied into several major debris fields, as this schematic diagram shows. (Authors' collection)

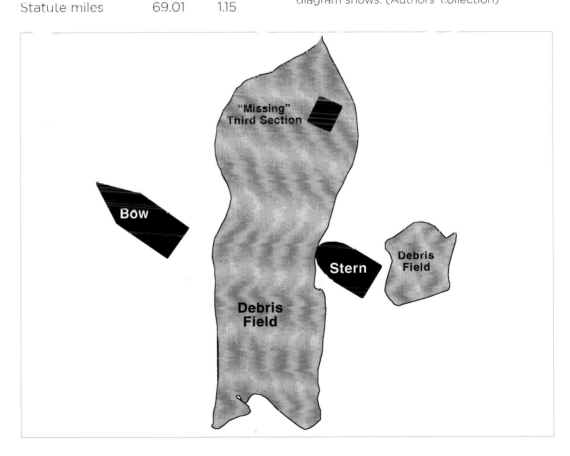

TOTAL ABOARD, LOST AND SAVED

THERE ARE NO FORENSICALLY accurate sources for the total number of passengers and crew who were aboard *Titanic* and, consequently, the total number lost.

Since it presumably was based on an actual head count, Captain Arthur Rostron's declaration (in a report dated 27 April 1912) of '705 living survivors brought to New York' can be accepted as the single true total. However, accounts of 'Aboard/Saved' gathered under more controlled circumstances show variations in this presumably infallible figure.

The United States Senate figures are remarkably accurate considering the short time available for their compilation. If only the five postal workers' names are added to 'total aboard', the number 2,228 is obtained; if the names of William Lyons (ship's crew/able seaman, saved but died aboard *Carpathia* 16 April) and the five postal workers are added to 'total lost', the figure reaches 1,513. Each figure, aboard and lost, is close to accuracy.

Even though a longer time has elapsed since the finalisation of the British Board of Trade figures, certain categories of passengers and crew are omitted from the list. Neither the names of the eight bandsmen nor six of the eight-member Harland & Wolff's 'guarantee group' appear on the Board of Trade's 'Final list' (BT334/052) dated July 1912, although the bandsmen's names are on the original ticketing list as Second Class passengers. As on the US Senate list, the five postal workers' names are not present.

Robert L. Bracken (trustee and treasurer of the Titanic International Society, Inc.) has spent many years consulting international archives and reliable documentation. With the co-operation of many leaders of the *Titanic* community, he has meticulously compiled a list of 'Total Aboard–Saved–Lost' passengers and crew. It is presented here for comparison with the United States Senate's and British Board of Trade's 'final figures'.

Neither the American Senate nor the British Board of Trade on-board figures for the crew include the postal workers. A number of crewmen signed on using false names, which makes name confirmation for all the lists difficult.[1]

		Aboard	Saved		Lost		Total	
			Psngrs	Crew	Psngrs	Crew	Saved	Lost
US Senate Report 28 May 1912	First	329}						
	Second	285}	492	214	832	685	*706*	*1,517*
	Third	710}						
	Crew	899						
	Total aboard:	2,223						
British Board of Trade Report 1912 30 July	First	325}						
	Second	285}	499	212	817	673	*711*	*1,490*
	Third	706}						
	Crew	885						
	Total aboard:	2,201						
Robert Bracken Research Study	First	324}						
	Second	284}	506	206	811	702	*712*	*1,513*
	Third	709}						
	Crew	908						
	Total aboard:	2,225						

1 Among the variables affecting the various counts of those on board: four American Line crewmen, ticketed as Third Class passengers, intending to meet a ship at New York, ate and lived with *Titanic*'s crew, but are mistakenly listed as 'crew' in the US Senate report. Others who sometimes are included, sometimes excluded from various counts include the two wireless telegraphists, the ship's eight bandsmen, several à la carte restaurant employees, six of the eight Harland & Wolff 'guarantee group' and eight Chinese seamen, also travelling in Third Class to meet a ship at New York.

TITAN/TITANIC

IT IS THOUGHT by many that *Titanic's* story really begins, not with the laying of her keel or the announcement of her construction, but with a book written in 1898 by the American writer of sea stories, Morgan Robertson.

The book concerns an April voyage of a great ship, the largest in the world, which strikes an iceberg during an Atlantic crossing and sinks. There is great loss of life due, in part, to a paucity of lifeboats. Perhaps the most remarkable coincidence is the mythical ship's name – *Titan*.

Prophetic? Paranormal? ESP? Telepathy? (If the latter, with what? With whom?)

Here are some comparisons between *Titanic* and *Titan*, between a real liner and a vessel fabricated in Robertson's story, written 14 years before the real ship's ill-fated voyage.

	Titan	*Titanic*
Description	'Largest liner ever built'	World's largest ship at time of launch
Length	800ft	882.5ft
Width	90ft	92.5ft
Displacement	70,000 tons	66,000 tons
Top speed	25 knots	23–24 knots
Watertight compartments	19	16
Engines	Three (triple expansion)	Three (two triple expansion, 1 low-pressure turbine)
Propellers	Three	Three
Masts	Two	Two
Capacity	3,000	3,250
Number aboard	2,000 passengers plus crew	2,225 passengers and crew
Lifeboats	24	20
Sailing date	April, from New York	10 April 1912, for New York

2   THE WRECK OF THE TITAN

From the bridge, engine-room, and a dozen places on her deck the ninety-two doors of nineteen watertight compartments could be closed in half a minute by turning a lever. These doors would also close automatically in the presence of water. With nine compartments flooded the ship would still float, and as no known accident of the sea could possibly fill this many, the steamship *Titan* was considered practically unsinkable.

Built of steel throughout, and for passenger traffic only, she carried no combustible cargo to threaten her destruction by fire; and the immunity from the demand for cargo space had enabled her designers to discard the flat, kettle-bottom of cargo boats and give her the sharp dead-rise—or slant from the keel—of a steam yacht, and this improved her behavior in a seaway. She was eight hundred feet long, of seventy thousand tons' displacement, seventy-five thousand horse power, and on her trial trip had steamed at a rate of twenty-five knots an hour over the bottom, in the face of unconsidered winds, tides, and currents. In short, she was a floating city—containing within her steel walls all that tends to minimize the dangers and discomforts of the Atlantic voyage—all that makes life enjoyable.

Unsinkable—indestructible, she carried as few boats as would satisfy the laws. These, twenty-four in number, were securely covered and lashed down to their chocks on the upper deck, and if launched would hold five hundred people. She carried no useless, cumbersome life-rafts; but—because the law required it—each of the three thousand berths in the passengers', officers', and crew's quarters contained a cork jacket, while about twenty circular life-buoys were strewn along the rails.

In view of her absolute superiority to other craft,

Page 2 of the text of Morgan Robertson's *The Wreck of the Titan* describes the safety devices of an actual ship that did not live and die for another 14 years. (Authors' collection)

	Titan	*Titanic*
Early incident	Collided at sea with a merchantman	Near-collision at Southampton with *Oceanic*
Route	Northern lane	Northern lane
Disaster	April, three days out of port of port (Queenstown)	14 April 1912, three days out
Iceberg	Pyramid-shaped, recently turned over	Pyramid-shaped, recently turned over
Involved crew	John Rowland, lookout, saved	Quartermaster George Rowe, on watch at the aft docking bridge, saved
Warning, as given	'Ice. Right ahead.'	'Iceberg right ahead.'
Damage	Bow raked by ice spur, starboard side near the bridge	Raked by ice spur, starboard side, 12ft above keel to a point just aft of the bridge

The *Titanic* disaster renews interest in Morgan Robertson's *The Wreck of the Titan*, and some American newspapers (like this one in Morristown, New Jersey, USA, in its 3 May 1912 edition) enthusiastically announce they will serialise the nearly forgotten work. (Authors' collection)

MOTION PICTURES FEATURING *TITANIC*

1912

SAVED FROM THE TITANIC (American)
Eclair Film Company, Fort Lee, New Jersey

Featured Miss Dorothy Gibson, *Titanic* survivor

Above Dorothy Gibson, star of *Saved From The Titanic*, is shown in a scene from the film. Miss Gibson is wearing the same clothing she wore when rescued. (Library of Congress/Authors' collection)

Left *Saved From The Titanic* (1912). (Library of Congress/Authors' collection)

IN NACHT UND EIS (German)
Continental-Künstfilm GmbH, Berlin
Script loosely based on testimony given during the US Senate investigation

In Nacht und Eis (1912). (Authors' collection)

1912

LOST YEARS
Rex Motion Picture Masterpiece Co.
(American)

Lost Years is the kind of picture that makes 'masterpiece' sound weak. The scene is the wireless room of the hapless ship sending the hopeless CQD, operated by a professional wireless operator, the startling scene of the blazing ship engulfed by waves, the thrilling and tense realism of the Robinson Crusoe-like existence on the desert island, the suggestive and compelling touch of real coconuts cast into the angry sea, all go to make this a picture that will be universally discussed and commended ...

Lost Years, a synopsis
First of all, he loved her, but he was already wedded to the sea; he was a naval officer – and naval officers' duties and desires don't often coincide. A few days before the date of the wedding, he was commissioned to go abroad on a secret assignment, so the happy, longed-for event was postponed.

On his return trip he sent a wireless to his fiancée, advising her that he would be home on the following Thursday, at two o'clock, and hinting that it would not be entirely objectionable to him if she was ready for the big occasion at that time. You can picture the happy excitement and the delightful frenzy at the girl's home.

Then fate and disaster. The ship sank, and the report had it that all on board perished. The girl, waiting in her bridal gown, heard the newsboys cry the dismal dispatch, and in a paroxysm of grief and despair, she lost her tortured, tottering senses.

There was one thought and one spark of intelligence still left on her sterile mind – the thought that he would be there at two o'clock. And every day she dressed in her bridal gown, waiting for the clock to strike the sound for sweeter bells. But her parents, fearful of the consequences should two o'clock come and go, turned the clock back. It was never two o'clock; he was never late; she never knew. But the months had passed hundreds of two o'clocks, and the years died.

The man, the sole survivor of the fated ship, had found his way on a raft to a desolate little island in the South Seas, and lived a sorrowful, solitary existence, hoping, despairing, praying, cursing, but always lingering longing that a ship might pass and rescue him. He threw cocoanuts into the sea, with a message of his identity and his whereabouts. In the fond, vain hope that a passing vessel might pick up.

After dreary years this hope was realized, and he was rescued and brought home. At two o'clock he met his waiting bride, and yesterday was the present. The girl went to his arms and his lips, and ten years ago was now.

(The Moving Picture News,
11 May 1912)

Beyond this single description in *The Moving Picture News* there is no further mention of the film, its producer, or its distributor. There is no local newspaper advertisement for its showing, no review, no critical appraisal – domestic or foreign.

Mme Trévoux (played by Renée Carl), her son (played by 'Le Petit Mathieu') and her godfather (Henri Julien) learn with dismay of *Titanic*'s sinking, perhaps with husband and father Mr Jean Trévoux on board, in a scene from the 1912 French film *La Hantise*. (Authors' Collection)

1912

LA HANTISE (*The Obsession*) (French)
Gaumont

A woman worries herself almost to death when a palmist tells her someone close to her will die and her husband books aboard the *Titanic*.

1913

ATLANTIS (Danish)
Nordisk Film Kompagni

A Danish doctor, whose wife is institutionalised with a brain tumour, pursues a young dancer to New York aboard the ship *Roland*, which sinks in mid-Atlantic after hitting an unseen object. This is the first Danish multi-reel film.

Government investigations into *Titanic*'s loss that had begun soon after the disaster now were concluded (28 May 1912 for the American inquiry, 30 July 1912 for the British). Public interest in the event began to wane.

Between 1914 and 1918, the Great War changed the world's face; people of the civilised world became aware of the people – the world – about them. Among the many changes was the manner in which people used their leisure time. In increasing numbers they began to attend motion pictures.

And motion pictures reached out for them. During the decade of the teens, motion pictures were modified from flickering, twelve- to fifteen-minute 'snapshots' to mature, well produced, multi-reeled portraits of the times, both present and past.

Because of the recent war, people were prepared to view disaster in their movies. But they wanted it tempered as comedy or as portrayed as part of the social scene.

Since the initial 1912–13 bloc of *Titanic*-inspired films, there is a fifteen-year hiatus during which there appears to be no ship disaster cinematic productions. Even following the cautious, even tentative, *Titanic*-related films of the 1920s and 1930s, it is not until 1943 that an attempt was made to film the disaster as a historic narrative – and even then it was made as a propaganda film by a totalitarian regime.

Today, there are two reasons for *Titanic*'s continued popularity: the November 1955 publication of Walter Lord's book *A Night to Remember*; and the 1 September 1985 discovery of *Titanic*'s wreck by an expedition co-led by Jean-Louis Michel and Robert D. Ballard.

Since 1955, *Titanic* has never been out of the public consciousness. It is the subject of seven films produced for theatrical release, countless books, and numerous television programmes.

It is the films – the motion – we shall now consider.

MOTION PICTURES PRODUCED FOR THEATRICAL RELEASE

Feature films containing significant segments related to or compared with *Titanic*

October 1927

EAST SIDE WEST SIDE (American)
Fox Film Corporation

A young man grows up in New York City and at sea in search of his father. There is a sinking ship related *loosely* to *Titanic*.

December 1927

BUTTONS (American)
Metro-Goldwyn-Mayer

A young street boy gets a job an ocean liner as a pageboy. The ship is wrecked at sea.

1929

ATLANTIC (British)
British International-Süd Film

First all-talking British film. Was shot with separate English- and German-speaking casts using the same sets and studio equipment.

1933

CAVALCADE (American)
Fox Film Corporation

Based on a 1931 British play by Noel Coward, there is a sequence depicting honeymooners aboard RMS *Titanic*.

1937

HISTORY IS MADE AT NIGHT (American)
United Artists

An eastbound Atlantic liner is threatened when it strikes an iceberg, but all aboard are saved when the bulkheads hold. ('Iceberg Ahead!')

1943

TITANIC (German)
Tobis Films

Vehemently anti-British propaganda film.

1953

TITANIC (American)
20th Century Fox

Clifton Webb and Barbara Stanwyck star. Excellently researched for its time

1958

A NIGHT TO REMEMBER (British)
The Rank Organisation
World premiere: 3 July 1958, Odeon Theatre, London

Based on Walter Lord's book, this classic film was the most detailed and accurate depiction of the disaster at the time of its release and well beyond.

1964

THE UNSINKABLE MOLLY BROWN
(American)
Metro-Goldwyn-Mayer

A fictionalised film biography of Mrs Margaret Tobin Brown, with a *Titanic* sequence, based upon the 1960 Broadway musical of the same name.

1979

SOS TITANIC (American)
ABC Television

Above *Atlantic* (1929): the doomed crew of the SS *Atlantic* stoically await their end. (Lumière Films/Authors' collection)

Below *Titanic*'s crew in the 1943 German propaganda film *Titanic* actively seek a safe exit from the sinking ship. (Private collection)

Above The 1953 Hollywood epic *Titanic* was well-researched for its period. (*TITANIC* © 1953 Twentieth Century Fox Film Corporation. All rights reserved)

1980

SOS TITANIC (British)
EMI Films

The April 1980 release in the UK of the theatre version (102 minutes) followed the September 1979 American television broadcast (140 minutes). The results in neither version were universally applauded.

1980

RAISE THE TITANIC! (American)
ITC Films/Marble Arch Production
Its script loosely based on the Clive Cussler novel of the same title, the movie's production costs were about $33 million. Its critical reception was less than enthusiastic, and its failure forced its maker, Lord Grade, to relinquish control of his entertainment empire.

1981

TIME BANDITS (British)
Avco Embassy Picture

A group of time-travelling zanies escape Mycenaean Greece to RMS *Titanic*. After the ship sinks, they bob around in mid-Atlantic planning their next move.

Right A model of the liner used in *Raise the Titanic!* depicts the ill-fated vessel as it emerged from the sea's depths, its only apparent damage being the missing second funnel. (ITC/Marble Arch Productions/ PolyGram Entertainment/Authors' collection)

Above Based on Walter Lord's book, and still considered by many to be the definitive *Titanic* film, *A Night to Remember* (1958) is notable for its many authentic action scenes. (Photo courtesy of Carlton International)

Left William MacQuitty, the film's producer, and his wife Betty were members of the 1996 Titanic Expedition Cruise. (Authors' collection © 1996 RMS Titanic, Inc.)

1981

SEARCH FOR THE TITANIC
Producers: Jack Grimm, Mike Harris

First shown publicly at its world premiere on 16 January 1981 in Abilene, Texas, but apparently not released commercially, this documentary film was narrated by Orson Welles. The 103-minute film depicts Texas oilman Jack Grimm's unsuccessful 1980 search for *Titanic*'s wreck aboard the research vessel *H.J.W. Fay*.

Two further unsuccessful expeditions by Grimm, later in 1981 and again in 1983, apparently were not filmed for theatrical release. *Search for the Titanic* became available on home video in 1998.

1992

TITANICA (Canadian)
An IMAX® Corporation Film
Stephen Low, Producer/Director; Dr Joseph MacInnis and André Picard, Executive Producers

A documentary film in the IMAX® film process, requiring special cameras that use the largest film frame in motion picture history, ten times the size of conventional 35mm film.

Public showing requires a specially designed projector and a specially constructed theatre to accommodate the seven-storey-high screen necessary for the oversize film's projection.

The underseas footage of the wreck site, while only a relatively brief part of the finished film, is striking for its illumination and detailed clarity.

Search for the Titanic (1981). (Courtesy of Mrs Jackie Grimm)

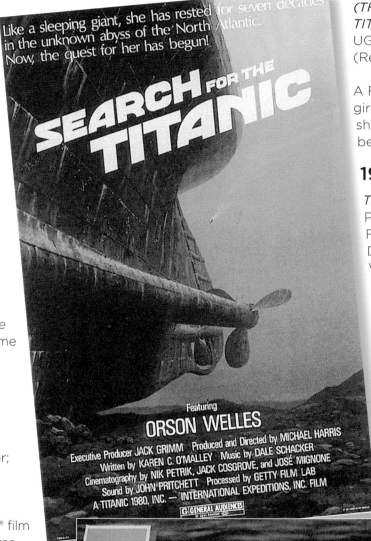

1997

LA FEMME DE CHAMBRE DU TITANIC (THE CHAMBERMAID ON THE TITANIC) (French–Italian–Spanish)
UGC YM (France) Production Company (Released 12 October 1997, Spain)

A French foundry worker sleeps with a girl who works on *Titanic*. When the ship sinks, his accounts of the liaison become increasingly elaborate.

1997

TITANIC (American)
Paramount Pictures and 20th Century Fox
Director: James Cameron
World premiere (Tokyo) 1 November
UK premiere (London) 18 November
USA premiere (Los Angeles) 14 December

This film describes in meticulous detail *Titanic*'s maiden voyage and the events leading up to its calamitous end.

Titanica (1992). (© IMAX Corporation)

Planning for this project began with a 1995 series of dives to the wreck, using Russian deep-sea equipment to photograph portions of the ship (qv).

The film's release was delayed past its scheduled July 1997 opening date because of post-production difficulties and its director's obsession with perfection.

The most expensive motion picture ever made – its costs exceed $200 million (£121 million) – the film required two major Hollywood studios to underwrite its completion and distribution.

Titanic received its world premiere on Saturday, 4 November 1997 at the 10th annual Tokyo International Film Festival, Japan. Although not accompanied by the traditional excitement that greets premiere showings of major films in America, the film was politely received by its Japanese audience.

The long-awaited American premiere, on 19 December 1997, was preceded by a publicity build-up of impressive proportions.

Although many of the disaster's historical details are sacrificed for dramatic content, and an overly prominent love story between two young passengers slows the story's continuity, the film was received with worldwide acclaim; during the first ten days of its American release it grossed $90 million (£54.5 million).

On Tuesday, 10 February 1998 the film received 14 nominations for awards given annually by the [American] Academy of Motion Picture Arts and Sciences, Hollywood, California. On Tuesday, 24 March James Cameron's film received 11 Academy Awards, including Best Picture and Best Special Effects. However, although nominated in ten categories at the annual British Academy Awards ceremony on Sunday, 19 April 1998, in London, England, *Titanic* failed to receive a single award.

In the United States, *Titanic* remained No. 1 on the box office list for a remarkable 15 weeks.

1998, 1 March: Sales figures indicate the film has earned more than $1 billion.

1998, 1 September: The film is released to the home video market. Its sales are more than $200 million; a Blu-ray version is added in September 2012.

2000, 26 November: NBC-TV's *Movie of the Week* televises the film, for which NBC pays $30 million for broadcast rights.

2012, 13–15 April: The weekend showing 100 years after the disaster brings *Titanic*'s worldwide distribution gross to more than $2 billion.

1999

LA LEGGENDA DEL TITANIC (THE LEGEND OF THE TITANIC) (Italian)
ITB Spain
Initial release date 17 April 1999

The history of *Titanic*'s sinking is loosely retold in this animated film.

2000

TITANIC: LA LEGGENDA CONTINUA (TITANIC: THE LEGEND GOES ON) (Italian)
Titanic Cartoons SRL Roma
Initial release date 15 September 2000

An animated film depicting *Titanic*'s maiden voyage.

2000

THE BOY WHO SAW THE ICEBERG (LA GARÇON QUI A VU L'ICEBERG) (Canadian)
National Film Board of Canada
Marcy Page, David Verrall
Initial release date 21 October 2000

An eight-minute animated film written and directed by Paul Driessen about a young boy's imaginary relationship with *Titanic*.

2003

GHOSTS OF THE ABYSS (American)
Walt Disney Pictures
Initial release date 11 April 2003

Using exploration techniques developed during the filming of *Titanic*, James Cameron visits the ship's wreck site and investigates the sunken liner's history and status.

2004

ALLA RICERCA DEL TITANIC (IN SEARCH OF THE TITANIC) (Italian)
Mondo TV
Initial release date 17 June 2004

An animated Italian film that loosely examines exploration of *Titanic*'s sunken wreck. (A sequel to the 1999 film *La Leggenda de Titanic*).

2010

TITANIC II (American)
The Asylum
Written, directed by and starring Shane VanDyke
Released 7 August 2010 to Australian television
9 August 2010 released in United Kingdom theatres

24 August 2010 released in the United States

Aboard a fictional replica of *Titanic*, the vessel's maiden voyage is taken along a reversed route from the original *Titanic*'s 100 years earlier, i.e. New York to Southampton. Global warming inflicts tsunamis and chunks of ice fall on the ship, causing an explosion that sets the ship afire.

2012

TITANIC IN 3-D
Lightstorm Pictures (with Paramount Pictures and 20th Century Fox)
Initial viewing at Royal Albert Hall, London, 27 March 2012
Public release (worldwide) 6 April 1912

A re-mastering, supervised by James Cameron, takes 60 weeks to produce, with a budget of $18 million. The original 1997 film is re-mastered to 4K resolution and post-converted to stereoscopic 3-D format. The release eventually earns more than $343 million worldwide.

A DVD is released 12 September 2012 by Paramount Pictures.

* * *

Many countries – the United States, England, Italy, France, Canada among them – have produced films about *Titanic* for theatrical release. Collectively, these feature films have included drama, comedy, animation, farce and adventure. But never has a country released a film that implied a *doctrinal* function.

On 22 August 1945, a Japanese ship, the *Ukishima Maru*, was repatriating Korean labourers to their homeland when it was mysteriously sunk by an internal explosion. The Japanese claimed there were 549 lost out of 3,275 aboard, and that the ship sank after striking an American mine; the Koreans claim there were 7,000 packed aboard, of whom up to 5,000 were lost following a deliberate explosion set by the Japanese (whose contempt for Koreans was well known). (The disaster had already been filmed by the Japanese in 1995 under the title *Asian Blue: The Ukishima Maru Incident*. It had also been published as a novel in North Korea.)

2000

SOULS PROTEST (*Sara-innun Ryonghongdul; Living Souls*) (North Korean)
Directed by Kim Chun-song
Cast: Ryon Hwa Kim; Chui Kim
Release date 2000
Running time 100 to 113 minutes

The film portrays thousands of Koreans returning joyously in August 1945 to their country whose liberation from brutal Japanese colonial rule had just been accomplished through the direct efforts of the Korean (Soviet-empowered) 'leader' Kim Il-sung.

The film's contents can be readily summarised by a view of the film:

On 15 August 1945, Japanese Imperialists were defeated and there echoed in Japan, too, the shouts of victory of thousands of Korean people who had been drafted to Japan. They joined in a repatriation group to return to their dear homeland. Because of their hatred for Koreans, the Japanese plot to blow up their ship, overloaded with twice as many passengers as it is registered to carry.

Ryon Hwa Kim and other Koreans, who are ignorant of this fact, set out with great joy and hope, talking and laughing. On the top deck two lovers exchange furtive glances and a weak smile passes between them.

The Japanese turn the ship to the port of Maizuru under the pretext of refilling the drinking water, and drive the Koreans below deck while preparing to blow up the ship.

An emaciated Korean woman tries to feed her baby while two Japanese sailors scurry past, saying they feel sorry for the infant. A terrible explosion shakes the ship and then another blast. Water spouts up and people tumble about. The ship breaks in half. Thousands of people disappear with it.

In 2000 – by splicing in scenes of rejoicing North Koreans celebrating

A publicity poster for the 2000 film *Souls Protest* from the People's Republic of Korea, which tells the story of the *Ukishima Maru*, sometimes called North Korea's *Titanic*. (Authors' Collection)

their freedom from the overbearing Japanese in 1945, and attributing it to the leadership of Kim Il-sung (who in 1945 was a Soviet puppet) – the North Korean Ministry of Propaganda saw the opportunity to help re-anoint Kim's right to govern and to justify the right he had already held for 15 years.

Hoping to gain not only international sympathy for the ill-used, North Korean wartime impressed workers, but also to coattail on the worldwide popularity of the 1997 Cameron film *Titanic*, the country's charismatic and jingoistic leader, seizing the opportunity to promote a political advantage, called the film (or caused it to be exploited as) 'The North Korean *Titanic*'.

The film was first shown internationally at a film festival in Moscow, held 21–30 June 2001, and simultaneously shown at Hong Kong from 27 to 29 June.

Little more has since been heard of – or from – the film.

* * *

It is not within this book's scope to consider the numerous films about *Titanic* – trivial as well as significant – produced solely for television broadcast.

Domestic and foreign, local and network, fiction and non-fiction – their descriptions represent a book-length project in themselves.

It is hoped that a perusal of the preceding listing of 'feature' motion pictures shall satisfy the curiosity of those who wish to venture beyond the printed page.

BIBLIOGRAPHY

BOOKS

Beesley, Lawrence *The Loss of the SS Titanic* (New York: Houghton Mifflin, 1912)

Bissett, Sir James *Tramps and Ladies* (New York: Criterion Books, 1959)

Eaton, John P. & Haas, Charles A. *Falling Star: Misadventures of White Star Line Ships* (Wellingborough: Patrick Stephens Ltd, Thorsons Publishing Group (UK)/W.W. Norton, Inc. (USA), 1989)

– *Titanic: Destination Disaster* (Sparkford, Somerset: Haynes Publishing Group, 3rd edition, 2011)

– *Titanic: Triumph and Tragedy* (Sparkford, Somerset: Haynes Publishing Group, 3rd edition, 2011)

Gracie, Archibald *The Truth about the Titanic* (New York: Mitchell Kennerley, 1913)

Harrison, Leslie *A Titanic Myth* (London: William Kimber, 1986)

Lord, Walter *A Night to Remember* (New York: Henry Holt & Co., 1955)

Lyons, Eugene *David Sarnoff* (New York: Harper & Row, 1966)

Marcus, Geoffrey *The Maiden Voyage* (New York: Viking Press, 1966)

Mead, Commander Hillary P. *Sea Flags* (Glasgow: Brown, Son & Ferguson Ltd, 1938)

Ocean Liners of the Past: Olympic and Titanic, Foreword by John Maxtone-Graham (Sparkford, Somerset: Patrick Stephens Ltd, Haynes Publishing Group, 1983)

Padfield, Peter *The Titanic and the Californian* (London: Hodder & Stoughton, 1965)

Reade, Leslie *The Ship That Stood Still* (Sparkford, Somerset: Patrick Stephens Ltd, 1993)

Rostron, Sir Arthur *Home from the Sea* (New York: The Macmillan Company, 1931)

Stenson, Patrick *Lights: The Odyssey of C.H. Lightoller* (New York: W.W. Norton & Co., 1984)

NEWSPAPERS AND PERIODICALS

The Belfast, Ireland, *Evening Telegraph*
The Belfast, Ireland, *News Letter*
The Brooklyn, New York, *Daily Eagle*
The Halifax, Nova Scotia, *Evening News*
The Halifax, Nova Scotia, *Herald*
The Halifax, Nova Scotia, *Morning Star*
Harper's Weekly
The Illustrated London News
L'Illustration
The London *Daily Mail*
The London *Daily Telegraph*

The Montreal *Gazette*
Motion Picture News, New York
Moving Picture News, New York
Nautical Magazine
The *New York American*
The *New York Herald*
The *New York Journal*
The New York *Morning Telegraph*
The New York Post
The New York Times
The *New York Tribune*
The Norfolk, Virginia, *Virginian-Pilot and the Ledger-Star*
Oceanus
The St John's, Newfoundland, *Evening Telegram*
Sea Classics
The Southampton, England, *Southern Daily Echo*
The Times, London
Voyage, the official journal of *Titanic* International Society Inc., Midland Park, NJ
Yau, Shuk Ting, 'Imagining Others: A Study of the "Asia" Presented in Japanese Cinema', in Nault, Derek M., ed., *Development in Asia: Interdisciplinary, Post-neoliberal and Transnational Perspectives* (Boca Raton, Florida, 2009)

DOCUMENTS AND REPORTS

US Senate, 62nd Congress, 2nd session, report number 806: *Titanic* disaster, Report of the Committee on Commerce, United States Senate, pursuant to Senate Resolution 283. Government Printing Office, Washington, DC, 1912. (1,145pp)

US Senate, 62nd Congress, 2nd session, document number 933: 'Loss of the steamship *Titanic*', Report of a formal investigation ... as conducted by the British Government. Government Printing Office, Washington, DC, 1912

In the Wreck Commissioner's Court, Proceedings before the Right Hon Lord Mersey ... on a formal investigation ordered by the Board of Trade into the loss of the SS *Titanic*. His Majesty's Stationery Office, London, 1912. (959pp +xiv pp appendices)

The 'Titanic' Relief Fund, Scheme of Administration (with schedules), Mansion House, London, 1913

Public Archives of Canada, Historical Resources Branch

The Department of Transport, Marine Accident Investigation Branch. 'RMS *Titanic*: Reappraisal of Evidence Relating to SS *Californian*'. Her Majesty's Stationery Office, London, 1992

PUBLIC COURT RECORDS

Great Britain:
In the High Court of Justice, Kings Bench Division

United States:
United States District Court, Southern District of New York
United States District Court, Eastern District of Virginia, Norfolk Division

ADDITIONAL READING

FOR FURTHER INFORMATION about *Titanic*, the ship and her people, as well as her ongoing history, readers may write for membership information to:

Titanic International Society, Inc.
PO Box 416
Midland Park,
NJ 07432-0416 USA
www.titanicinternationalsociety.org

ACKNOWLEDGEMENTS

THROUGHOUT THE completion of this work, the authors have received the kind assistance and selfless cooperation of many individuals and organisations on both sides of the Atlantic and the Pacific. Two simple words, 'thank you', form the basis for these pages. But *Titanic: A Journey Through Time* owes so much to these individuals and organisations that 'thank you' seems both incomplete and insufficient. To these very special people and many other friends who have offered advice, support, assistance, time and effort on the book's behalf, the authors express their sincere appreciation and gratitude.

In the United Kingdom, our thanks to T. Kenneth Anderson and Michael McCaughan, Ulster Folk and Transport Museum, Holywood, Co. Down; Philip Armstrong, Una Reilly, Stephen Cameron and the members of the Belfast Titanic Society; Geoff Whitfield, the late Steve Rigby, David Hill and the members of the British Titanic Society; Capt. and Mrs. Thomas Barnett; Capt. and Mrs. James deCoverly; Patrick Bogue, Onslow's Auctions, Ltd; Alan Geddes; Simon Hashim, Director, Putford Enterprises Ltd; David F. Hutchings; Gillian Hutchinson and David Taylor, National Maritime Museum, Greenwich; Michael Malamatenius; Tim Padfield, copyright officer, and the ever-helpful reference and reading room staffs at The National Archives, Kew, Richmond, Surrey; the always-obliging staff of the British Library Newspaper Library, Colindale; Peter Pearce; Jonathan Perchal, PolyGram Filmed Entertainment, London; Richard Whitaker, Ian Frater and Margaret Saunders, CGU plc, London; Janet Cook and Janet Heaney, *Newcastle Chronicle and Journal, Ltd*; Stuart J. Farr, *The News*, Portsmouth; and Andrew Aldridge, Henry Aldridge and Son, Auctioneers.

For the beautiful artwork that graces these pages, our admiration and gratitude to E.D. (Ted) Walker – a very special friend, indeed – and the gifted Simon Fisher.

Elsewhere in Europe, our thanks go to our dear friends Dr. Stéphane Pennec and his heroic colleagues at Atelier LP3 Conservation, Semur-en-Auxois, France; Günter Bäbler, Wald, Switzerland and Claes-Göran Wetterholm, Stockholm, Sweden; our appreciation also to IFREMER, Toulon, France; the Sea Museum, Malmö, Sweden and the Stockholm Maritime Museum.

In Canada, we recognise with thanks Alan Hustak, *Montreal Gazette*; Garry Shutlak and Dan Conlin of the Public Archives of Nova Scotia; the Maritime Museum of the Atlantic; Henrietta Mann, Dalhousie University, Halifax; the Halifax (Nova Scotia) Public Library; the St. John's, (Newfoundland) Public Library; Wayne Sturge, Provincial Archives of Newfoundland and Labrador; the Vancouver Maritime Museum; and Sue Mander, Jennifer Fraser and Brenda Kirke, IMAX Corporation, Toronto.

In Japan, our special gratitude to the family of Masafumi Hosono, and to Matthew Taylor.

At sea and ashore, we salute the officers and crews of *Ocean Voyager*, *Nadir*, *Nautile* and *Abeille Supporter* for enduring our countless questions, continual intrusions and endless appetites.

In the United States, we express our gratitude to the late Frank O. Braynard, Sea Cliff, NY; Norman Brouwer and Madeline Rogers, South Street Seaport Museum, New York City; Glen A. Campbell, Wonders, Memphis, TN; the Department of Oceanography at Texas A&M University; Bob Forrest; Edith Gamba; William H. Garzke, Gibbs and

Cox, Inc; Judy Geller; Mrs. Jackie Grimm; Claudia Jen and her colleagues at the Mariners Museum, Newport News, VA; Doug Johnson, New York City; Paul F. Johnston, Smithsonian Institution, National Museum of American History/Transportation, Washington, DC; Marian H. Kelley, Tracor, Inc; the staff of the Periodicals Division of the Library of Congress, Washington, DC; Lamont-Doherty Geological Observatory, Palisades, NY; Shelley Lauzon and Kathy Patterson, Woods Hole Oceanographic Institution, Woods Hole, MA; Joan Marcus, New York City; the Naval Historical Society, Washington; Bonnie N. Pryor, McGuire Woods Battle and Boothe, LLP, Norfolk, VA; Jamie Roberts; Suzanne Tighe, Dodger Endemol Productions; Matthew Tulloch; the US Senate Historical Office, Library of Congress; the Morris County (New Jersey) Public Library; the New Jersey and Washington staffs of Representative Rodney P. Freling-

huysen; Joel Perry of OceanGate, Inc.; and Alex Klingehofer, Premier Exhibitions, Inc.

A special acknowledgement goes to the trustees and members of the Titanic International Society, Midland Park, New Jersey, and in particular to Michael V. Ralph, Michael A. Findlay, Robert M. DiSogra, Deborah Lamoot, the late Joseph A. Carvalho and Bill and Susan Willard for their contributions to this work.

We pause to remember, too, the late Frank P. Aks, *Titanic* survivor, and his lovely wife Marie and their family; the late Matthew Russell Lownds and Mrs. Lownds; the late George Fenwick and his thoughtful wife Mary Lou. Their willingness to share enriched us all.

We express our gratitude to the administration and the custodial staff of Randolph High School, Randolph, NJ, to Bonnie Baumert of the Randolph High School Modern and Classical Language

Department for her invaluable translation assistance, and to the Randolph Township (NJ) Board of Education for its continuing support.

We remember with gratitude the late William MacQuitty, whose remarkable film remains unsurpassed in portraying *Titanic* and her people, and to the equally remarkable Betty MacQuitty, who inspired all who knew her.

A warm and personal thanks to three very special men and their families, without whom much of this book would have proven impossible. To George and Cindy Tulloch, to Paul-Henri and Florence Nargoolet, and to Allan and Diane Carlin, our love, our best wishes for smooth sailings always, and our abiding gratitude.

And finally, to Rian Keating we extend our deepest thanks; to the late Beatrice Haas, who always was there for us, we express our eternal love.

INDEX

Page numbers in *italics* denote illustrations or photographs.

THE TITANIC COLLECTION

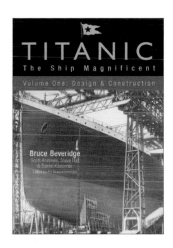

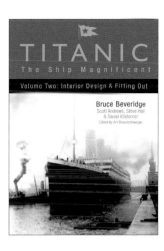

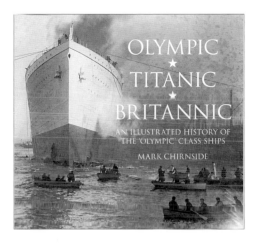

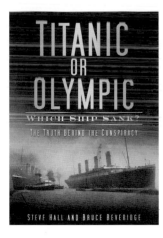

For the full *Titanic* experience visit The History Press website and follow the *Titanic* link

www.thehistorypress.co.uk